ENDING HOMELESSNESS?
The Contrasting Experiences of Denmark, Finland and Ireland

Mike Allen, Lars Benjaminsen,
Eoin O'Sullivan and Nicholas Pleace

First published in Great Britain in 2020 by

Policy Press
University of Bristol
1–9 Old Park Hill
Bristol
BS2 8BB
UK
t: +44 (0)117 954 5940
pp-info@bristol.ac.uk
www.policypress.co.uk

North America office:
Policy Press
c/o The University of Chicago Press
1427 East 60th Street
Chicago, IL 60637, USA
t: +1 773 702 7700
f: +1 773 702 9756
sales@press.uchicago.edu
www.press.uchicago.edu

© Policy Press 2020

British Library Cataloguing in Publication Data
A catalogue record for this book is available from the British Library.

Library of Congress Cataloging-in-Publication Data
A catalog record for this book has been requested.

ISBN 978-1-4473-4717-0 (hardback)
ISBN 978-1-4473-4718-7 (ePdf)
ISBN 978-1-4473-4719-4 (ePub)

The right of Mike Allen, Lars Benjaminsen, Eoin O'Sullivan and Nicholas Pleace to be identified as authors of this work has been asserted by them in accordance with the Copyright, Designs and Patents Act 1988.

All rights reserved: no part of this publication may be reproduced, stored in a retrieval system or transmitted in any form or by any means, electronic, mechanical, photocopying, recording or otherwise, without the prior permission of Policy Press.

The statements and opinions contained within this publication are solely those of the authors and not of the University of Bristol or Policy Press. The University of Bristol and Policy Press disclaim responsibility for any injury to persons or property resulting from any material published in this publication.

Policy Press works to counter discrimination on grounds of gender, race, disability, age and sexuality.

Cover design by Robin Hawes
Printed and bound in Great Britain by CPI Group (UK) Ltd, Croydon, CR0 4YY
Policy Press uses environmentally responsible print partners

Contents

List of figures and tables		iv
Acknowledgements		vi
1	Ending homelessness? Policy and progress in Denmark, Finland and Ireland	1
2	Before the goal of 'ending homelessness': the evolution of policy	29
3	The strategies described	47
4	Trends in homelessness in Denmark, Finland and Ireland	73
5	Explanations: housing matters	103
6	Explanations: welfare and politics matter	139
7	Conclusion	159
References		179
Index		195

List of figures and tables

Figures

4.1	Annual number of homeless shelter users in Denmark, 1999–2018	76
4.2	Homeless people recorded in the Danish homelessness counts, 2009–2019	78
4.3	Young homeless people, 18–29 years old in the Danish homelessness counts, 2009–2019	80
4.4	Long-term homelessness in Finland, 2011–18	83
4.5	Living rough and in shelters/accommodation for homeless people in Finland, 2008–18	84
4.6	Homeless people living temporarily in institutions in Finland, 2008–18	85
4.7	Homeless families in Finland, 2008–18	86
4.8	New adult presentations to homeless services in Ireland, Q1 2014–Q4 2018	89
4.9	Exits from emergency accommodation to housing (local authority, approved housing body, private rented sector and HAP), Q1 2014–Q4 2018	90
4.10	Number of adults in emergency accommodation in Ireland for longer than six months, Q1 2014–Q4 2018	91
4.11	Number of adults in section 10 emergency and temporary accommodation in Ireland, April 2014–December 2018	92
4.12	Expenditure on homelessness services in Ireland, Q1 2013–Q4 2018	96
4.13	Households experiencing homelessness and staying in temporary and emergency accommodation in Denmark, Finland and Ireland, 2008–19	100
4.14	Households experiencing homelessness and staying in temporary and emergency accommodation in Denmark, Finland and Ireland per 1,000 households, 2008–19	101
4.15	Households experiencing homelessness and staying in temporary and emergency accommodation in Helsinki, Dublin and Copenhagen as a percentage of total households experiencing homelessness, 2008–18	101
5.1	Single adult homelessness and Y Foundation apartment procurement and building in Finland, 1987–2016	121
5.2	Dwellings completed in Denmark, 2007–18	124
5.3	Social housing provision in Ireland, 2008–18	128

| 5.4 | Stock of social housing in Ireland, 2008–18 | 129 |
| 5.5 | Rent indices, Ireland, Q3 2007–Q4 2018 | 134 |

Tables

| 1.1 | ETHOS | 25 |
| 4.1 | Individuals by homelessness situation, Danish homelessness counts, 2009–19 | 79 |

Acknowledgements

We would like to thank the editorial team at Policy Press for their support and forbearance. We would also like to thank Daniel Hoey and Courtney Marsh for their valuable editorial assistance, and the members of the European Observatory on Homelessness, Isabel Baptista, Volker Busch-Geertsema, Nora Teller and Freek Spinnewijn for their collegiality while we worked on this book.

1

Ending homelessness? Policy and progress in Denmark, Finland and Ireland

Introduction

In recent years, across Europe, North America and the Antipodes, a significant number of countries, states and regions have devised strategies that aim to end long-term homelessness and the need to sleep rough (Parsell et al, 2012; Owen, 2015; O'Sullivan, 2017a; Lee et al, 2018).[1] Long considered an intractable or 'wicked' social problem, the notion that homelessness could be ended represents a significant sea change in conceptualising and responding to homelessness, what Henwood et al (2015: 3) call a 'fundamental shift in expectations'. The idea of ending homelessness has, in the words of Baker and Evans (2016: 25) 'gone from politically unthinkable to politically mainstream'.

The growth in the numbers experiencing homelessness, particularly since the early to mid-1980s saw an expansion of the number of shelter beds in most cities in Europe, North America and the Antipodes, with transitional housing added later, resulting in a largely unplanned, reactionary and complex system of various forms of emergency and temporary accommodation, in many cases, with on-site or linked psychosocial supports.

Crucially, there was emerging evidence that existing service responses were not reaching some individuals whose homelessness had either been triggered by high and complex needs, or who had developed such needs in association with their homelessness becoming prolonged or recurrent. Innovations such as Critical Time Intervention and, particularly, Housing First, initially in the US, showed that this high-cost, high-risk population of people experiencing homelessness could be reached, and that their homelessness could be ended. Both an enhanced, nuanced and evidence-based understanding of homelessness and a new and more effective toolkit for ending homelessness had become available, changing the context in which policy was being developed.

In a review of over 60 plans and strategies in North America, Europe and Australia, it was noted that while there was little consistency in how ending homelessness was operationalised, the majority of plans and strategies had a broadly similar objective of ending homelessness, using a 'functional zero' definition. This approach recognises that an 'absolute zero' attempt to completely eliminate people experiencing homelessness in all circumstances at all times may not be possible, albeit that Finland, one of the countries discussed in this book, is now openly talking about achieving 'absolute zero'. 'Functional zero' aims to ensure that:

> there are enough services, housing and shelter beds for those who need it, creating a dynamic equilibrium in which services can stop homelessness from building up because they can react immediately as soon as homelessness occurs. In this approach, emergency shelters are meant to be temporary and the goal is permanent housing. (Turner et al, 2015: 5)

Despite the widespread adoption of these ambitious strategies, over the past decade, homelessness has increased in most European Union member states and the Antipodes (Busch-Geertsema et al, 2014; Australian Bureau of Statistics, 2018), and remains at stubbornly high levels in the US, albeit that the overall figure conceals a dramatic decline of 48 per cent in the number of veterans experiencing homelessness between 2009 and 2018 (Department of Housing and Urban Development, 2018). On the face of it, there appears to be a disjuncture between the adoption of these plans to end homelessness and the fact that the numbers of people experiencing homelessness are rising or, at best, remaining stable in the majority of countries, provinces and regions where reasonably robust and consistent data are available. However, a key driver for states, regions and municipalities to devise plans to end homelessness, and an optimism that this policy objective can be achieved, is that there is an increasing research evidence base on what works to end homelessness. This increasingly sophisticated research evidence covers both the prevention of homelessness in the first instance and the support mechanisms that can ensure sustainable exits and stable, secure accommodation for people who have experienced homelessness (Pauly et al, 2012). However, in the European context, it should be borne in mind that much of the research evidence drawn on originates in North America (for further elaboration on this point, see Pleace, 2016b).

Strategies are increasingly devised on the basis of this research evidence, rather than simply a praiseworthy desire and hope to reduce homelessness. Evidence on what does not work, and the pitfalls to avoid along the way, is becoming increasingly sophisticated (for a recent overview, see FEANTSA and FAP, 2018: 22–35), in particular, the extensive and expensive use of congregate emergency accommodation to contain people experiencing homelessness rather than ameliorating their homelessness (Serme-Morin and Coupechoux, 2019: 9–41). While 'ending homelessness' may appear to have a utopian ring to it, in reality, these various homeless strategies and plans consist of essentially evidence-based, pragmatic, relatively modest and realisable targets.

This book explores these issues through a detailed comparison of the experiences of Denmark, Finland and Ireland over recent decades. As will be expanded on in the remainder of the book, it has become increasingly clear that services that concentrate on preparing people experiencing homelessness to live in housing in advance of providing the housing are considerably less successful in ensuring sustainable exits from homelessness than services that provide housing and supports simultaneously. As Parsell (2017: 150) puts it, this knowledge 'provides rigorous and compelling evidence to underpin our philosophical desire to change inequitable systems rather than change people'. Equally, the proliferation of street-based services that provide subsistence-type services in the form of food, beverages and hygiene have been criticised for undermining the well-being of those who are experiencing literal homelessness (Parsell and Watts, 2017), rather than ameliorating their objectively degrading position.

Managing homelessness

Until relatively recently, the dominant response for the last 200 years at local and national governmental levels was to 'manage homelessness', which generally involved local municipalities and non-state bodies providing rudimentary and temporary shelter, usually bleak congregate facilities, for the unfortunate few that descended into homelessness. These basic services, generally linked to various Poor Law facilities and the need to provide for 'itinerant labourers', provided the initial basic framework of provision for those experiencing homelessness. Governments had also taken a particular punitive interest in the vagrant populations of the 19th and early 20th centuries due to their potential disruption of their developing industrial economies, and in a number of European countries, particularly Germany, Switzerland and Belgium, vagrant colonies were established to contain and restrain this mobile population (Busch-Geertsema, 2001; Maeseele et al, 2014). The gradual growth of welfare supports in the first half of the 20th century, and the establishment of more or less comprehensive welfare states in the second half, effectively managed the tensions generated by market economies and put in place a series of programmes 'to render market capitalism habitable for humans and compatible with modern democracy' (Garland, 2016: 137).

However, despite the broad and often comprehensive welfare programmes associated with welfare states, particularly after the Second World War, they failed to provide for a relatively small residual population of largely single homeless men; referred to as 'NFAs' (those of 'no fixed abode') or simply 'vagrants' in Europe, and 'skid-rowers' in North America. In addition to the existing municipal provision, a range of non-state bodies, either as part of their overall charitable endeavour or established specifically to work with this group, responded to the inability of universalistic welfare services to meet their needs (Wallich-Clifford, 1974; Stewart, 1975). For example, in the early 1980s, there were 47 institutions providing 2,383 shelter beds for adults in Denmark (Borner Stax, 1999: 94), and in Dublin, there were nearly 20 public and largely private institutions providing 1,400 shelter beds for adults (Housing Centre, 1986), as well as 2,121 shelter beds in Helsinki (Y Foundation, 2017).

This was a particularly gender-blind understanding of homelessness, with women only occasionally appearing in eccentric supporting roles to this male world (for further details, see O'Sullivan, 2016b). Thus, during the 'golden age' of the welfare state, homelessness policy, albeit largely implicit, was to allow various non-state actors to provide residual services for a residual population, which was expected to gradually fade away due to its age and disabilities. However, by the early 1980s, and most visibly in the US, it became clear that homelessness had not faded away with the advance of welfare states, but due to reconfigurations in welfare provision from the mid-1970s onwards, particularly in liberal welfare regimes, appeared to be growing and was no longer experienced almost exclusively by single, white males. Referred to in the US as the 'new homeless' (Shlay and Rossi, 1992; Lee et al, 2010), those experiencing homelessness were increasingly families with child dependants, young people and minority groups. In Europe, the first synthesis report on homelessness in the European Union (containing 12 member states) in the early 1990s described homelessness as a 'rising tide' (Daly, 1992), albeit based on less than robust data. Not only were the numbers experiencing homelessness growing across the European Union, but similar to the US, those experiencing homelessness were increasingly women and those aged between 20 and 35 (Avramov, 1995).

These increases in the numbers experiencing homelessness were broadly associated with economic and social changes: the hyper-casualisation of labour markets (the loss of full-time, relatively well-paid work and the increase in more casual, low-paid, part-time work); drops in the supply of affordable housing; and cuts to welfare systems. There were also social and cultural changes in society creating shifts in extended family structures, social cohesion and social networks, which could remove the informal supports that had previously helped to prevent and end homelessness.

As the numbers experiencing homelessness grew during the 1980s and 1990s, the basic model of provision that had prevailed for single males for most of the 19th and 20th centuries – the provision of congregate shelter facilities providing basic subsistence infused with various strands of rehabilitative, religious and redemptive assumptions – was expanded and modified to cover new groups. For example, youth homelessness was identified early on in a number of countries as a distinctive cohort of the 'new homeless', and the provision of shelter or other forms of residential services was a common response to youth homelessness. A remarkably consistent finding of studies into the operation of such facilities is the belief that young people needed structure in their lives to reverse their homelessness, and that congregate residential facilities could best instil the required structure and discipline. Even as the edifice of emergency shelter and transitional accommodation responses to homelessness was rapidly expanding for single adults, families and youth, increasingly sophisticated research into the dynamics and drivers of homelessness was questioning these policy responses to homelessness.

Understanding the dynamics and drivers of homelessness

The underlying ideology of the shelter-based response was that people should be provided with immediate relief for literal or street homelessness; then, once sheltered, a range of other services could be put in place to prepare those experiencing homelessness for housing through a series of self-improving measures, such as ensuring sobriety or abstinence from drugs and providing treatment for the symptoms of mental ill health, addiction, physical ill health, limiting illness or other disabilities. Despite a broad academic consensus that structural factors were driving the increase in the number of people experiencing homelessness, services largely responded to homelessness as a set of personal inadequacies and deficiencies that required addressing and resolving before any attempt would be made to house them. The logic was that services were only setting people 'up for failure' if housing was provided without the underlying personal inadequacies being addressed. After these personal issues were confronted, acknowledged and resolved, individuals could then move through a series of transitional and short-term rental contracts, determined by their level of engagement with their psychiatrist, therapist, counsellor and/or social worker, and if such engagement was determined to be satisfactory, there was the possibility of a secure rental contract at the end of process. This Housing Ready or Staircase model, necessarily simplified in this description because practice varied enormously by services and jurisdiction, was based on an understanding of people experiencing homelessness as deficient in a number of personal domains, which required various expert interventions to remedy along a continuum of temporary, usually congregate, accommodation before achieving independent housing. In practice, it was often difficult to identify Housing Ready services that conformed to all the characteristics described earlier, but the use of the term signalled a broad ideological disposition to understanding homelessness as resulting from various personal deficiencies that required managing and resolving prior to consideration for housing.

This understanding of homelessness, and thus the construction of the service response, was not all that surprising as it was based on the observed characteristics of those who were presenting as homeless, and those who were entrenched in emergency shelter services or literally homeless. Irrespective of country or city investigated, shelters for people experiencing homelessness were invariably full of individuals, largely single males, exhibiting symptoms of alcohol/drug abuse and/or mental/physical ill health. While the service response to homelessness for much of the 20th century in Europe and North America was not explicitly based on research evidence, the service response nonetheless chimed with the known characteristics of people experiencing homelessness. The research from cross-sectional surveys of those experiencing homelessness clearly showed that a high proportion of people in shelters or rough sleeping exhibited a range of disabilities, often long term and profound. These disabilities explained both their entry into homelessness and their restricted exit options until these underlying disabilities were addressed (Shlay and Rossi, 1992).

From Los Angeles to London, from Dublin to Düsseldorf, and from Texas to Tallinn, those experiencing homelessness, particularly the visible homeless, seemed remarkably similar in their characteristics. For example, in one of the first accounts of homeless men in London, it was noted that homeless men could easily be identified by their physical characteristics: 'Filthy and dishevelled, with face often blackened by the smoke of fires which are lit in derelict houses or bombed sites, the Skid Row alcoholic is not difficult to recognise' (Edwards et al, 1966: 249). In Dublin, Kearns (1984: 227) described the majority of the homeless population as 'completely disaffiliated from family and friends and suffering emotional and psychological disorders; all have some difficulty in the coping with the daily demands of life'. Studies from the 1960s from the US also suggested that much homelessness was quasi-voluntary, being a 'way of life', as suggested in the classic account by Wallace (1965) in the 1960s, or a process of 'disaffiliation' (Bahr, 1973) from the norms and structures of society, requiring containment and management by the police (Bittner, 1967). In this context, the provision of shelters and hostels that would provide rudimentary sleeping and eating facilities, with defined geographical areas, was an appropriate response to the very basic needs of these deviant, disabled, deranged and drunken individuals that existed outside of the mainstream of society.

Managed primarily by non-state bodies, some believed that securing release from skid row could only come through the salvation of the soul, and hence had a strong evangelical emphasis; for others, the more secular 'disease of alcoholism' was the cause of their downfall, and salvation could only be attained through the treatment of the 'disease' (Garret, 1989). In brief, literal homelessness was perceived as the outcome of a gradual process of withdrawal from the norms and conventions of society that was largely voluntaristic but often exacerbated by various diseases and disabilities, particularly the 'disease of alcoholism'. Curing or controlling these disabilities and diseases was logically the first step in assisting their return to mainstream society; however, despite the intensive interventions of pastors, police, counsellors and carers, their efforts were largely unsuccessful. In reality, a closer historical reading shows much more heterogeneity among those experiencing homelessness, rather than the stereotypical drunk and/or discharged mentally ill patient (Stark, 1992); the archetypal 'skid row wino' was, in reality, a stereotype that obscured 'the differences to be found among the men on skid row' (Peterson and Maxwell, 1958: 308).

Alternative interpretations of homelessness: ethnographic and longitudinal research

By the 1980s, both ethnographic and longitudinal studies of people experiencing homelessness were increasingly highlighting the limitations of cross-sectional research (Koegal, 1992) as the basis for formulating policy responses to those experiencing homelessness. Snow et al (1994), utilising ethnographic data from Austin, Texas and Los Angeles, argued that cross-sectional research methods were unwittingly distorting the reality of homelessness, resulting in a truncated, decontextualised and over-pathologised picture of the homeless. Not only did this picture tell us relatively little about life on the streets as it is actually lived; it also glossed over the highly adaptive, resourceful and creative character of many of the homeless, some of which may be mistaken as pathological (Snow et al, 1994: 473). Thus, in hindsight, a distorted and skewed understanding of homelessness emerged from the 'skid row' studies of the 1950s and 1960s, and this heavily pathologised portrayal of homelessness, with its population of drunken, deviant, damaged and disaffiliated males supplemented with a small number of 'shopping-bag ladies', persisted among the public and policymakers well after the disappearance of skid rows. On the other hand, interventions by service providers to rehabilitate homeless people through religious conversion was deemed a failure 'on a colossal scale' (Rooney, 1980: 904) and managing and reducing problematic alcohol consumption could best be achieved through housing with support in the community, rather than in 'treatment centres' for alcoholics (Stark, 1987; Hopper, 1989).

The limitations of cross-sectional research were also apparent in the debates from the 1970s onwards in understanding the links between psychiatric deinstitutionalisation, mental ill health and homelessness. The deinstitutionalisation of patients from psychiatric hospitals from the 1960s onward was often cited as a contributor to the emergence of the 'new homelessness' from the early 1980s (Shlay and Rossi, 1992; Lee et al, 2010). If, indeed, many of those appearing on the streets were those discharged from psychiatric institutions, then the provision of congregate shelter provision for them made some intuitive sense as it simply replaced one form of institutional care with another. In the US, and no doubt elsewhere, the perception of the causes of homelessness also had important financial implications. As Stern (1984) notes, if homelessness was a consequence of psychiatric deinstitutionalisation, it was therefore a mental health issue and the responsibility of the state; if it was a housing and welfare issue, it was the responsibility of the city budget rather than the state budget. However, ethnographic work by Snow et al (1986) and by Hopper (1988) cast significant doubt on the psychiatric discharge thesis, and more rigorous analyses demonstrated the difficulty of 'making empirical connections between deinstitutionalisation and homelessness' (Montgomery et al, 2013: 61). Crucially, this research identified the difficulty of distinguishing between the symptoms of mental illness and behaviours that reflected an adaptation to living in public spaces or congregate shelters, thus potentially leading to bias in attributing homelessness to mental ill health due to inadequate diagnostic assessments. Claims of high rates of mental illness among those experiencing homelessness arose from the limitations of the predominantly cross-sectional methodology, and 'confounded the understanding of those who became homeless with those who remained homeless' (Montgomery et al, 2013: 64).

A further strand of research identified that access to services for people experiencing homelessness, particularly access to housing services, often required a formal diagnosis of serious mental illness. Homeless outreach workers thus 'fitted' their clients to meet the criteria for housing, artificially constructing a high rate of serious mental illness among those experiencing homelessness (Smith and Anderson, 2018). Overall, in a review of research on deinstitutionalisation, serious mental illness and homelessness, Montgomery et al (2013: 68) concluded that 'the research supports there being nothing inherent to serious mental illness that leads to homelessness, rather this link is mitigated by the economic difficulties that often accompany living with mental illness in the community'.

The distorting influence of cross-sectional research in terms of policy design and service provision was starkly highlighted in the pioneering work of Culhane and colleagues in the 1990s, utilising longitudinal shelter data. Cluster analyses of time-series data on shelter admissions in New York and Philadelphia showed a clear pattern whereby approximately 80 per cent of shelter users were transitional users, in that they used shelters for very short periods of time or a single episode and did not return to homelessness. A further 10 per cent were episodic users of shelters, and the remaining 10 per cent were termed chronic or long-term users of shelter services. Although a relatively small percentage of single homeless people, these chronic or long-term users occupied half of all bed nights, in addition to being heavy users of criminal justice and emergency health services, and had high rates of mental health and substance abuse treatment (Kuhn and Culhane, 1998). Conversely, the largest group of transitional users had low rates of mental health or substance abuse treatment and were younger than the chronic users, and their single shared characteristic was poverty (Burt, 2001).

What this research made apparent was that cross-sectional research was capturing the 'demographics and disabilities' of the minority 'chronic homeless' population but failing to adequately capture the majority of people who experienced homelessness over a period of time. This pattern of shelter use first identified by Kuhn and Culhane has been replicated in similar analyses of longitudinal data in, for example, Denmark, Canada and Ireland (see Aubry et al, 2013; Benjaminsen and Andrade, 2015; Waldron et al, 2019).

For example, the case of Dublin shows that long stay or chronic shelter users, comprising 12 per cent of all users, occupied 50 per cent of all bed nights between 2012 and 2016. Episodic users, accounting for 10 per cent of shelter users, consumed 15 per cent of bed nights. Thus, 22 per cent of shelter users, the chronic and episodic, accounted for 65 per cent of all bed nights between 2012 and 2016 (Waldron et al, 2019). However, the pattern for families is appreciably different from the pattern exhibited by single adults. The numbers of long-term, chronic users are significantly higher, at 25 per cent of all family users of services for homeless people, or 1,726 families, staying an average of 407 nights and consuming 60 per cent of family bed nights. Only 2 per cent were in the episodic category and the remaining 73 per cent used the services on a temporary basis, staying an average of 80 days.

In the case of Denmark, episodic users accounted for 7 per cent and chronic users accounted for 16 per cent of all shelter users, but this 23 per cent occupied 75 per cent of all bed nights, though in a context in which larger-scale homelessness associated with poverty appeared to be largely prevented via an extensive welfare system. However, in contrast to the US data, a high proportion of shelter users in Denmark have complex support needs, among both long-term and short-term shelter users. The high share of homeless people with either mental illness or substance abuse problems reflects the fact that in a country like Denmark with a relatively low level of poverty and with an extensive welfare system, fewer people become homeless solely due to poverty and housing unaffordability (Benjaminsen and Andrade, 2015). Thus, while the *pattern* of shelter use is remarkably similar across a number of countries with very different welfare systems, the *characteristics* of shelter users vary considerably, as demonstrated by the Danish data, where the transitional shelter users show similar rates of disability to the chronic and episodic users, unlike the case in the US. The pattern of shelter use in Ireland is similar, but data are not available on the characteristics of shelter users in terms of support needs, and in the case of Finland, no data are available on the patterns of shelter use. However, it seems plausible to suggest that the profiles of shelter users in terms of support needs, particularly the transitional shelter users in Finland, are more likely to be similar to the Danish transitional shelter users than the American transitional shelter users.

This chronic population of people experiencing homelessness has three main characteristics. The first is that existing services only partially meet their needs, fail to meet their needs altogether or cannot engage with them properly to begin with. The second is that they can be financially expensive; those who are in the category of chronic homelessness also have an increased use of emergency health, mental health and addiction services, as well as an increased use of ambulances and hospitals, and, in some cases, keep getting picked up and processed by criminal justice systems. Alongside this, some of this population get stuck in homelessness services, staying for prolonged periods in, what are meant to be, temporary support and accommodation services, or moving from one homelessness service to another on an unending loop. The third characteristic is the most important: the effect on individual mental and/or physical health and on relationships, both in terms of stigmatisation and in terms of very early mortality, can be catastrophic (Pleace and Culhane, 2016).

Therefore, residential instability due to periodic shortages of affordable housing, rather than individual-level disabilities, was seen as explaining why the majority of individuals entered homeless services, particularly in the US. Nonetheless, in countries like the US, UK, Denmark and Ireland, between 20 and 25 per cent of those who enter emergency homeless shelters stay for considerable periods on a consecutive or intermittent basis, and are people who do, indeed, have a range of disabilities but become 'stuck' in existing services and/or refuse to enter such services. In addition, as noted earlier, while a high proportion of transitional shelter users in Denmark had a substance misuse or mental health issue, they did not get 'stuck' in the shelter system, suggesting that extensive welfare services resulted in their shelter use being transitional rather than chronic or episodic. Long-term shelter users and those literally homeless on the streets are also high-volume and costly users of a range of other emergency services.

This issue of cost is crucial to understanding homelessness policy in recent years. Chronically and episodically homeless people in the US, where this research originated, who looked very like the long-term homeless Finns, Danes and Irish, were hugely expensive for American taxpayers, and the media story of 'Million Dollar Murray', on whom various elements of the US government and public services had spent around US$1 million but who still died on the street (Gladwell, 2006, was backed up by hard research (Culhane, 2008). However, there were not very many people actually in this group: they were around 10–20 per cent of the homeless population in the US, Denmark and Ireland. This created a powerful financial incentive to reconsider homelessness policy towards a target population that was not overwhelming in size, which meant that it was practical to consider the revision of existing policy.

Cross-sectional research thus failed to capture the dynamics of homelessness, unwittingly conflating the chronic homeless as representative of all of those experiencing homelessness, and failing to grasp that the majority of people who experienced homelessness exited from homelessness relatively quickly, requiring little social support in doing so, and did not return to homelessness. It also crucially failed to capture women's experience of homelessness as women had a greater tendency to use a range of informal supports rather than enter emergency accommodation, or as the emergency accommodation that they utilised, for example, refuges for those escaping gender-based violence, were often not categorised as accommodation for those experiencing homelessness (Bretherton, 2017). Thus, a focus on both emergency accommodation and literal homelessness, allied to the inability of cross-sectional research to uncover the dynamics of homelessness, resulted in a misleading picture of those experiencing homelessness as being largely single males with a range of disabilities, rather than a relatively heterogeneous population in terms of gender, disabilities and duration of homelessness. This, of course, is qualified by the conclusion, based on longitudinal data in the UK, that the risk of experiencing homelessness is 'systematically structured around a set of identifiable individual, social and structural factors, most of which, it should be emphasized, are outside the control of those directly affected' (Bramley and Fitzpatrick, 2018: 112). Culhane et al (2013) have identified a cohort effect in the US whereby those born during the period 1945–64 (particularly the late 'baby boom' generation), through a combination of factors, were at heightened risk of entering and remaining homeless, particularly single people, as evidenced by the ageing of those experiencing homelessness.

In understanding the drivers of homelessness, it was also increasingly clear that depending on the type of data utilised, very different interpretations of homelessness were possible. Individual-level data consistently showed that the single most important factors determining entry to homelessness were personal, while area-level data highlighted the significance of housing and labour markets, eschewing personal characteristics (O'Flaherty, 2004). In Australia, the Journeys Home study was the first study to link individual- and area-level data to understand entries to and exits from homelessness (Johnson et al, 2015). These data show that tight housing markets and high rates of unemployment do matter, but that they matter in different ways for different groups. Single individuals with various social and health issues are at a higher risk of homelessness irrespective of the nature of housing and labour markets; however, for families and couples with these personal issues, housing and labour markets matter a lot.

In brief, over the past 20 years or so, our understanding of entries to and exits from homelessness has been shaped by increasingly sophisticated methodological approaches, in particular, the use of longitudinal administrative and survey data (Culhane, 2016), in addition to randomised control trials (RCTs), particularly in researching the effectiveness of Housing First versus Housing Ready approaches to resolving homelessness (for further details on Housing First, see later). However, much of the research on homelessness in Europe suffered from the same methodological limitations as the North American research: a predominance of cross-sectional methods meant longitudinal and ethnographic work was still relatively rare.

Critique of service responses

As the numbers of people experiencing homelessness grew from the 1980s onwards in the majority of Western countries, a model of service provision gradually evolved that saw large congregate shelters as the front-line response for people experiencing homelessness. Such shelters provided a basic humanitarian response which ensured that people were not literally on the streets: they provided what the Americans termed 'three hots and a cot', as well as a place and a space to assess the needs of the person using the service in order to understand the reasons for their homelessness and what remedies were required for them to exit homelessness. Some countries, including Sweden and the US, had a formal 'continuum of care' (Hoch, 2010) or 'staircase of transition' (Sahlin, 2005) where homeless people with high and complex needs were moved from congregate shelters to various forms of transitional accommodation designed to prepare them for their eventual self-contained accommodation. Other countries had more informal and heterogeneous provision, which included elements that were housing led, in that housing solutions were prioritised, and Housing Ready-type services, which focused on enhancing personal capacities; however, the provision of usually congregate emergency and temporary accommodation on various scales was, and remains, the fundamental response in all countries.

The role of congregate institutional shelters, hostels and/or lodging houses in providing emergency and temporary accommodation for people experiencing residential instability has a long history (see, for example, Hopper, 1990a, 1990b; Busch-Geertsema and Sahlin, 2007). While the popularity of congregate emergency and temporary accommodation as a response to homelessness has ebbed and flowed it has shown remarkable resilience, remaining a constant presence and the default position for responding to periodic surges in residential instability in the majority of Western countries. Such services are currently provided by a range of agencies, including municipal authorities, private for-profit providers and non-profit providers, which often have a strong presence of religiously inspired organisations but 'vary substantially in terms of size, client group, type of building, levels and nature of support, behavioural expectations, nature and enforcement of rules, level of "professionalization" and seasonal availability' (Mackie et al, 2017: x). Despite extensive critiques of the limitations of this form of congregate accommodation as a response to residential instability, and the largely negative experience of those who reside in such facilities, this form of congregate accommodation remains the single most significant intervention in the lives of people experiencing homelessness in a majority of Western countries, even though they have been described in a recent report as 'oversubscribed, insecure and unsuitable' (Serme-Morin and Coupechoux, 2019).

Earlier debates, particularly centred around New York, on the concept of 'shelterisation' – the idea either that congregate institutional emergency accommodation created various forms of deviancy or that deviants were attracted to such accommodation (Marcus, 2003) – have largely been replaced with several critiques. First, there is the inherent contradiction of imposing rules and regulations that restrict individual autonomy, and are often infantilising in tone, in shelters whose overt objective is to promote autonomy in order to facilitate exiting the shelter, thus acting to create a 'role conflict' that allows shelter users to survive shelter life but limits their ability to achieve sustained exits to independent accommodation (Gounis, 1992; Stark, 1994; Lyon-Callo, 2000; Wallerstein, 2014). Second, the worldview of shelter providers sees homelessness as a result of individual pathology and designs services around treating these ostensible pathologies, rather than seeing shelters as a temporary respite from bouts of residential instability (Wasserman and Clair, 2013). Third, despite the rules and regulations, the violence and intimidation often evident in such congregate settings can result in some of the most vulnerable people rejecting entreaties to enter shelters. Fourth, the objective of providing care in shelters is 'severely adulterated' (Ranasinghe, 2017: 8) by the problematic and often provocative provision of 'security' (Hansen Löfstrand, 2015), and the legal rules governing the running of the shelter always take precedence over the provision of care. Fifth, those with the most complex needs and who do enter shelters are often excluded because they pose difficulties in meeting managerial targets, thus receiving less professional support (Quirouette, 2016). Sixth, shelter usage reflects broader policies in housing, social and health systems, and the role of shelters is 'tied to the functioning of the social welfare system and will be more determined by its policies than the policies that govern the behaviour of shelter clients and providers' (Culhane, 1992: 439). Finally, managing homelessness through the provision of emergency congregate shelters is extraordinarily expensive, and a minority of shelter users also make extensive use of other expensive emergency health services (Culhane, 2008) as they traverse through institutional circuits of short stays in various services without ever resolving their residential instability (Hopper et al, 1997).

Just as the role of congregate institutional emergency accommodation was critiqued and the limitations of such accommodation were laid bare, the role of transitional accommodation equally came under scrutiny and the limitations of this form of accommodation were identified, with Gerstal et al (1996) describing such facilities for families experiencing homelessness as a form of 'therapeutic incarceration'. Furthermore, the development of these residential services for people experiencing homelessness were often accompanied by the provision of mental health, addiction and other social services, leading Culhane and Metraux (2008: 112) to argue that the continuum of care policy in the US 'institutionalised a parallel social welfare system' that allowed mainstream services 'to largely ignore their clients' housing problems, a situation which limits their effectiveness and mitigates their accountability'.

The archetypical service responses that appeared when homelessness services began to focus more on support were the Housing Ready, 'treatment-led' or Staircase models. These were designed to 'correct' behaviours, particularly addiction, that were thought to trigger and sustain homelessness. Further, they aimed to treat the diseases and illnesses, particularly poor mental health, that were also thought to trigger and prolong homelessness, and to produce individuals who were capable of living largely or wholly independent lives once they had finished with the services. Homeless people using these services completed a series of steps that involved transitioning from a state of being defined as not being ready to live independently, through to, eventually, being judged 'housing ready'.

These services were suspended somewhere between the essentially surveillant responses of the 19th and early 20th centuries. They were designed to contain and discipline a population that was seen as disruptive, criminal and excluding itself from mainstream society for its own ends, for example, to live an itinerant alcohol-dependent lifestyle. There was also a re-conceptualisation of homelessness that medicalised the problem, positing that homeless people were homeless because they were mentally ill.

Multiple challenges stemmed from these Housing Ready approaches emerging from the 1990s onwards. Gaining traction throughout the 2000s, the service models were increasingly criticised as dehumanising, surveillant, costly and, all too often, relatively ineffective (Sahlin, 2005). While there are arguments that, in some instances, these services failed because they were not standardised, properly tested or properly resourced (Rosenheck, 2010), failures still outnumbered successes (Pleace, 2008). The Housing Ready model had been adopted from mental health services but the original Staircase model for former psychiatric patients had been abandoned in favour of a 'supported housing' model that would go on to be the basis of Housing First (Ridgway and Zipple, 1990; Tsemberis, 2010a).

As the response to the increasing numbers of people experiencing homelessness focused on the provision of further institutional beds, in New York, an alternative and evidence-based response to homelessness, specifically, the chronic, long-term homeless, was emerging through a programme entitled Pathways to Housing led by Sam Tsemberis (the programme was later to become popularly known as Housing First). This approach demonstrated that individuals with significant disabilities experiencing long-term homelessness were capable of retaining their accommodation if they were provided with independent housing, given choice and control in their lives, and provided with floating support services for any addiction, mental health or other disability. In the case of a minority of the high-risk and/or high-cost users, this also resulted in significantly less use of costly health and criminal justice services (Padgett et al, 2016). Additionally, treatment for addiction or mental ill health was not a prerequisite for successful housing retention (Hall et al, 2018). The knowledge of the costs of effectively maintaining people in homelessness, via the provision of congregate emergency and temporary accommodation, demonstrated that it was both fiscally responsible and ethically justifiable to provide evidence-based housing responses to homelessness, with support where necessary; this was based on the financial costs to the government and damage to the capabilities and productivity of individuals if their homelessness was not ended (Parsell et al, 2017; Pleace and Culhane, 2016.

The emergence of Housing First

The emergence of Housing First as an evidence-based response to the needs of those experiencing homelessness with high support needs is emblematic of this shift and a response to the critique of the utility of the shelter system. Housing First uses housing as a starting point rather than an end goal, providing both housing and support services simultaneously, enabling someone to successfully live in their own home as part of a community and aiming to improve the health, well-being and social support networks of the homeless people it works with. This is very different from homelessness services that try to make homeless people with high support needs 'housing ready' before they are rehoused.

However, the term Housing First is used in a fairly promiscuous manner, particularly by service providers, with some services providing services that they term 'Housing First' bearing only a very tangential resemblance to the Housing First model pioneered by Sam Tsemberis and Pathways to Housing in New York (Padgett et al, 2016). This has resulted in a debate on the importance and appropriateness of fidelity to the original model, the degree of variation that is possible to reflect local housing markets and social service provision, and, indeed, whether the adoption of Housing First policies in certain countries, particularly Finland, bore any relationship to the model developed in New York. In addition, following the European Consensus Conference in 2010, organised by the European Federation of National Organisations Working with the Homeless (FEANTSA) and the Belgian presidency of the European Commission, the term 'housing-led' was used to refer to the development of *policies* to address homelessness, rather than *programmes* to address homelessness, such as Housing First.

The initial results from Housing First in the US were very impressive. In the 1990s, existing Staircase model services in New York were losing 40 per cent of service users before they were rehoused, compared to 15 per cent for Housing First, at two years of service contact. What was more, Housing First appeared to be significantly more cost efficient than existing Staircase services (Tsemberis and Asmussen, 1999). Over time, the evidence about the Tsemberis model of Housing First increased and those involved in the development model began to talk in terms of Housing First creating a paradigmatic shift in strategic as well as service delivery-level responses to homelessness (Padgett et al, 2016).

Housing First, as designed by Tsemberis, was targeted on homeless people with a psychiatric diagnosis, including those who were also presenting with addiction. The Housing First model employed Intensive Case Management (ICM) and Assertive Community Treatment (ACT). The former can be summarised as giving social and practical support, and coordinating existing services together. The latter ACT model is characterised as an interdisciplinary group of health, addiction, mental health and homelessness professionals; both used mobile support teams. There were also peer support workers and a team focused on finding and securing the housing that was needed, working mainly with private landlords.

Beyond the use of ordinary housing and mobile support, the employment of a harm-reduction approach, an emphasis on service-user choice and control, and the separation of housing and support were all quite radical in the US. As noted, the majority of existing services required abstinence from drugs and alcohol; they did not seek to reduce harm, nor did they offer open-ended support. Housing was conditional on abstinence, treatment compliance and conditionality linked to behavioural change. Further, a homeless person was not given a home that was independently theirs, regardless of whether or not they were compliant with service requirements.

By European standards, the original US Housing First programme was not quite as relaxed and empowering as it sometimes portrayed itself. There were, and are, deep-seated American ideas about the nature of the individual and society, and how social problems should be responded to, engrained in how Housing First operated (Hansen Löfstrand and Juhila, 2012). There was a requirement for people to engage with Housing First front-line workers and the integral 'recovery orientation' meant that the service was still working towards behavioural change around addiction, treatment compliance and other issues that were seen as undermining someone's capacity to maintain an independent home. Housing First also tended to not offer direct tenancies to service users, instead using subletting arrangements, which meant that they did not have the same housing rights as an ordinary citizen. The service also ran people's bank accounts, ensuring that all service users' bills were paid before giving them what was, in effect, an allowance or pocket money (Tsemberis, 2010a, 2010b). The original Housing First was something of a revolution but it also had restricted tenancy rights, exercised financial controls over service users and had an overall goal centred on behavioural modification that did not look all that progressive to some European eyes (Hansen Löfstrand and Juhila, 2012).

The expansion of Housing First across the US that happened during the 2000s was not necessarily an organised process. Federal funding, the requirements for which did not go into a great amount of detail about what Housing First should be, became available but the lack of precision about what Housing First was, combined with significant public money being available for service development, led to inconsistencies. There were congregate models using dedicated apartment buildings, shared housing models, scattered housing models and services that varied in the intensity and underlying philosophy of the support that they provided from the original Tsemberis model (Pearson et al, 2009). Critics began targeting Housing First as being an inconsistent set of services that lacked clarity in design and objectives. The outcomes being achieved by Housing First were also questioned, particularly as evidence of 'success' did not really extend beyond good rates of getting people into housing and keeping them there, whereas improvements in physical and mental health, addiction, and socioeconomic integration were less evident (Kertesz et al, 2009; Tabol et al, 2009; Stanhope and Dunn, 2011). A reality of programme drift was firmly in place by the late 2000s and 'Housing First' referred to more than one kind of service in the US (Pleace, 2011).

A group of US, European and Canadian academics moved to counteract these criticisms and argue that in order to work properly, a Housing First service had to closely replicate the original Pathways to Housing model created by Sam Tsemberis in the early 1990s (Greenwood et al, 2013a; Padgett et al, 2016; Aubry et al, 2018). The Canadian and French national Housing First programmes, At Home/ *Chez Soi* and *Un Chez-Soi d'Abord*, were highly influenced by these arguments for preserving fidelity with the original version of Housing First. Both countries pursued the development of high-fidelity models, using well-resourced pilot programmes tested by RCTs, led by public health agencies and targeted towards homeless people with a diagnosis of severe mental illness. In both cases, a national programme was rolled out following the completion of successful piloting (Tinland et al, 2013; Aubry et al, 2015).

Meanwhile, elsewhere in Europe, experiments were happening with Housing First services that were not very high fidelity in terms of the detail of their operation. These services used social housing, offering full tenancy rights to service users, and created their own versions of high-intensity support services, rather than precisely following the ICM and ACT mental health models used by the original Housing

First service (Busch-Geertsema, 2013; Pleace and Bretherton, 2013). These versions of Housing First, in the Netherlands and the UK, were also targeted differently, being aimed at all long-term homeless populations, not just people diagnosed with a severe mental illness.

In the context of the comparatively much more extensive social protection and public health systems of North-Western Europe, Housing First was sometimes being organised as a highly flexible, intensive case-management service using social housing, without the onus on behavioural modification and with full housing rights with the people they worked with. Some emerging European services were low fidelity in respect of their detailed operation. However, these European versions of Housing First did retain a high degree of philosophical consistency with the original model, emphasising service-user choice and control, harm reduction, and independent housing. Success rates also appeared comparable to those for services that more closely matched the original Tsemberis model (Pleace and Bretherton, 2013).

A later exercise attempting to reconcile different versions of Housing First across Europe in order to produce broadly applicable guidance was conducted in 2015 and 2016. This produced a somewhat more flexible set of principles for Housing First in Europe (Pleace, 2016b: 28): 'housing is a human right; choice and control for service users; separation of housing and treatment; recovery orientation; harm reduction; active engagement without coercion; person centred planning, and flexible support for as long as is required'.

Operational details as to whether or not housing is privately rented or socially rented, as well as the degree and level of expectations placed on service users in terms of maintaining contact with the Housing First service, were left fairly open. The targeting of Housing First was not specified. However, the approach being described in the pan-European guidance was still relatively directive in respect of 'active engagement without coercion' and a 'recovery orientation', compared to some of the emergent European Housing First services, which were more relaxed about whether behavioural change needed to be encouraged (Busch-Geertsema, 2013; Pleace and Bretherton, 2013).

However, variation remained widespread. France has high fidelity to the original model (Rhenter et al, 2018), as does the Housing First service in Dublin (Manning et al, 2018), as well as some, though importantly not all, Danish services (Benjaminsen and Knutagård, 2016; Bretherton and Pleace, 2015). By contrast, Italian, British and Swedish experiments with Housing First tend to have much lower budgets and follow the broad philosophy rather than the operational details (Knutagård and Kristiansen, 2013; Lancione et al, 2018). There are also relatively well-resourced services that follow an ICM-only model, for example, in the Netherlands (Wewerinke et al, 2013).

The best-known example of a Housing First approach to ending homelessness in Europe is that of Finland (Y Foundation, 2017). Although the Finns chose to describe their approach to ending homelessness as 'Housing First', and it does reflect a number of common values and insights, there are some aspects of confusion in policy terms. Finland developed their approach to tackling homelessness before they discovered the 'model' of Housing First developed in New York. Hence, it is a mistake to see the Finnish case as an example of 'policy transfer' as the Finnish approach developed separately. The differences in practice are discussed in Chapter 5, but the distinction is between Housing First as a programme (based on the Pathways model) and Housing First as a system (as in the Finnish model).

Rethinking homelessness services: research and practice

The implications of this new understanding of homelessness as a dynamic and fluid process pointed to the provision of preventive services and rapid rehousing for those individuals who did experience homelessness as the most effective policy and service responses, rather than the construction of multilayered, intensive remedial services. There was also a growing awareness that in the US, the majority of those experiencing homelessness had few, if any, disabilities; rather, the insufficiency of income to access market-rented housing or the lack of priority for social housing, particularly for single people, largely explained their entries into homelessness. The profile of people experiencing homelessness in more generous and extensive welfare systems showed higher rates of disability among shelter users; however, some four decades after the emergence of the 'new homeless', a range of evidence-based differentiated responses to those experiencing homelessness is nonetheless increasingly apparent across North America, Australia and Europe.

These evidence-based responses to homelessness for those experiencing chronic or literal homelessness stress, above all, the need for preventive services in the first instance, rapid rehousing with income support for those entering homelessness for the first time and permanent housing, with support as required, not temporary shelter in congregate facilities (Culhane and Metraux, 2008; Mackie et al, 2017; Pleace, 2018). The form of housing (social, private, scattered site and so on) and models of tenancy support, from ACT to ICM, varies significantly, but they can all be described as 'housing-led' responses to long-term homelessness. In many cases, these evidence-based differentiated responses operate alongside traditional congregate shelter-based services, and in most countries, shelter-based services remain the dominant response for people experiencing homelessness.

Ending homelessness: policy and progress in Denmark, Finland and Ireland

Despite the persistence of traditional responses, by the beginning of the 21st century, much of the pessimism and fatalism associated with resolving homelessness was dissipating, albeit with significant geographical variation and pace, as sustainable solutions to homelessness were proliferating across Europe and North America. This book aims to explore in detail the experience of three relatively small members of the European Union – Denmark, Finland and Ireland – that adopted strategic plans in 2007/08 to end homelessness, understood as achieving a 'functional zero'. In the Irish case, 'functional zero' meant that no person would be in emergency accommodation for more than six months and the need to sleep rough would be eliminated. In the case of Denmark, the maximum time spent in a hostel should be reduced to three to four months, and in Finland, the numbers experiencing long-term homelessness should be reduced by half by 2011 to achieve 'functional zero'. In their strategic plans, the three countries also endorsed a policy shift in the way in which services for people experiencing homelessness were provided, arguing for a shift from the dominance of shelter-led provision to the provision of housing with support as the primary response. All three countries also have comparatively sophisticated and reasonably accurate means of measuring the trends in homelessness on a point-in-time, time-series basis, and some data on measuring intervention outcomes, thus allowing us to measure the degree to which the strategies were effective on their own terms.

In the case of Finland, the 2008 strategy had the goal of halving long-term homelessness by 2011. However, a second strategy in 2012 aimed to eliminate long-term homelessness by 2015. A third strategy, covering 2016–19, had a focus on prevention, and continued building new dwellings. The target is to build or allocate 3,500 dwellings over the period for people that are homeless or at risk of becoming homeless (Pleace, 2017). All three strategies adopted key elements of the Housing First approach, albeit with a distinctive Finnish flavour, building services that were found to be similar to the original Pathways model of Housing First but not directly derived from it, prompting discussions with, rather than inspiration from, North Americans. The Finns also took the broader concept of 'Housing First' in the sense of emphasising the human right to an adequate home, and they built an entire strategy around it, a truly housing-led response to all forms of homelessness. As such, Finnish references to 'Housing First' are both about a type of homelessness service and a broader 'Housing First' philosophy (Y Foundation, 2017; Fredriksson, 2018, cited in Ranta, 2019), which we will discuss in further detail in subsequent chapters.

Following the first national homelessness count that took place in 2007, a Danish national homelessness strategy was adopted for 2009–13 (Ministry of Internal and Social Affairs, 2009). A key element of the strategy programme was developing and testing evidence-based floating support methods (ACT, ICM and Critical Time Intervention) in municipal social services, with funding provided from the central government (Benjaminsen, 2013). The strategy programme was succeeded by a follow-up programme, 'The Implementation Programme', from 2014 to 2016 that aimed at anchoring Housing First and the floating support methods in local welfare services in the municipalities that participated in the strategy programme, as well as extending the Housing First approach to other municipalities (Benjaminsen et al, 2017). A third-stage programme from 2017 to 2019, 'Extending Housing First', has a similar objective. However, whereas the strategy programme had substantial funding from the central government, the succeeding programmes had much less funding attached as they mainly provided implementation support from central government agencies to municipalities, which had to finance services out of their local budgets.

In Ireland, an early adopter of homeless strategies from 2000, a comprehensive strategy was published in 2008, entitled *The Way Home*, which aimed to ensure that by 2010, 'long-term homelessness and the need for people to sleep rough will be eliminated throughout Ireland'. This strategy implicitly adopted a housing-led approach to ending homelessness, and a review and restatement of the strategy in 2013 explicitly adopted a housing-led approach (O'Sullivan, 2016a) that aimed to end long-term homelessness by 2016. It is also of note that the three countries embraced broadly social inclusionary models of responding to homelessness, and largely eschewed exclusionary means of managing homelessness through punitive responses, such as the criminalisation of rough sleepers. Although the extreme case of penalising homelessness in Hungary (Udvarhelyi, 2014), for example, has gained much attention, it is nonetheless a clear outlier in terms of responding to homelessness, with the majority of member states responding with various inclusionary policies.

From the position in 2008 to the end of 2018, the numbers living rough and in temporary and emergency accommodation (broadly equivalent to the European Typology of Homelessness and Housing Exclusion [ETHOS] categories 1–3 and hence excluding those living with family and friends)[2] (see Table 1.1) showed a decline of 72 per cent in Finland, while the number of households in emergency accommodation increased by 300 per cent in Ireland; in Denmark, the number of adults in emergency accommodation increased by 12 per cent over the shorter time period of 2009–17. The purpose of this book is to offer explanations for stark variations in these outcomes despite similar starting points.

Methodologically, the book adopts a case-oriented approach to comparative research, where we take a small of number of cases – three countries – and look at their policies in relation to homelessness in depth within a historical context. The book seeks only to provide limited generalisability, rather than a broader generalisability as is the case with variable-oriented comparative research, and to provide a narrative that relates 'concrete knowledge about specific processes' (Della Porta, 2013: 203) in relation to the formulation and implementation of policies that sought to end homelessness in Denmark, Finland and Ireland.

The adoption of policies and programmes to end homelessness in the three countries coincided with the onset of the Great Financial Crisis, and we discuss how the crisis impacted on the ambition to end homelessness in Chapters 5 and 6 in particular. In the case of Denmark, 'welfare for the poor has become increasingly weak' (Goul-Andersen, 2019: 208), whereas in Finland, 'the universal welfare state was able to cushion most of the economic shock and guarantee security when most needed' (Kangas, 2019: 173–4). In Ireland, the crisis resulted in a deterioration of already-weak welfare services, particularly housing (Daly, 2019).

In Chapter 2, we provide a detailed analysis of the emergence and content of the homeless strategies in Denmark, Finland and Ireland. While all three countries had various homelessness policy statements and strategies prior to 2008, in all three cases, their 2008/09 strategies were the most ambitious, aiming to end long-term homelessness and the need to sleep rough. Chapter 2 will review the sequence of events that led to the radical shift in policy that aimed to end homelessness and the assumptions about the causes of homelessness in each strategy.

Table 1.1: ETHOS

Conceptual category	Operational category		Living situation	
ROOFLESS	1	People living rough	1.1	Public space or external space
	2	People staying in a night shelter	2.1	Night shelter
HOUSELESS	3	People in accommodation for the homeless	3.1	Homeless hostel
			3.2	Temporary accommodation
			3.3	Transitional supported accommodation
	4	People in a women's shelter	4.1	Women's shelter accommodation
	5	People in accommodation for immigrants	5.1	Temporary accommodation, reception centres
			5.2	Migrant workers' accommodation
	6	People due to be released from institutions	6.1	Penal institutions
			6.2	Medical institutions
			6.3	Children's institutions/homes
	7	People receiving longer-term support (due to homelessness)	7.1	Residential care for older homeless people
			7.2	Supported accommodation for formerly homeless persons
INSECURE	8	People living in insecure accommodation	8.1	Temporarily with family/friends
			8.2	No legal (sub)tenancy
			8.3	Illegal occupation of land
	9	People living under threat of eviction	9.1	Legal orders enforced (rented)
			9.2	Repossession orders (owned)
	10	People living under threat of violence	10.1	Police-recorded incidents
INADEQUATE	11	People living in temporary/non-conventional structures	11.1	Mobile homes
			11.2	Non-conventional building
			11.3	Temporary structure
	12	People living in unfit housing	12.1	Occupied dwelling unfit for habitation
	13	People living in extreme overcrowding	13.1	Highest national norm of overcrowding

Chapter 3 provides a detailed description of the strategies to end homelessness. The strategies of the three countries were published within a relatively short period of each other. The Finnish strategy, *Paavo I*, was launched in February 2008, while the Irish national homeless strategy, entitled *The Way Home: A Strategy to Address Adult Homelessness in Ireland, 2008–2013*, was launched in August 2008 and the Danish strategy, *A Strategy to Reduce Homelessness in Denmark, 2009–2012*, was launched in October 2009. We argue that the three strategies can each be seen to have distinct phases of announcement and implementation. In the case of the Finnish strategies, these build upon each other through a series of achievements and refined objectives, while in the Irish case, the strategies change considerably in format and scope, reflecting the broader economic and political crisis that engulfed the country. The Danish strategy and succeeding programmes fall in between the other two cases, as there is a clear objective and commitment to Housing First across the different stages, whereas the Danish programme did not have as strong an emphasis on general housing provision as the Finnish programme.

In Chapter 4, we outline trends in recorded homelessness in the three countries between about 2008 and 2018. The chapter first explores in some detail how homelessness is measured in each of the three countries as the three countries use a variety of methodologies to measure homelessness and it is important that the strengths and limitations of these different approaches are understood, particularly in relation to their comparability. Having explored the full range of data on homelessness in each country, we then focus on those living rough, in emergency accommodation and in accommodation for the homeless, and data on these forms of homelessness are presented for the three countries. It is important to note that while the comparative figures used in this chapter include only those sleeping rough or in emergency accommodation, this is a pragmatic, rather than an ideological, decision done only because Ireland does not adequately capture the 'hidden homeless', that is, 'people living in insecure accommodation'.

We then turn our attention to explanations in Chapters 5 and 6. These chapters explore how three countries that started the 21st century with relatively modest and similar numbers of homeless households, and expressed similar levels of ambition to reduce homelessness, ended up with very different experiences in the second decade. In Chapter 5, we explore the role of Housing First and then the broader housing market, particularly social housing, in explaining these variations in outcomes, while the impacts of welfare policies and political choices are explored in Chapter 6. Finally, Chapter 7 draws together some of the lessons that can be learned from the experiences of three small European countries in responding to homelessness. It is clear that responses to homelessness are embedded and enmeshed in the political and administrative culture of the individual countries, particularly the role of the state, both centrally and locally, in the provision of housing, welfare, social services and so on. Homelessness cannot be responded to as a separate issue from this broader context, and this is particularly the case in Finland and Ireland, where the roles of the state and market are understood very differently. For example, in Ireland, Housing First is understood in policy and practice as a specific programme for a specified number of people experiencing long-term homelessness (a subgroup of the thousands in emergency accommodation) funded by the state but provided by a non-governmental organisation (NGO). However, in Finland, Housing First reflects an understanding of responding to homelessness with housing as the default position, not the provision of shelter accommodation.

Notes

[1] In the European Union, Portugal, Ireland, Spain, Italy, Norway, Finland, Denmark, Sweden, the Netherlands, Luxembourg, France, Flanders, the constituent members of the UK and the Czech Republic have all produced homeless strategies.

[2] ETHOS was developed as a means of allowing meaningful comparative analysis on the extent of homelessness across different jurisdictions (Busch-Geertsema, 2010).

2

Before the goal of 'ending homelessness': the evolution of policy

Introduction

This book is focused on the formulation and delivery of strategies to end homelessness that the three countries adopted from around 2008. However, it is useful to reflect briefly on the recent history of responses to homelessness in each country as these histories influenced the ways in which the early 21st-century strategies were framed and developed.

The 20th century

Most economically developed countries in Europe, including the three that are the subject of this book, initially pursued policies that were grounded in assumptions about homelessness that began with a picture of lone, economically marginalised, adult men who had, in some way, chosen an itinerant lifestyle, often linked to alcohol dependency. Over the last three decades of the 20th century, homelessness policy was characterised by an increasing emphasis on treatment and support. This shift reflected broader trends across the economically developed world as homelessness came to be seen as associated with sets of shared characteristics such as addiction, alcoholism and severe mental illness.

Finland (Y Foundation, 2017; Fredriksson, 2018, cited in Ranta, 2019), Denmark (Kolstrup, 2014) and Ireland (O'Brien, 1981; Kearns, 1984) all experienced this transition, although the details and time frames varied somewhat across the three countries, as is described later. All three countries also saw the development of social housing at scale. Social housing was seen as an integral part of wider social policy, designed to increase affordable housing supply rather than the pursuit of free market housing policy.

The first phase in homelessness policy was surveillant: an attempt to contain, control and discipline. The second phase stemmed from medicalisation, emphasising the need to treat and support, but this was framed in the context created by the first phase. As the three countries developed their homelessness strategies at the beginning of the 21st century, a third phase in which services started to be modelled differently was underway. Choice, recovery and strength-based approaches, and housing-led models that included, but were not restricted to, what became the global Housing First movement, were gaining momentum.

Denmark

In Denmark, rapid economic growth from the 1960s onwards saw a significant expansion of the welfare state, alongside major shifts in how welfare systems operated. Repressive 'worthiness laws', which applied moralistic conditionality rules for social assistance, were abolished and replaced with the universal principles of support that became a landmark of the Danish, and Scandinavian, welfare state. Systems that had been focused on labour market activation were reoriented towards care and support, creating a network of homeless hostels and shelters that still exist at the time of writing. Public housing expanded rapidly during the 1960s and early 1970s, and today comprises 21 per cent of the total Danish housing stock. This expansion helped alleviate the severe housing shortages of the 1950s and 1960s. Thus, access to housing played an import role in the expansion of the welfare state. The 'Golden Age' of the Danish welfare state culminated with the General Support Act 1976 and its far-reaching rights to income and support given to citizens, depending on their needs.

The public housing sector is non-profit, subsidised and open to everyone, regardless of income level, with access coming through general waiting lists (Skifter Andersen, 2010). Individuals on transfer incomes pay rent directly from their benefit, and supplementary housing benefits are available to a wider group of individuals with low income. According to the Act on Social Housing, municipalities are able to allocate up to 20 per cent of all flats in public housing that become vacant each year to individuals in acute housing need. In the capital, Copenhagen, where the demand for public housing is high, the allocation of one third of vacancies has been negotiated between the municipality and public housing organisations.

However, when the realities of the financial crisis in the 1970s set in, the now extensive welfare system increasingly came under pressure. Although there was an economic recovery in the mid-1980s, welfare reforms and cutbacks began that would continue into the 1990s, resulting in a constriction of services. The completion of new public housing units fell dramatically in the 1980s compared to earlier decades. The general pressure on welfare services meant that the deinstitutionalisation of psychiatric hospitals from the late 1970s was not accompanied by sufficient mobile and floating support services to reintegrate people with complex support needs into the local community. These complex changes to welfare, housing and treatment systems coincided with new influxes of hard drugs. Although no homelessness statistics were yet being collected, by the late 1980s, homelessness, including visible street homelessness, appeared to be increasing in Denmark.

In Denmark, before the first count in 2007, the only national statistics available on homelessness were administrative data on people using the shelter system, which had been collected since 1999. These showed that a quite stable number of about 6,000–7,000 people used the 2,000–2,100 beds in the homeless shelters on an annual basis[1]; each bed was used by approximately three homeless people a year. The fact that these were longitudinal data was important because it showed that actual homelessness was at a higher level than service provision on its own would suggest, and that there were transitional elements in the population. The data were robust, each individual being identified by their personal number, the equivalent of a social security or national identity number in other countries. As administrative data focused on shelter users, the data were restricted in scope. Hidden homelessness (people sofa/couch surfing or staying with friends or relatives because they had nowhere else to go) and people living rough were not being counted.

The first national homelessness count was conducted in 2007 (Benjaminsen and Christensen, 2007). The count took place over one week and the methodology that was employed has been repeated on a biennial basis during the same calendar week in February every second year. The definition of homelessness used in the count was inspired by the European Typology of Homelessness and Housing Exclusion (ETHOS),[2] which was explained in Chapter 1. The 2007 count and the subsequent biennial counts thus included rough sleepers and homeless shelter users, but also hidden homeless people who were staying temporarily, without any legal right to their accommodation, with family or friends (the sofa/couch-surfing population), who are not enumerated in most countries (Busch-Geertsema et al, 2014a).

The methodology is an extended service-based count, which in addition to homelessness services, also includes a wide range of other welfare services such as psychiatric services, addiction treatment centres, municipal social offices and job centres, which all report on clients in a homelessness situation. Hidden homeless people are enumerated via their contact with other types of services outside the homelessness sector.

The Danish homelessness counts have also provided a profile of people affected by homelessness in Denmark. The counts have shown that a high proportion of homeless people have a mental illness or a substance abuse problem. In total, almost four out of five homeless people recorded in the counts have either a mental illness, substance abuse problems or both, with about a third having a dual diagnosis of both mental illness and substance abuse problems.

There appeared to be important differences between the homeless population in Denmark and those in some other countries. Work in the US found that point-in-time counts, like the Danish national count, could seriously overestimate the proportion of homeless people with high and complex needs as there was a significant population with lower needs whose homelessness appeared to be transitional and most clearly associated with poverty (Kuhn and Culhane, 1998). However, the high share of homeless people with mental illness or substance abuse problems in Denmark has been corroborated by research using longitudinal data from the shelter system, showing that a high share of shelter users have a mental illness or a substance abuse problem *regardless* of the duration that they have been in a shelter (Nielsen et al, 2011; Benjaminsen, 2016).

The Danish strategy at this time reflected the patterns of need that were found in the population experiencing homelessness. Better data, as well as changing practice elsewhere in the world, resulted in a move towards services that *enabled* access to sustainable housing within choice-focused service models, and away from the treatment-led approaches that tried to modify behaviour, treat and support in order to *make* someone 'housing ready'. Yet, Denmark did not have the stronger version of the Treatment First or Staircase model that was found in neighbouring Sweden (Sahlin, 2005), as well as in Finland. Instead, the situation before the homelessness strategy came into place was marked by an unsystematic and incoherent approach to rehousing homeless people, both in terms of providing housing and regarding the provision of adequate support when homeless people moved out of shelters.

In Denmark, relatively generous social benefits for households with dependent children, in combination with the possibility of municipalities giving prioritised allocation to one out of four vacancies in social housing, seems to have had a significant effect on levels of family homelessness. Levels were not high, nor did they seem to be increasing. International research generally shows that women and women with children may react to homelessness by seeking informal solutions, temporarily accommodating themselves with friends, relatives and acquaintances, and/or not presenting at homelessness services, which are often designed for and populated by single homeless men (Pleace, 2016a). This pattern of avoidance and concealment may be linked to: broader tendencies for women and men to react to homelessness in different ways; the risks associated with homelessness for women; and the strong tendencies for family homelessness to be experienced by lone mothers who are escaping domestic violence (Baptista et al, 2017; Bretherton, 2017). Nevertheless, Danish experience and data were not suggesting high levels of family homelessness.

However, although a high proportion of Denmark's homeless people had complex support needs, low income and the lack of affordable housing still potentially played an important role in explaining why people with complex support needs became homeless in the first place. Dependency on social assistance benefits due to long-term exclusion from the labour market, combined with a growing lack of affordable housing, was still likely to affect people with support needs harder than most other groups, thus increasing their risk of being exposed to homelessness compared to broader low-income groups.

In Denmark, the period before the 2009 strategy programme was characterised by a number of programmes aimed at strengthening social services for marginalised groups. For instance, the City Programme (*Storbypuljen*) from 2003 to 2005 also involved initiatives for homeless people, as well as services for other marginalised groups.

A range of services relevant for homeless people are specified in the Law of Social Services. In particular, section 110 in the Law of Social Services obliges municipalities to provide temporary accommodation for people who have no place to live or cannot stay at the place they live due to social problems. About 70 homeless shelters are operated nationwide under this section. The Law of Social Services also obliges municipalities to operate general floating support services aimed at supporting people with support needs in their own home due to, for instance, mental illness or substance abuse problems. Thus, the new interventions that were initiated with the strategy were built not only on the general welfare service, but also on top of services that, to some extent, were already based on principles of recovery and social rehabilitation that had already taken root in social and psychiatric services.

Finland

In Finland, by the early 1970s, associations between high and complex needs and long-term homelessness brought about a policy shift, and the problem of homelessness began to be defined more in terms of the support needs of lone men presenting with alcohol addiction, severe mental illness and disability. Homelessness started to be defined as a social care and health services challenge (Fredriksson, 2018, cited in Ranta, 2019) and services were designed on that basis. However, much of what was happening in Finland was still a 'warehousing' approach. There were still big shelters operating in Helsinki that despite having nominal roles in the resettlement of homeless people, were actually accommodating individuals with complex needs in supposedly 'emergency' and 'temporary' services for years on end (Kärkkäinen, 1996).

Spending more on these services did not seem to do very much to stem an upward trend in homelessness, and the population on which these services had been targeted, mainly lone men with support needs, seemed to be getting larger rather than smaller. In 1985, numbers of lone adult homeless people in Finland peaked at some 20,000 people, 90 percent of whom were male (Y Foundation, 2018).

In 1987, which was the 'international year of the homeless', the Finnish Government announced its first plans to eradicate homelessness in Finland. At that point, it was estimated that Finland had some 20,000 people experiencing homelessness and one of the most important policy decisions taken was to start enumerating and estimating that population. The annual count established at that time is still being conducted at the time of writing and while, as we will see later in the book, the data are not perfect, Finland has been able to track the impact of successive homelessness policies and strategies with a dataset that has been in place for over 30 years.

In the 1987 plan, the Finns put in place a major building programme, aiming to deliver 18,000 homes specifically aimed at the 20,000 of their citizens who were estimated to be experiencing homelessness (Kärkkäinen, 1996). However, the policy emphasis on homelessness was not to last as Finland found itself facing recession, and while some spending continued, priorities shifted elsewhere.

As one of the first to declare a national goal to end homelessness, the Finnish state realised that it had to set about defining what it meant by homelessness, counting that population and tracking the extent to which the five-year plan to end homelessness was being achieved. The statistics were based on data collection, using a point-in-time methodology (an annual count at the same point in time) to track progress. In addition to counting lone adults who were sheltered (in services) and unsheltered (sleeping rough), data were also collected on concealed/hidden homelessness (defined as living involuntarily with friends or relatives because there was nowhere else to go) and on family homelessness. Importantly, the methodology for the count included (and still includes) some numbers that are based on estimates by some municipalities rather than actual data (Pleace et al, 2015).

The Finnish annual homelessness survey is conducted on a single day. There is no longitudinal element and nor, at the time of writing, has Finland proposed the development of the kind of administrative data merging that enables the tracking of the homeless population seen in Denmark. The Finnish survey is completed by a wide range of homeless services and other welfare services. The survey also includes people who are in nursing homes, institutional settings and hospitals (on a temporary basis) who will lack housing on leaving as 'homeless' (Benjaminsen and Dyb, 2008). This is in line with ETHOS but not established practice elsewhere in Europe.

Finland saw other significant changes in homeless policy from the mid-1980s. Of particular importance was the creation of Y-Säätiö (the Y Foundation) in 1985, which was initially designed to acquire small rented apartments for single homeless people from the existing housing stock. Initially, the Y Foundation bought housing for lone homeless people on the open market, although this role was later extended to include the building of new apartments (Y Foundation, 2017). At the time of writing, the Y Foundation has been operational for 33 years and describes itself as the fourth-largest landlord in Finland, with housing in more than 50 municipalities and 16,650 apartments. These are managed by the Y Foundation itself and let to municipalities and other organisations, which then sublet them as social housing (Y Foundation, 2017).

The development of the Y Foundation in 1985 represented what was, in effect, the creation of dedicated social housing supply targeted towards lone homeless people. By 1985, Finland was trying to end lone adult homelessness by creating a specific housing supply for homeless individuals at a strategic level (Kärkkäinen, 1996).

The numbers of homeless people in Finland fell. In Helsinki, for example, the 1985 reported estimate was 6,700 homeless individuals, of whom around 200 were outside, 2,000 were in hostels and 3,500 were living with friends and relatives. Strategies linked to the 1987 commitment had a significant impact on the number of people who were living rough, or were in homelessness services and in institutions, with numbers dropping by two thirds between 1987 and 1995. The first national survey in 1987 counted and estimated a population of 4,700 people living rough and in shelters (broadly equivalent to ETHOS categories 1–3); by 1995, this had reached 1,710, 36 per cent of the level that it had been.

However, following this point, the number began to plateau. In 2000, the figure was at 1,790, 38 per cent of the 1987 level, while by 2008, the number was 1,520 – lower, but at 32 per cent of the 1987 level, not very much lower than it had been 13 years earlier. Lone adult homelessness in institutional settings, with the important caveat that, by some definitions, *potential* homelessness was also being counted, also fell, but again that fall stalled after the mid-1990s. In 1995, it was 44 per cent of the 1987 level, and by 2008, it was still at 34 per cent of the 1987 level.

Putting these figures into perspective is important. These numbers were quite small, even for a country with a population of 5.3 million in 2008. The numbers experiencing homelessness had not been very high in the late 1980s, and a sustained effort, combining service integration, the important initiative of the Y Foundation creating social housing for lone homeless adults and the funding of extensive homelessness services, had reduced this number still further. By 2008, the risks of living rough or in shelters and/or being homeless in an institutional setting were low, with 7,690 people representing 0.14 per cent of the Finnish population.

By 2008, Finland had achieved further successes. According to the annual point-in-time count and estimates, levels of lone adult hidden homelessness had fallen until 2005 and were 63 per cent of 1987 levels in 2008. Family homelessness had also fallen fairly steadily: by 2008, it was around one fifth of the levels being reported in 1987 (from 1,370 families in 1987 to 300 in 2008). This pattern of relatively lower – indeed, apparently much lower – levels of family homelessness compared to lone adult homelessness is also reported in many other European countries (Baptista et al, 2017). Family homelessness did not involve a very large population to begin with and it had been brought down further by 2008. As in Denmark, there were potential risks of undercounting, but, again like Denmark, neither experience nor the available data suggested that levels of family homelessness were high.

The area of policy that presented the most obvious and pressing problem was the persistence of lone adult homelessness. Despite what was then a textbook example of homelessness policy, including dedicated housing provision from the Y Foundation, municipalities being encouraged to develop integrated responses to homelessness, the coordination of housing, health and social work services, plus the funding that was going towards homelessness services, following the internationally recognised Staircase model, Finland had seemingly not been able to reduce lone adult homelessness beyond a certain point.

Existing systems were also sometimes struggling. While levels of homelessness had fallen, the provision of emergency shelters had also declined markedly, so that Helsinki found itself having to open winter emergency shelters during 2005 and 2006 because existing provision was being overwhelmed. There was evidently an insufficient supply of affordable housing, particularly in the capital, but the data were suggesting something else about why homelessness was not being brought to an end (Tainio and Fredriksson, 2009).

Homeless people were becoming stuck in services that had been designed for emergency and temporary use, which were supposed to resettle people into settled housing but were instead 'warehousing' them. Just as research in the US had been showing for some time (Kuhn and Culhane, 1998), there was a chronic homelessness problem in Finland: the reason homelessness was not falling was because it was sometimes persistent.

The answer to Finnish homelessness, at least in part, lay in reducing what the Finns termed 'long-term' homelessness, which was seen as creating a hard core of homelessness. This meant reducing the population of long-term homeless people who numbered around 3,600, some 45 per cent of the total homeless population. The Finnish definition of long-term homelessness comprised people who were homeless, or who were likely to be homeless, for prolonged periods for health and for social reasons, with combinations of support and treatment needs that could often include severe mental illness and addiction. The specific definition of long-term homelessness was that someone had been homeless for at least one year or they had been homeless several times in the last three years (Tainio and Fredriksson, 2009; Y Foundation, 2017).

The initial Finnish approach to this group of some 3,600 people who had been homeless for a year, or repeatedly homelessness over the last three years, and who had high and complex support and treatment needs was to develop new forms of congregate services. Towards the end of the 1990s, services with a harm-reduction framework developed a different system that dropped the requirements found in Staircase services, namely, that service users be drug- and alcohol-free. Smaller units with 20–30 people met with some successes where they were working with alcohol-dependent older men and had a high staff ratio, but the services were less successful with younger people. The existing array of Staircase services – with their requirements of abstinence and compliance with behavioural change in order to complete the steps to independent housing – were not ineffective, but the long-term homeless population was not being engaged with successfully; however, just shifting the Staircase approach to harm reduction was not delivering an end to homelessness either (Tainio and Fredriksson, 2009).

This growing awareness of the ineffectiveness of existing services for stopping longer-term homelessness came along with the realisation that homelessness was potentially *costing* more than it should (Tainio and Fredriksson, 2009; Fredriksson, 2018, cited in Ranta, 2019). Eviction was also more expensive than prevention: each eviction was costing around €7,000–7,500 by the 2010s (Pleace, 2014), and it was evident that preventive services could bring that cost down, having stopped 2,000 evictions in Helsinki by 2014.

As has been noted elsewhere (Pleace, 2008; Rosenheck, 2010), and as was reflected in the Finnish experience, this situation was not one in which Staircase services were constantly failing: when individuals could engage with their requirements, these services were routinely providing an end to homelessness. When deployed in place of Staircase services, Housing First is sometimes portrayed as replacing darkness with enlightenment, catastrophic failure with unqualified success, but the realities are more nuanced and complex (Pleace, 2016b; see also later). Finnish Staircase services were working, but there was a significant section of the lone adult homeless population, perhaps as much as 45 per cent, that they were not reaching; instead, that population had entered long-term homelessness (Tainio and Fredriksson, 2009). Existing systems were also inconsistent: it was not just that the Staircase services had limitations, Finland was also still using emergency shelters and hostels, which were doing little more than warehousing the problem of lone adult homelessness. It was in some of these settings that long-term homeless people were living. Finland needed a new strategy.

Doing something about housing supply, even focusing a specific supply of social housing on homelessness, did not look like it was going to get the job done, and so the Finns began to look at how their services were working. As Finland's homelessness strategy developed, municipalities had been encouraged to ensure that relevant services were working together, which involved health, social welfare and social landlord services, with tackling homeless increasingly being defined as a core function of local government and other public services. In Helsinki, a single hub for homelessness services was developed, while the Y Foundation created the opportunity to employ scattered, ordinary housing to which housing-led (floating or mobile support) could be delivered. There was also an array of homelessness services being funded, providing a mix of emergency accommodation and Staircase model services (Tainio and Fredriksson, 2009).

There is a narrative that describes the Finns 'finding' Housing First and adopting it as the core of a new homelessness strategy to address long-term and recurrent homelessness, which mirrored the potential of the approach that had been seen in the US (Pleace, 2011). Parallels with the American model of Housing First were recognised and the Finns began dialogue and sharing practice, but they did not 'import' Housing First (this is discussed in more detail in Chapter 5). A shared direction of travel with Denmark was evident: not only was homelessness being defined increasingly in terms of a need for holistic services among a high-need group whose needs were not being met by existing services; it was also being seen as a problem that was going to be solved most effectively through the use of services that placed choice and control in the hands of homeless people.

Importantly, while the rationale behind the broader Finnish strategy was to reduce the human costs of homelessness, following a Finnish 'Housing First' philosophy that focused on the human right to a decent home – a truly housing-led approach to homelessness policy – the Finns were still aware of the cost-saving potential in changing strategy and services (Y Foundation, 2017). Finnish Housing First and similar service models had lower operating costs than some existing services and reduced long-term homelessness, and expenditure could be directed more effectively (Pleace et al, 2015, 2016; Fredriksson, 2018, cited in Ranta, 2019).

Ireland

In Ireland, the first survey of services for people experiencing homelessness was conducted by the newly formed Simon Community in Dublin in 1971 (O Cinneide and Mooney, 1972).[3] The survey identified 14 shelters/hostels providing just over 1,300 beds for adults experiencing homelessness, with over 75 per cent catering for men, and less than 10 per cent provided by statutory health or local government providers. They also identified 196 rough sleepers, either on the streets or who were intermittently using shelters, of whom 16 were female.

Following a similar pattern of shelter development as Finland, and most other Western economies, by the mid-1980s, there were approximately 1,500 shelter beds available across Ireland for adults experiencing homelessness, with more than half in Dublin. Just under

80 per cent were for males. There was remarkable consistency in terms of service providers, with a number of non-governmental organisations (NGOs) of varying ideological dispositions, as well as in the nature of the service provided: congregate facilities where shelter users had to vacate the premises during the day.[4]

A visiting American academic described the physical conditions of hostels in Dublin as ranging from 'primitive to appalling', 'managed by kind, but often inexperienced, volunteers and … typically understaffed, under-financed, and poorly equipped' (Kearns, 1984: 226). The single most important change in this period was the phasing out of casual wards, that is, units that provided temporary accommodation for 'casuals' or homeless people, attached to what were formerly workhouses, which was an approach to homelessness that had been inherited on Irish independence in 1921. Although no accurate data existed, campaigning groups usually gave an estimate of 3,000 people experiencing homelessness, the majority of whom were single males.

A lack of clarity about the responsibilities of health services and municipalities was a focal point of the early campaigning work in Ireland. The public health authorities were required to provide 'institutional assistance' to people experiencing homelessness, or to provide funding to voluntary bodies aiding the homeless under the provisions of the Health Act 1953, while the municipal authorities were to provide housing for those 'in need of it or who were unable to provide it from their own resources' under the Housing Act 1966. This ambiguity led to different health and municipal authorities adopting varying levels of responsibility, resulting 'in homeless people being shunted from health board to local authority and vice-versa' (Shannon, 1988).

In Ireland, campaigns from the mid-1980s for legislative change culminated in the Housing Act 1988. The new Act was preceded by a number of attempts to bring in legislation to create clear statutory responsibilities that failed due to the instability and short tenures of governments during this period. The political debates on this legislation revolved around the question of whether there should be a statutory responsibility on local authorities to house people who were homeless and whether people who were deemed to have made themselves 'intentionally homeless' should be excluded from such a responsibility; both questions were features of the neighbouring UK's initial legislative attempt to reduce homelessness, the Housing (Homeless Persons) Act 1977.

In the event, the Irish legislation that was signed into law as the Housing Act 1988 contained neither of these provisions, opting instead for 'more discretionary provisions which would not give homeless persons a right to accommodation superior to that of all other persons in need of housing'. The rationale for this policy change was that then Minister Padraig Flynn did not:

> Regard as prudent to impose a statutory obligation on housing authorities to secure accommodation for homeless persons when the resources necessary to discharge that obligation would not be available to the authorities. In addition, with reduction in the availability of local authority accommodation, a statutory obligation to secure accommodation for homeless persons would create a premium on being adjudged homeless. This could result in applicants who are frustrated at delays in securing accommodation seeking to be housed as homeless persons with the likely outcome that few, if any, applicants would ultimately be rehoused from the normal waiting lists.[5]

Under the terms of the Act, local authorities have significant discretion in determining if a person is homeless, and broad options for how they should address the housing needs of homeless people. Section 10 of the Act created a legal basis on which central government and local authorities could fund emergency services for people who were homeless. It was only with this 1988 Act that the Irish government repealed the 'wandering abroad' section of the Vagrancy Act 1824, inherited from UK law.

In Ireland, by the mid-1980s, it was estimated that between 3,000 and 5,000 people were experiencing homelessness, primarily single homeless males residing in an 'institutional circuit' (Hopper et al, 1997) of hostels, casual units and psychiatric units. While no explicit policy determined provision, in practice, it was a mixture of simply providing rudimentary, temporary and emergency accommodation services and attempting to access health, particularly detoxification and in-patient psychiatric, services for the users of these shelters.

Data on the extent and nature of homelessness during this period were scant. Around the same time that Finland was introducing its first count, the 1988 Act intended to introduce the first systematic measurement of the number of people who were homeless and using emergency shelters; however, this initiative failed to create the same level of reliable data. It quickly became apparent that there was considerable variation in how local authorities defined homelessness and, consequently, the provision of services to people experiencing homelessness. The assessments of homelessness conducted in 1989 and 1991 by the local authorities were also seen as inconsistent (Dillon et al, 1990; Kelleher, 1990; Nexus Research, 1992).

Following the third Assessment of Housing Need and Homelessness in 1993, the Department of Environment commissioned an independent research body, the Economic and Social Research Institute (ESRI), to inquire into the 'adequacy and accuracy' (Fahey and Watson, 1995: 12) of the assessments. In relation to assessing the extent of homelessness, the ESRI found that a significant number of authorities recorded nobody experiencing homelessness in their functional area, despite the presence of shelter services, and concluded that an undercount had taken place. This, they explained, was due to local authorities restricting their response to their traditional role of providing long-term housing to households without any ongoing support, thus excluding single persons who had support needs.

The first three assessments of homelessness simply gave the total number of adult individuals by local authority area; however, the 1999 assessment provided a breakdown by male and female adults and child dependants. This is the first relatively modern figure that gives us an insight into the extent of homelessness in Ireland. The assessment recorded 3,743 households who were deemed homeless by local authorities, comprising 2,593 adult males and 1,399 adult females, with 1,242 child dependants, and with over two thirds recorded in the Greater Dublin region. The 2002 assessment of homelessness recorded little change, with 3,773 households, or 4,176 adults, identified, with 1,405 accompanying child dependants, and with two thirds of the households recorded in Dublin.

Unlike Finland and Denmark, Ireland adopted a method of counting the number of homeless people that was based on administrative data from local authorities. This approach is exclusively concerned with a narrow definition of homelessness and gives little insight into the numbers who were 'hidden homeless'. During this period, Ireland had a significantly less developed welfare state and social care system than either Finland or Denmark; however, Irish data give no insight into the impact of this on the proportion of the homeless population who had complex support needs. Nevertheless, the institutional debate about whether homelessness should be the responsibility of the health or housing authorities reflects the debate in the other two countries.

In Ireland, it was not until the mid-1990s that policymakers and senior administrative managers in central government and in regional health and local government came to increasingly recognise that homelessness was a question of both housing supply and the provision of health and allied services. In particular, for people to successfully exit homelessness on a sustained basis, the coordination of health, housing and social services was identified as requiring urgent attention. Established in Dublin in October 1996, the 'Homeless Initiative' had the objective of ensuring that services for homeless people were more effective, particularly by improving their planning, coordination and delivery, as well as by ensuring the development of responses that enabled people to settle in secure accommodation, moving them out of the cycle of homelessness. The establishment of the Homeless Initiative in Dublin was a crucial catalyst in devising new ways of responding to homelessness at a national level, and in August 1998, a Cross-Departmental Team on Homelessness was established with representatives from all central government bodies providing services to those experiencing homelessness, tasked with developing an integrated national strategy.

Some traditional shelter providers, particularly in Dublin, were closing or refurbishing their shelters, leading to the loss of approximately 150 shelter beds. The remaining shelters were rudimentary; in a review of facilities in eight of the main shelters, half still provided dormitory-style accommodation (Hennessy, 1993) and were 'becoming a catch-all solution for a very diverse range of problems' (Kelleher et al, 1992: 18). This decline, allied to the lack of places for families, particularly with children, saw the growth in the use of 'bed and breakfast' (B&B)-type accommodation for such households experiencing homelessness. In 1994, 718 households were placed in such accommodation, 474 of them in Dublin, up from five households in 1990 (Moore, 1994). By 1999, the number of households placed in B&Bs had increased to 1,202 at a cost of €5.9 million, compared to the €660 spend on the five households in 1990. The length of time spent in such forms of emergency accommodation also rose during this period from an average of 12 nights in 1992 to 81 nights in 1999 (Houghton and Hickey, 2000).

In 2000, the Cross-Departmental Team published their deliberations, *Homelessness – An Integrated Strategy*, which noted the limitations of previous approaches to responding to homelessness. In the Cross-Departmental Team's view, this necessitated a 'new approach to the provision of a range of housing for individuals and families as well as addressing their health and welfare needs' (Department of the Environment and Local Government, 2000: 7). The committee also discussed ongoing difficulties in determining whether statutory responsibility for those experiencing homelessness fell to the health or housing authorities. The report clarified that 'local authorities will have responsibility for the provision of emergency hostel and temporary accommodation for homeless persons as part of their overall housing responsibility; health boards will be responsible for the health and in-house care needs of homeless persons' (Department of the Environment and Local Government, 2000: 30). The committee also proposed that both housing and health authorities, in conjunction with relevant NGOs, draw up action plans on homelessness in each local authority area, alongside the establishment of homeless forums in every county. In addition, in 2002, a Homelessness Preventative Strategy was published.

Thus, the previous ad hoc system – in which either health or housing authorities might fund, or decline to fund, NGO-provided shelters and hostels – was replaced with a clear understanding that this was now exclusively a local authority function. As we will see later, this was to contribute to the rapid increase in section 10 funding during the 2000s. However, in addition, the committee noted that additional services were required to meet the needs of those experiencing homelessness, and that capital and current funding would have to increase substantially, requiring an estimated additional €7.6 million per annum for both local authority and health services, with a further €25.3 million in capital funding.

An independent review of the government's Homeless Strategy was published in February 2006. It systematically reviewed the 43 specific policy proposals identified in the two strategies and put forward 21 recommendations to aid the implementation of the strategies, which were all accepted by government. In relation to the integrated strategy, the consultants suggested that over 60 per cent of the objectives outlined were either fully or significantly progressed. In relation to the preventive strategy, just under 30 per cent were fully or significantly progressed. While these outcomes were broadly positive, the review noted that a dominant feature of homeless services was the inconsistency of approach and organisation throughout the country. This was particularly the case outside of urban areas and this inconsistency resulted in a 'lack of equality in the treatment of homeless persons in different areas' (Fitzpatrick Associates, 2006: 28).

To deal with these inconsistencies, the review recommended that the production of locally based homeless action plans should be put on a statutory basis. The report argued that while the provision of emergency accommodation in Ireland was now sufficient, the key challenge for the future was to refocus attention on the provision of long-term housing options and to 'develop appropriate short and long term care mechanisms that prevent institutionalisation in "emergency" accommodation and limit the recycling of homelessness' (Fitzpatrick Associates, 2006: 32). The report argued that in moving the homeless strategies forward, each agency working in this area needed to refocus its energies to make 'itself largely obsolete, which should, after all, be its overarching goal' (Fitzpatrick Associates, 2006: 128).

Following the review of the earlier strategies, in August 2008, a revised strategy, entitled The Way Home: A Strategy to Address Adult Homelessness in Ireland 2008 – 2013 (Department of the Environment, Heritage and Local Government, 2008) was published which aimed to end long-term homelessness (i.e. in emergency accommodation for more than six months) and the need to sleep rough by 2010.

This 2008 commitment to end long-term homelessness, coming 20 years after a similar commitment was made in Finland, was the first time that a specific time limit was placed on achieving an end to homelessness in Ireland. The 2008 Assessment of Housing Need brought some further changes to the methodology for assessing the extent of homelessness, recording 1,394 households who were homeless, with just over half in the Greater Dublin area. The adjusted comparator figure for 2005 was 1,987 households, but irrespective of the comparator figure, the 2008 figure suggested a significant decrease in the numbers experiencing homelessness at the time of the publication of the revised strategy, hence the optimism that homelessness could be ended within a relatively short time frame.

Conclusion

For much of the early part of the 20th century, the three countries shared a similar view of homelessness: it was a problem largely associated with lone adult men with mental health or addictions issues, and shelter and surveillance were the best responses. The organised responses to homelessness at governmental and NGO levels diverged significantly, reflecting the particular legal, religious and social histories of the countries, but there is little evidence that these histories exerted significant differences in later developments. From the 1970s, a medical/treatment-based approach started to emerge in all three countries. These approaches developed earlier and more consistently in Denmark and Finland than in Ireland. This more supportive approach to homelessness is closely linked to the developments in the welfare state in each country during this period, and differences between the countries in this respect can be seen as accounting for much of the differences in developments in homeless provision.

This shift towards medicalised responses to homelessness initially delivered some reduction in the numbers who were homeless, particularly in Finland, where explicit public policy initiatives emerged earliest. However, it soon became apparent that such approaches were not reducing homelessness below a certain level. This failure can be ascribed to shortcomings in the 'Staircase model' that was used in some services, or more generally to the fact that services had no effective model and were simply 'warehousing' people with complex support needs. The shift to a medical supportive response to homelessness had involved significant increases in public expenditure and the fact that it was not resulting in an equivalent reduction in the number of people needing that support was a concern of policymakers in all three countries.

The first coherent efforts to count the number of people who were homeless emerged during this period, and the nature of these counts both reflects the historical approach to homelessness in each country and influences the way in which it is subsequently seen. Finland was the first to introduce its annual count in 1987, reflecting a broad concept of homelessness, and despite the limitations of the methodology, Finland has maintained the annual count since. Ireland made its first attempt to formally count homelessness around the same time; however, even though the definition to be used was extremely narrow, the early triennial counts were undermined by conflicting and confused applications of the definition and frequent changes in methodology. Denmark's first count came with the introduction of its strategy in 2007, and although only biennial, it provides the most robust and inclusive of the three.

In each of the three countries, the particular needs of people who were long-term homeless, had high support needs and appeared to be trapped in a cycle of homelessness emerged as a concern that needed a more strategic approach – one that would bring together policies and agencies responsible for welfare, health and, crucially, housing. Chapter 3 will look at the content of those strategies as they developed over the following decade.

Notes

[1] Bed levels had increased to reach 2,200 places in 2018.
[2] See: www.feantsa.org/en/toolkit/2005/04/01/ethos-typology-on-homelessness-and-housing-exclusion
[3] The Report of the Commission on the Relief of the Sick and Destitute Poor, including the Insane Poor, requested the Garda Siochana (Police) to carry out a one-night census 'of homeless persons observed wandering on the public highways in a single night in November 1925'. A total of 3,257 adults and children were identified, primarily in rural areas, but the majority were itinerant workers.
[4] Of the 14 shelters identified in 1971 in Dublin, eight of them were still operating in 2018.
[5] National Archives of Ireland, 2017/11/600, Department of Taoiseach, Housing (Homeless Persons) Bill 1983.

3

The strategies described

Introduction

The strategies of the three countries were published within a relatively short period of each other. The Finnish Strategy, *Paavo I*, was launched in February 2008, while the Irish national homeless strategy, entitled *The Way Home: A Strategy to Address Adult Homelessness in Ireland, 2008–2013*, was launched in August 2008, and the Danish *A Strategy to Reduce Homelessness in Denmark, 2009–2012* was adopted in August 2007 and published in October 2009.

When considered in retrospect over the period 2008–18, the three strategies can each be seen to have distinct phases of announcement and implementation. In the case of the Finnish strategies, these build upon each other through a series of achievements and refined objectives, while in the Irish case, the strategies change considerably in format and scope, reflecting the broader economic and political crisis that engulfed the country. The development of the Danish strategy falls in between the other two cases.

The initial strategies

The Danish homelessness strategy

In Denmark, following the first homelessness count in 2007, a national homelessness strategy was adopted by the Danish government. The strategic programme succeeded earlier programmes aimed at strengthening social services for marginalised groups. For instance, the City Programme (*Storbypuljen*) from 2003 to 2005 also involved initiatives for homeless people, as well as services for other marginalised groups. At the same time, the strategy built on top of existing services in the general welfare system.

Four overall goals were set in the programme and operational targets attached to each goal were set at the local level. The four goals were:

1. to reduce rough sleeping;
2. to provide solutions other than shelters to homeless youth;
3. to reduce time spent in a shelter; and
4. to reduce homelessness due to institutional release from prison and hospitals without a housing solution.

A range of services for homeless people, and vulnerable people in general, was already specified in social services legislation. In particular, section 110 in the legislation obliges municipalities to provide temporary accommodation for people who have no place to live or who cannot stay at the place where they live due to social problems. About 70 homeless shelters nationwide operate under this section of the law. Social services legislation also obliges municipalities to operate general floating support services aimed at supporting people with support needs in their own home due to, for instance, mental illness or substance abuse problems. Thus, the new interventions that were initiated with the strategy programme built upon services that were, to some extent, already based on principles of recovery and social rehabilitation that had already taken root in social and psychiatric services. Yet, the strategy also added new perspectives on housing and support interventions for homeless people by adapting new knowledge, for example, on Housing First and on Critical Time Intervention (CTI) that was emerging at that time on how to approach the rehousing and reintegration of homeless people into the local community.

The homelessness strategy programme consisted of several initiatives aimed at strengthening social services for homeless people. One of the largest initiatives was a Housing First programme in all the municipalities that participated in the strategy programme. However, there were also other initiatives at the local level, reflecting specific local priorities, such as strengthening street outreach work or other services for particular groups.

Funding of DKK500 million (€65 million) was allocated to the strategy programme over a period of four years from 2009 to 2012. As in the Finnish and Irish strategies, local plans were at the heart of the approach. Eight municipalities, which had 54 per cent of the total homeless population in Denmark and included the largest cities in Denmark, Copenhagen, Aarhus and Odense, were invited to participate in the programme. Most of the funding was allocated to these municipalities. In a later round, other municipalities could apply for the remainder of the funding. Nine further municipalities, mainly medium-sized towns, were selected to participate in the programme and DKK30 million (€4.55 million) of the total funding was allocated to these nine municipalities.

Due to the emerging evidence on Housing First from other countries, it was decided from the inception of the programme that Housing First should be the overall principle of the Danish homelessness strategy. A main emphasis of the programme was to provide access to permanent housing with intensive social support. An important part of the programme was to apply the evidence-based support methods that had been used in Housing First programmes in the US and to develop and test these methods in a Danish setting.

Three support methods were included in the Danish Housing First programme: Assertive Community Treatment (ACT), Intensive Case Management (ICM) and CTI. The ACT and ICM methods are well-established practices in the Pathways Housing First programmes in the US, but CTI, as a 'time-limited' intervention, does not correspond to a key principle in Pathways Housing First of providing intensive support for as long as needed. The reason for including the CTI intervention into the Danish programme next to ACT and ICM was to further differentiate the provision of support to different groups depending upon need. CTI was intended to be given to homeless people with less intensive support needs than the individuals who were the target group for ACT or ICM support. However, in practice, the intention of using different support methods according to support needs was only partly met. Only one municipality made use of the ACT method, and some municipalities made use of either the ICM or the CTI methods, whereas only a few municipalities implemented both of these methods. The ICM programme was the largest sub-programme, with about 700 individuals receiving ICM support, whereas about 300 individuals received CTI support through the programme. In contrast, only one ACT team was established, in the city of Copenhagen, with about 90 individuals receiving ACT support (Rambøll and SFI, 2013).

Housing for the Danish Housing First programme was mainly provided through access to public housing, either through municipal prioritised allocation or through general waiting lists. Only a minority of the participants were housed in the private rental sector. Denmark is an example of implementing Housing First in a European context and, more specifically, in a social-democratic welfare system according to Esping-Andersen's (1990) typology, where public housing plays a much larger role than the private rental sector in providing housing for low-income and vulnerable groups.

In Denmark, despite the positive results in rehousing people with the Housing First method, the four aggregate goals set up for the strategy for 2009–12 were generally not met (Benjaminsen, 2013; Rambøll and SFI, 2013). In regard to the first goal of reducing rough sleeping, the homelessness counts documented an increase in the number of rough sleepers, even in the municipalities that had operational goals set for this target, as the number of rough sleepers in these municipalities increased from 307 in 2009 to 351 in 2013. For the second goal of providing alternatives to staying in a shelter for homeless young people, only a minor reduction in the number of 18- to 24-year-old shelter users was achieved, from 345 in 2007, increasing to 433 in 2010, and then decreasing to 343 young shelter users in 2012 for the municipalities with targets set for this goal. Yet, under the strategy, a number of shielded shelter places for young homeless people were established, and when these places are excluded from the statistics, the number of young homeless people in regular shelters fell to 223 in 2012. However, it must also be taken into consideration that the majority of young homeless people in Denmark do not stay in homeless shelters, but rather 'sofa surf' with friends or family, and as previously mentioned, the number of young homeless people generally increased sharply during this period.

For the third Danish goal of reducing the number of long shelter stays, statistics from the municipalities with goals set on this target showed that the number of long shelter stays increased slightly, from 903 in 2007 to 988 in 2012. Only for the fourth goal of reducing homelessness due to institutional discharge, or release from prison, without a housing solution could a reduction be observed. Numbers fell from 106 persons in the count week in 2009 to 65 persons in the count week in 2013 within the municipalities with goals set for this target.

There are many factors that may explain why the aggregate targets set for the strategy were not met. Among the most important reasons were a lack of a clear connection between these targets, the scale of interventions and the impact of wider barriers to ending homelessness, such as general changes in housing markets and welfare policies.

The Finnish Paavo I strategy

There are several descriptions of the development of the current Finnish homelessness strategy that all tell a similar story (Busch-Geertsema, 2010; Pleace et al, 2015; Y Foundation, 2017). In 2007, *Ympäristöministeriö*, the Finnish Ministry of the Environment, created a working group of four experts – the director of Helsinki's social services, a Bishop, the chief executive officer (CEO) of *Y-Säätiö* (the Y Foundation) and a doctor who was also a well-known civil activist – which drew on support from other key individuals and agencies. This working group delivered what was to become a key report, referred to as the *Name on the Door* report, which was to shape Finnish homelessness policy for the next decade and beyond. The report drew up what has been referred to as a 'Finnish Housing First Principle' (Y Foundation, 2017: 19): 'Solving social and health problems is not a prerequisite for arranging housing, but instead housing is a prerequisite that will also enable solving a homeless person's other problems.'

This housing-led approach to homelessness marked a transition away from a Staircase-based, 'housing-last' system and towards a Housing First model. Investment was significant. In 2008, €80 million was allocated to structural investment and €10.3 million for hiring support staff, with funding being roughly divided between central government and the municipalities. A further €18 million came from *Raha-automaattiyhdistysthe* (RAY) (the Finnish Slot Machine Association), essentially a reinvestment of gambling profits in social projects (Tainio and Fredriksson, 2009).

Finnish thinking at the time was that they were developing a Finnish version of Housing First, which drew on their own experiences and ideas. Finnish Housing First was always intended to operate within a wider, integrated strategy that was described as following a set of key principles (Tainio and Fredriksson, 2009: 189). In many respects, this is different from the development of Pathways Housing First in the US. The differences between the two approaches to Housing First are extremely important in understanding the Finnish project and the development of Housing First in other countries. This is discussed in detail, along with the implications for policy, in Chapter 5.

Paavo I, which ran from 2008 to 2011, had one main target: to reduce long-term homelessness. Specifically, the goal was to halve the estimated population experiencing long-term homelessness (some 3,600 people) within three years. The four main elements of *Paavo I* were as follows (Luomanen, 2010):

- Action plans and letters of intent from the participating cities – the plans had to be ready by March 2008 and the letters of intent signed by May 2008.
- Designated funding from the Criminal Sanctions Agency, Housing Finance and Development Centre of Finland (ARA), RAY and the Ministry of Social Affairs and Health.
- The development of a dedicated project to provide supported housing for ex-offenders (former prisoners) at risk of homelessness.
- New systems centred on the prevention of homelessness, including a young person's supported housing project and a national scheme for providing housing advice to people at risk of homelessness, organised by municipalities and funded by central government.

Focusing on the goal to end long-term homelessness, *Paavo I* had resources to deliver at least 1,250 new homes, including supported housing units, for long-term homeless people in the ten cities. Importantly, there was a simultaneous goal to stop using shared and communal emergency accommodation and to replace them with these 1,250 new homes.

Around €21 million in subsidies was granted for housing construction between 2012 and 2013, with a further €13.6 million being granted for developing and delivering services, a total of €34.6 million. The municipalities also provided significant matched funding, increasing the overall level of investment. Total investment in the programme was reported at some €170 million, including all state, RAY and municipality funding. It is worth briefly pausing to consider the amount of money invested relative to the population being targeted: there were 7,960 lone homeless people counted by ARA in 2008, less than half of whom (an estimated 3,600 people) were in the target group of long-term homelessness (Pleace et al, 2015).

In this first phase, all three elements of Finnish thinking were in evidence. First, *Paavo I* was integrated at the strategic, local and service-delivery levels. Second, *Paavo I* was housing led: there was to be the focus on Housing First that the *Name on the Door* report had emphasised, but the strategy was not just implementing a new *service* design, but building and converting the necessary housing stock to do it. Third, *Paavo I* was not tokenism: this was a serious level of investment for a three-year programme, targeted as it was on a relatively very small group of homeless people.

The Irish strategy: The Way Home

In August 2008, the revised national homeless strategy, entitled *The Way Home: A Strategy to Address Adult Homelessness in Ireland, 2008–2013*, was published, setting out six strategic aims:

1. prevent homelessness;
2. eliminate the need to sleep rough;
3. eliminate long-term homelessness;
4. meet long-term housing needs;
5. ensure effective services for homeless people; and
6. better coordinate funding arrangements.

A more detailed implementation plan was published in early 2009, which included a further two strategic aims: data/information strategy; and monitoring/implementation.

As noted in Chapter 2, the 2008 Assessment of Housing Need suggested that there had been a significant decrease in the numbers experiencing homelessness at the time of the publication of the revised strategy, hence the optimism that homelessness could be ended within a relatively short time frame.

The broad ambition of the plan was to ensure that nobody would remain in emergency accommodation for more than six months by the end of 2010 and no one would need to sleep rough. These objectives were to be achieved by increasing the supply of long-term social housing in each local authority area and providing the necessary social and health supports required to maintain these tenancies. Although not explicitly stated, the ideological thrust of the strategy was clearly housing led.

Like the Finnish and the Danish strategy, local homeless action plans were at the heart of the plan. The first set of local action plans were drawn up covering the years 2009–13, with a second set of plans to be drafted to cover the period 2014–17. Unlike the earlier action plans that had been proposed under *Homelessness – An Integrated Strategy* in 2000, these action plans were put on a statutory basis via section 37 of the Housing (Miscellaneous Provisions) Act 2009.

This plan was conceived during a period of rapid economic growth, but by the time of its publication in 2008, the Irish economy had started to contract. In 2008, the Irish government and most commentators were predicting a 'soft landing' for the economy after years of rapid growth (Honohan et al, 2010), but in late 2010, the Irish government was forced to secure a loan, formally known as a 'Programme of Financial Support', from the European Union and the International Monetary Fund. As part of the loan agreement and underpinned by earlier and later treaties, the amount of public spending on capital projects such as social housing was severely restricted.

Although hampered by the lack of robust consistent data on the extent and duration of the experience of homelessness, it was clear by 2010 that the target of eliminating long-term homelessness had not been achieved. The 2011 Assessment of Housing Need, which once again changed the methodology for assessing housing need, making strict comparisons with previous assessments problematic, recorded 2,348 households as homeless, an increase of 68 per cent on the 2008 figure of 1,394.

There was no ring-fenced budget for the implementation of the strategy; rather, the funding available to local authorities was modestly increased, and despite the imposition of substantial austerity budgets from 2009 onwards, the amount available for homelessness from central and local government services averaged over €100 million per annum between 2009 and 2018. Capital and current expenditure on social housing declined from nearly €1.2 billion in 2008 to €269 million in 2014, with capital expenditure constituting 40 per cent of the diminished budget compared to 95 per cent in 2008.

Management of the strategies

The question of how the different strategies related to central and local government, how they were managed, and who was involved in that process will come up on a number of occasions in assessing why they all turned out so differently. Therefore, it is useful to set out some of the key elements of these structures as they were envisaged in the first phase of the strategies.

In Denmark, the homelessness strategy and succeeding programmes were anchored at the Ministry of Social Affairs. The implementation of the programme was the responsibility of the National Board of Social Welfare, which is an agency under the ministry responsible for the implementation of social programmes. This agency generally works closely with municipalities, which are responsible for local welfare services and thus key actors in implementing the programmes in practice. The support from the ministerial agency to participating municipalities generally involved extensive process support, such as workshops, network and training activities, with a key focus on supporting the shift towards Housing First in daily practice. Although a considerable number of homeless shelters in Denmark are operated by non-governmental organisations (NGOs), in many cases, municipalities are also direct service providers of homeless shelters. Moreover, the new ICM, ACT and CTI services established through the programme were often directly provided by municipalities, although there were also examples of anchoring such services at NGO-run shelters. Like in Finland, the Danish strategy and succeeding programmes did not encompass all Danish municipalities; rather, a selection of larger and medium-sized municipalities that represented a substantial part of homelessness at the national level were included.

Paavo I was led by the Ministry of the Environment, but implementation involved many arms of the Finnish state, including, *Sosiaali-ja terveysministeriöthe* (the Ministry of Social Affairs and Health), the ARA, RAY and the Y Foundation (see Chapter 2). Strictly speaking, the programme was not a *national* strategy, being focused on the ten cities with the largest percentages of homeless people, although these urban areas also contained the bulk of the Finnish population.

The cities of Helsinki, Espoo, Vantaa, Tampere, Turku, Lahti, Jyväskylä, Oulu, Joensuu and Kuopio were the sites chosen for *Paavo I* (Pleace et al, 2015, 2016).

In describing the processes involved in delivering *Paavo I*, it is important to note the degree of political effort that was involved in building a really quite radically different national homelessness strategy, using a distinctly Finnish 'Housing First' philosophy. Two individuals in particular, Peter Fredriksson (a senior adviser to the Ministry of the Environment) and Juha Kaakinen (CEO of the Y Foundation), were instrumental in mobilising support for the *Name on the Door* report and building up a consensus for action following its publication, which quickly became *Paavo I* (Pleace et al, 2015; Y Foundation, 2017).

Alongside orchestrating cooperation between central government and other relevant national bodies, the Finns secured local authority (municipality) cooperation by creating a standardised set of requirements that the ten cities were required to sign up to via a 'letter of intent' to collaborate to deliver *Paavo I*. Alongside this, the non-governmental bodies working with homeless people were also actively encouraged to sign up, which included a mix of charities and faith-based organisations. Central government, national agencies, municipalities and the homeless sector were all integrated into *Paavo I*.

In Ireland, as was noted in Chapter 2, a Cross-Departmental Team on Homelessness had been established in 1998, with representatives from all central government bodies providing services to those experiencing homelessness. A National Homelessness Consultative Committee (NHCC), which was established in April 2007 and chaired by the Assistant Secretary for Housing in the Department of Housing, with membership comprised of central and local government representatives and NGO providers, was an important forum for the discussion and sharing of information on homelessness. This committee was merged with the pre-existing Cross-Departmental Team, which had comprised only public servants from 2009. Between 2007 and 2013, the committee met on 19 occasions.

While the government-only Cross-Departmental Team led the formulation of the 2008 strategy, the strategy was broadly the product of a consensus between government and NGO service providers that homelessness could be ended. However, it has been noted (Brownlee, 2008) that impediments to that consensus included a perception from central government that NGO service providers were reluctant to configure their services towards eventual dismantlement and overly negative to the new strategy. The NGOs, on the other hand, believed that while they embraced a partnership-based approach to ending homelessness, as evidenced by their participation in the NHCC, they had no meaningful input into the 2008 strategy, with central government, and particularly the Ministry of Environment, being resistant to genuine collaborative partnership.

While key local authorities were required to commit to the *Paavo I* programme in Finland, in Ireland, legislation was introduced that directed local authorities in each of the nine regions to work together, with one of the local authorities taking the lead role. Each region was required by law to establish a management group that would prepare and review a homelessness action plan, and to generally advise the local authority on services and funding for such services. To aid this management group, a homelessness 'Consultative Forum' whose aim was to provide advice to the management group in their drafting of the action plan was also provided for in the Act, which included not only statutory organisations, but also representatives of locally active NGOs. The Act also provided that these structures could be established jointly in regions rather than in every local authority. Every local authority was required to establish its own structure or participate in a regional structure, irrespective of the extent of homelessness in its own city our county area. With some significant regional variations, these groups met on a regular basis, providing a useful forum for the sharing of information.

The second phase: 2012–15

Denmark

While the aggregate targets of the 2008 homelessness strategy were generally not achieved in Denmark, the results clearly showed that on an individual level, the combination of access to permanent housing and intensive support given according to the Housing First approach had very positive outcomes for the homeless people who received these interventions. Following these positive outcomes, a follow-up programme, 'The Implementation Programme', was initiated from 2014 to 2016.

The follow-up programme had the purpose of further anchoring the Housing First programme in the municipalities that participated in the strategy programme and to extend the programme to new municipalities. While only a few of the municipalities involved in the earlier programme did not participate in the follow-up programme, 24 municipalities participated in the new programme. However, the funding structure of the programme was fundamentally different. Whereas interventions were mainly funded by the central government under the homelessness strategy, for the follow-up programme, municipalities had to fund interventions largely out of their own local budgets.

During the period from 2014 to 2016, about 350 individuals were rehoused under the follow-up programme. The results for the individuals who received the interventions in the follow-up programme closely resembled the results of the earlier strategy programme, with a high housing retention rate and very few people losing their housing over the observation period (Benjaminsen et al, 2017). Although a high housing retention rate was generally observed, the evaluation research also showed that there was a smaller group of participants who eventually dropped out of support services, either by not wanting any further support or because support workers were no longer able to get in touch with them anymore, despite several contact attempts.

However, the results were generally in line with findings from the first stage of the programme and the international research literature as about 10–20 per cent of those receiving the Housing First approach did not exit homelessness and may need other services such as supported accommodation or alternative long-stay housing. Like the international evidence, the Danish data showed that Housing First should not be seen as a universalistic method, and a range of differentiated options needs to be in place. Thus, Housing First cannot replace institutionalised forms of accommodation, such as social-psychiatric supported housing, for those who need this type of care. Yet, it is a powerful result of both the first and second stage of the Danish programme that a high share of about 80–90 per cent of homeless people with complex support needs are able to exit homelessness through the combination of access to permanent housing and intensive support that are the key components of Housing First.

Finland

Paavo II was envisaged well before *Paavo I* came to an end. The objective of *Paavo I* had been to halve long-term homelessness, and following the 28 per cent reduction that was achieved, *Paavo II* was designed to end it altogether. The goals were as follows (Pleace et al, 2015):

- the elimination of long-term homelessness by 2015;
- the reduction of the risk of long-term homelessness by improving the efficiency of social housing management; and
- the creation of more effective measures for preventing homelessness.

The same basic principles from the *Name on the Door* report, with a housing-led approach, and the Finnish 'Housing First' philosophy informing every aspect of strategy and service design were ingrained in *Paavo II*. The new programme worked with 11 cities, with a plan to develop 1,000 new homes, of which at least 500 were intended to be scattered housing, within the broader objective of facilitating wider access to general needs (ordinary) social housing for long-term homeless people. The plans for each city were to be more specifically tailored to their particular needs and there was a greater emphasis on the development of preventive services. Alongside these goals, there was an expectation that *Paavo II* would end the provision of emergency shelters across Finland.

Over the course of 2012–13, 1,057 additional housing units were brought into use, including 294 for young people with support needs; a further 652 homes were allocated for use as scattered housing. Across *Paavo II*, some €21 million was allocated for the construction and procurement of housing, with an additional €13.6 million for support services, totalling €34.6 million.

The most obvious difference from *Paavo I* was that rather than looking to convert and repurpose existing homelessness services, the Finns were also looking to develop and purchase scattered housing at scale, in parallel with improving access to the existing, ordinary social housing, which comprised around 12 per cent of total housing stock (Luomanen, 2011). Finnish social housing is not exactly 'scattered' as it tends to be built in blocks or across neighbourhoods in relatively high concentrations, but it was scattered in the sense that using this form of housing stock meant that long-term homeless people were living alongside ordinary Finns renting social housing. In contrast, some of the homes purchased by the Y Foundation are scattered among privately rented and owner-occupied housing.

In practice, Finland pursued a mixed approach to implementing its own version of Housing First, using a mix of congregate and scattered housing. This was not incompatible with the definition of Housing First being used: the congregate schemes remained a core component of national strategy but the Finns were not locked into any single approach to their version of Housing First. The emphasis remained on a housing-led approach to tackling all forms of homelessness. Floating (mobile) support being delivered to people with support needs living in ordinary housing was long established as a service model in Finland, being used by harm-reduction-focused addiction services and mental health services (Pleace et al, 2015).

Paavo II also saw an increased focus on homelessness prevention. Finland had been moving towards a more preventive approach for some time in the major cities, including Helsinki, which had been progressively investing more and more in stopping homelessness from occurring in the first place, but *Paavo II* increased preventive efforts at the national level. This echoed national strategy in Wales and England, which have since gone further than the Finns in reorienting towards a largely prevention-led approach at a strategic level (Mackie et al, 2017) in some respects, as well as the broad orientation of homelessness policy towards increased prevention in Scotland, Northern Ireland and parts of the US (Culhane et al, 2011). Again, however, there was a distinctly Finnish take on what was meant by homelessness prevention, with an emphasis on the idea of 'housing social work'. This meant scalable, responsive services that could provide housing advice and information but that were also able to triage individuals and step up the level of support provided when necessary. As with the broader strategy in *Paavo I*, *Paavo II* was again focused on the 'Housing First' philosophy that the Finns had developed: a housing-led and housing-focused approach that saw affordable housing supply as the central response to homelessness. In 2014, a Finnish policymaker described this thinking in the following terms (Pleace, 2014): 'We have realised there is a huge group of people with very low income who can't afford a reasonable flat … it is important also to focus on this group, I see it as part of the prevention of homelessness.' Work continued on youth homelessness prevention, with a goal to build 600 housing units and provide housing support services to 500 young people. This element of *Paavo II* was led by the Finnish Youth Housing Association (NAL) and funded by RAY. The development of specific provision for potentially homeless former offenders also continued.

Ireland

While changes in government and ministers do not feature strongly in the Finnish and Danish strategies, they deserve some mention in Ireland. The government that had approved the 2008 strategy continued to hold office during the period of the economic crisis and the arrival of the Troika (the European Central Bank, the International Monetary Fund and the World Bank). A general election in early 2011 saw a completely new government elected and a new Minister of State for Housing appointed, but this incoming government remained broadly committed to objectives set out in the 2008 strategy.

In late 2012, it was clear that the six objectives set out in the 2008 strategy were not being fully met, although in the absence of robust means of measurement, the extent of the shortfall was hard to quantify. At the same time, there was greater knowledge, awareness and dissemination of housing-led and Housing First approaches among NGOs and central and local government, particularly following the European Consensus Conference on Homelessness organised by the European Federation of National Organisations Working with the Homeless in December 2010.

As a result, a Housing First demonstration project was established in Dublin in April 2011. At the central government level, a view was taken that although there were difficulties in fully realising the six strategic objectives, they remained valid; however, housing-led and Housing First principles and approaches required enhancing. A review of these approaches was commissioned by the Department of the Environment, Community and Local Government (O'Sullivan, 2012).

This review ultimately culminated in the publication of a revised *Homelessness Policy Statement* in February 2013 (Department of the Environment, Community and Local Government, 2013). In contrast to the strategy adopted in 2008, it was a brief document. It aimed to end long-term homelessness and the need to sleep rough in Ireland by the end of 2016.[1] Long-term homelessness was later defined as living in emergency accommodation for longer than six months, but no data for the number of people falling into this category were available until the following year. The *Homelessness Policy Statement* proposed to end homelessness by adopting a 'housing-led' approach, which was defined as 'the rapid provision of secure housing, with support as needed to ensure sustainable tenancies' (Department of the Environment, Community and Local Government, 2013: 2).

The Assessment of Housing Need in 2013 showed an increase of 20 per cent in the number of households recorded as homeless, from 2,348 to 2,808 households. Despite the increases recorded between 2008 and 2013, the number of households recorded as homeless was relatively low, and with a targeted housing-led approach, there remained optimism that the number of households experiencing homelessness could be lessened and the numbers staying in emergency accommodation for more than six months could be significantly reduced.

The 2008 strategy was drafted during a period when house building was at record-high levels. After two years in which almost 90,000 homes were built in each year, housing construction slightly slowed in 2007 to just under 78,000 completions of houses and apartments

(CSO, 2008: 33). This amounted to 18 new homes for every 1,000 of the population, as compared to less than 7:1,000 in Finland and less than 6:1,000 in Denmark (CSO, 2008: 7) in the same year. Even though fewer than 9 per cent of these units were built by local authorities or voluntary housing associations, there were good reasons why accessing new housing units did not feature as a problem in the 2008 strategy. By the time of the new *Homelessness Policy Statement* in 2013, the impact of the economic crisis meant that new house construction had fallen to fewer than 5,000, with only 1,800 of these in urban areas (the balance being largely one-off rural constructions) (CSO, 2019). In response to this lack of new housing supply, the target of ending long-term homelessness was to be met primarily by bringing a large number of void social housing back into use and by redirecting these and casual social housing vacancies to people who were experiencing homelessness on a long-term basis.

To assist the minister in monitoring and measuring progress towards ending homelessness in 2016, a three-person Homelessness Oversight Group, comprising a senior social policy academic, a retired former senior civil servant and a partner in a private sector accountancy firm, was established. Some ten months later, in December 2013, the group produced its first, and ultimately only, report (Homelessness Oversight Group, 2013). The report noted that, in the absence of robust data, it was difficult to determine if progress was being made in reducing long-term homelessness, but that from the limited data available to them, the rate of reduction was 'too little and at too slow a pace' (Homelessness Oversight Group, 2013: 10) to achieve the policy objective of ending long-term homelessness in 2016. Despite this caveat, the report commented that given the relatively limited scale of long-term homelessness in Ireland, which they estimated at between 1,500 and 2,000, the target of ending long-term homelessness and the need to sleep rough by 2016 was realistic.

In addition, the government approved the establishment of a Homelessness Policy Implementation Team and a Central Implementation Unit in February 2014, charged with implementing the Homelessness Oversight Group's *First Report*. Whether the 2013 *Homelessness Policy Statement* replaced or augmented the 2008 strategy was not clear, nor was the relationship between the new Homelessness Policy Implementation Team and Homelessness Oversight Group with the NHCC or Cross-Departmental Team on Homelessness.

In May 2014, a detailed *Implementation Plan on the State's Response to Homelessness* was published by the Department of the

Environment, Community and Local Government (2014) (the lead government department with responsibility for homelessness policy). The implementation plan contained 80 specific actions that the department believed were required to end homelessness by the end of 2016. The implementation plan contained the first governmental reference to Housing First, noting that following a successful demonstration project in Dublin (Greenwood, 2015), a Dublin Housing First project targeting 100 rough sleepers, which was ultimately delivered by two NGOs, would be launched at the end of 2014 (Quinn, 2018).

In July 2014, a cabinet reshuffle led to the appointment of a new minister responsible for housing. Reflecting a growing political awareness that housing and homelessness were emerging as problems, responsibility for housing was upgraded from being the responsibility of a junior Minister in the department to being the responsibility of the full cabinet minister.

In April 2014, the current series of homelessness statistics was published for the first time, showing that 2,477 adults were living in emergency accommodation during the final week of the previous month. In early December 2014, a special 'summit' on homelessness was convened by the Minister for the Environment, Community and Local Government following the death of a man sleeping rough in the vicinity of the Irish Parliament. The outcome of the summit was a new *Action Plan to Address Homelessness*, which identified a further 20 actions aimed at ending homelessness, giving a total of 100 actions. These 100 action points included: identifying vacant housing units and making them available for homeless and other vulnerable households; prioritising homeless households for social housing allocations; putting in place protocols in relation to discharge from institutions; and securing rent supplements for homeless households. It was unclear whether the 100 action points agreed under the new minister augmented or replaced the 80 actions agreed under the previous junior minister, or how these related to the unfinished action points in the 2008 strategy. The minister appointed in 2014 did not reconvene the Homelessness Oversight Group.

In early 2015, the minister issued a legally binding directive to the larger urban local authorities requiring them to increase the proportion of new social housing tenancies (either arising from cyclical vacancies or voids that had been refurbished) that were allocated to homeless households. The Dublin local authorities were to allocate 50 per cent while the other larger towns were to allocate 30 per cent.

The third phase: 2016–18

Denmark

Despite the positive outcomes for individuals receiving the interventions, a major challenge for the second stage of the programme was that it did not achieve a significant level of scale. The overall number of citizens (about 350) rehoused through the programme was quite modest compared to the overall extent of homelessness at the point-in-time homelessness count in week six of 2015, showing that 6,138 individuals were in a homelessness situation at that time, increasing to 6,635 individuals at the count in week six of 2017 when the second-stage programme period had ended. The evaluation research pointed to various barriers to upscaling interventions. In particular, the lack of access to affordable housing was a main factor in almost all the municipalities that participated in the programme. The local provision of intensive support interventions such as ACT and ICM was also quite modest in scale compared to the overall number of homeless people and given the relatively high proportion with complex support needs among homeless people in Denmark (Benjaminsen and Enemark, 2017; Benjaminsen et al, 2017). As previously mentioned, the funding structure for the follow-up programme was different than for the initial strategy programme as in the follow-up programme, municipalities had to fund interventions out of their own local budget. Yet, in a context of generally tight municipal budgets, with local competition for spending in different areas of welfare services, an unintended consequence may have been that the scale of the programme turned out to be less ambitious than intended.

On the other hand, the positive results of the Housing First interventions in Denmark led to the continuation of Housing First as a leading principle of interventions in the third stage of the homelessness programme that was decided on in 2016, running from 2017 to 2019. The title of this programme was 'Extending Housing First'. The focus of this programme is generally in line with the second stage of the Danish programme ('The Implementation Programme') as the emphasis is on supporting municipalities in implementing the Housing First approach in their local welfare services by applying the basic principles of the approach and making the necessary changes to support this implementation, for example, in local housing allocation systems, the provision of floating support services and so on. In addition, an 'Action Plan' to alleviating homelessness, was initiated in 2017, running from 2018 to 2021 and with funding of DKK154 million (€20.5 million) attached to the plan. The action plan continued the ambition from previous programmes to extend Housing First interventions to a wider part of people experiencing homelessness as well as emphasising other elements such as the prevention of homelessness.

Finland

Both *Paavo I* and *II* had objectives of increasing preventive activity and this approach reflected longer-standing practice. For example, in Helsinki, in a context where the city's housing supply was coming under increasing pressure, there was a shift towards prevention as a means to try to reduce the need for emergency accommodation for families and other homeless people. The 2016–19 action plan (there was not to be another '*Paavo*' strategy) was introduced at a point where homelessness was already at very low levels and where the composition of the homeless population had changed, with the bulk of homelessness being made up of people living temporarily with friends or family, including most of those people classified as long-term homeless. As is discussed later in the book, Finland was reliant on essentially one main data source, which was a partially estimated annual survey; however, there was again the broad sense across the various agencies involved in homelessness that the numbers were continuing to fall.

In moving further towards a preventive approach, and bearing in mind that Finland had been pursuing prevention both before 2008 and during both *Paavo I* and *II*, Finland was again in line with broader international trends. While the Irish government published its 'Homelessness: A prevention strategy' in 2002, it can be argued that the first real shift towards action prevention happened in England in the mid-2000s, influencing American practice, and reached what may be its extreme with the prevention-led, Welsh strategy (Mackie et al, 2017 and subsequent 2017 English legislation). However, as with their use of a Housing First model, the Finns have taken their own path towards homelessness prevention, particularly around the concept of housing social work within preventive services.

Prevention was being pursued by attempting to build a comprehensive early warning system that operates across all public agencies that might be in a position to detect the risk of homelessness. Housing, health, social work and employment/welfare services are all to be involved in a multidisciplinary plan to orchestrate the relevant services when homelessness is threatened. Housing advice services are to be extended, there are specific provisions to reduce evictions among younger people and a *Pienlaina* (micro-lending) system offering very small loans to stop low-income households becoming overwhelmed by debt has been introduced, alongside existing municipal systems designed to stop eviction due to debt and poverty (Ympäristöministeriö, 2016).

Alongside this, the strategy has identified three further priorities, which are to: better understand and respond to gender issues in homelessness, which is a new element to the Finnish strategy that received less attention in *Paavo I* and *II*; continue the existing work on youth homelessness; and tackle migrant homelessness (Ympäristöministeriö, 2016). In part, these objectives were influenced by the 2014 international review (Pleace et al, 2015), which highlighted gender and also drew attention to very limited service provision for homeless migrants without the right of residence in Finland (which is a pan-European issue [see Baptista et al, 2017]). Equally, the shift in emphasis was also influenced by data from the annual survey, which reported that, in 2016, 23 per cent of lone homeless adults were women (ARA, 2017).

Concerns about the outcomes for people for whom Finnish Housing First did not work out, raised by the 2014 international review, were to be addressed by a system called *Pienet Tuvat* (Small Places), which appears to mirror the Danish *Skæve Huse* model, a form of small, sheltered congregate housing for formerly homeless people with high support needs, which offers a tolerant system of support (Ympäristöministeriö, 2016). The specifics of this approach have not been detailed in English and no results are available at the time of writing.

The action plan remains consistent with the Housing First approach first specified in the *Name on the Door* report, emphasising that housing must be secured at whatever point someone who is homeless or at risk of homelessness is encountered by public, NGO or charitably run services. Specific groups are specified but essentially include any and all populations potentially at risk of homelessness. A budget of €78 million was announced in 2016, of which around 70 per cent was to be spent on housing supply, with the remainder to be focused on services. The goal for housing development is to build 2,500 new housing units, concentrated in Helsinki but extending into other cities, and there is to be specific housing provision for young people, as under *Paavo I* and *II*. There are specific provisions to attempt to prevent migrant homelessness. At the time of writing, research and reviews on improving homelessness services for women were ongoing (Ympäristöministeriö, 2016; Pleace, 2017).

Alongside the emphasis on prevention, the new building of social housing, the development of services for women and people with complex needs for whom Finnish Housing First does not work, and the continued emphasis on youth homelessness, the 2016–19 action plan also emphasises service-user involvement, 'experts by experience' being the Finnish term. Formerly homeless people are being consulted about service design and approach, and there is also an emphasis on recruiting formerly homeless people as peer support workers in services; however, as yet, no results are available (Ympäristöministeriö, 2016).

Ireland

As the 2016 target date for ending long-term homelessness approached, it was clear not only that the target would not be met, but also that it was becoming increasingly irrelevant in the face of an emerging rapid rise in the number of adult individuals and families entering homelessness services. The second phase came to an end with an election in which the Labour Party (which had held the housing portfolio in the outgoing government, first, at minister of state level and, from 2014, at cabinet minister level) lost three quarters of its seats and no party had a majority in the Dail (Parliament).

The process of forming a new national government, composed of a Fine Gael (Christian-democrat)-led coalition, occurred during the period February to May 2016. An indication of the degree to which housing and homelessness were a priority for all political parties was the rapid establishment of an All-Party Committee on Housing and Homelessness in mid-April, which met in parallel with negotiations between the parties to form a new government. Having taken submissions from a wide range of interest groups, they produced a 157-page report on 17 June (Houses of the Oireachtas, 2016). On homelessness, it recommended that the government: increase the social housing stock by an average of 10,000 units per year for five years; increase security of tenure and protection from evictions for tenants in the private rented sector; reinstate the policy of ring-fencing 50 per cent of local authority allocations to the priority list in Dublin and other areas where homelessness is acute, which was introduced in January 2015 but had lapsed in April 2016; ensure that no homeless shelters are closed until alternative accommodation is available elsewhere; significantly expand Housing First; and enhance cooperation between homeless services and mental health services.

In May 2016, a new government was formed with *A Programme for Partnership Government*, which stated that '[i]t is not acceptable in 2016 to have families living in unsuitable emergency accommodation or to have people sleeping rough on our streets' (Government of Ireland, 2016: 19). In a further indication of the increasing political impact of the housing and homelessness issue, the government department was renamed the Department of Housing, Planning, Community and Local Government. The programme committed to: publish a new action plan for housing within 100 days; increase the rent limits on the rent supplement scheme; and substantially increase the social housing output. The document also promised that the action plan on housing would contain specific measures to prevent homelessness and to end the use of hostels and 'bed and breakfast' (B&B)-type accommodation as long-term emergency accommodation, primarily through the provision of rapid-build housing (Government of Ireland, 2016).

On 19 July, and within 100 days of the formation of the government, an action plan for housing and homelessness, entitled *Rebuilding Ireland* (Department of Housing, Planning, Community and Local Government, 2016), was launched. The plan stated that the 'long-term solution to the current homelessness issue is to increase the supply of homes' (Department of Housing, Planning, Community and Local Government, 2016: 33). The plan promised to: limit the use of hotels for accommodating homeless families by mid-2017; increase Housing First tenancies in Dublin from 100 to 300 by 2017; extend tenancy sustainment services across the country; and increase the amount of rent subsidy available to homeless households.

On 22 September 2016, an elaboration of the homelessness actions was published that, in addition to the earlier actions, promised to accelerate the rapid-build programme to ensure the provision of 1,500 units by the end of 2018, and to add 200 emergency beds for rough sleepers by the end of 2016. It is of note that the *Rebuilding Ireland* action plan does not contain a commitment to ending homelessness, in contrast to the 2008 and 2013 strategies.

Reviewing Rebuilding Ireland

In June 2017, a cabinet reshuffle led to a new Minister for Housing, Planning and Local Government being appointed. This new minister announced a review of the *Rebuilding Ireland* strategy and sought submissions in relation to 'what further action should now be considered in order to prevent homelessness, to find more permanent solutions for those in emergency accommodation and to help individuals and families to remain living in their own homes' (Department of Housing, Planning, Community and Local Government, 2017: 7). The deadline for submissions was 11 August 2017, but at the time of writing, the review has not been published. Two months later, in September, the minister called a 'Housing Summit' with the chief executives of the local authorities, which concluded with agreement, among other things: to provide an additional 200 shelter beds in Dublin by the end of December 2017; to provide additional funding in the amount of €10 million for family hubs; to provide increased funding for health services for those experiencing homelessness; to establish the Homeless Interagency Group to coordinate and deliver services to people experiencing homelessness[2]; to appoint a national director of Housing First; and to shift expenditure in social housing to direct-build programmes rather than acquiring existing properties to rent.

Shelters, hubs and managing homelessness

These multiple reports had a significant degree of overlap, both in analysis and in the measures announced. Increased provision of social housing and measures to address rent inflation in the private rented sector were central to all the reports. While many of the reports contain 'something new', for example, rapid-build housing or an extension of the Housing First project, the reports ultimately conclude that increasing the supply of housing, both public and private, is fundamental to reducing homelessness. The sundry plans provide slightly different timelines and output figures, as well as revisions of earlier objectives, but from the enormous pile of reports, the core recommendation of increasing the supply of housing remained the common denominator.

One significant development, not explicitly mentioned in these strategy documents, was the establishment of what were termed 'Family Hubs' in 2017 (O'Sullivan, 2017b). In relation to the *Rebuilding Ireland* commitment that homeless families should no longer have to be accommodated in commercial hotels, the strategy had stated that 'their needs will be met through the enhanced Housing Assistance Payment (HAP) scheme … and through general social housing allocations, as well as by tapping into wider housing supply' (Department of Housing, Planning, Community and Local Government, 2016: 36). However, by early 2017, less than six months after the publication of *Rebuilding Ireland*, a decision was taken by the Dublin Municipal Authorities to manage homeless families through the provision of what were initially termed 'Family Transition Hubs', with a capacity for 500 families and a budget of €25 million.

In these Hubs, families share various facilities (see Hearne and Murphy, 2018), described euphemistically as 'co-living' in the promotional video for the Hubs, and the length of stay is limited to six months. The first Hub was opened in March 2017, operated by the voluntary housing association Respond, and was described in the press release as 'our humanitarian response to address the needs of homeless families in Ireland today'.

By the end of 2018, there were 26 such Hubs in operation, with 22 in Dublin alone, having a capacity for 564 families (six Hubs are operated by private providers, with the remaining 16 operated by six NGOs). Most of the Hubs have a capacity of less than 40, but one, a former hotel converted into a Hub in Dublin city centre, has a capacity for 98 families.

There is no published rationale for the establishment of essentially congregate transitional supervised accommodation for homeless families, but it does seem to depart from the stated objective of homelessness policy in Ireland to move to a housing-led approach that would eschew the use of congregate emergency and transitional accommodation. The ideology supporting the Hubs appears to be based on a view of homeless families as families that have underlying psychosocial dysfunctions that require therapeutic intervention to ensure that they are adequately prepared for housing at the end of what is intended to be a six-month stay.

Thus, between 2008 and 2018, homelessness in Ireland became an increasingly significant social and political issue. More reports, strategies, reviews and analyses were produced by central and local government during that period than from the foundation of the state to 2008. The early optimism that long-term homelessness could be ended was increasingly replaced by narrower targets; however, as detailed Chapter 4, as the numbers of adults and children in emergency accommodation increased each month, even more modest targets, such as reducing the use of hotels and B&B-type accommodation by a certain date, were quietly abandoned.

Conclusion

In a reflective essay on the review and aftermath of the 2008 Irish strategy, one of the authors of the review of the initial homeless strategies noted that the ambition to end homelessness was 'feasible' due to, among other things: '[the] relatively small scale and concentrated nature of the problem; widespread agreement around the solutions that are necessary to address the problem; [and] the fact that if resources are pooled and deployed more effectively they should be largely sufficient to provide such solutions' (Brownlee, 2008: 40). This reflection could apply to all three countries.

While all three strategies, of course, built on preceding work, the groundwork for the Finnish strategy was more extensive, and the succeeding objectives, implementations, learnings and new objectives appear to build upon each other coherently. At the outset, all three strategies had one objective in common: to reduce the length of time that people remained in homeless accommodation. In the Irish and Finnish cases, this was expressed specifically as ending 'long-term homelessness', while in the Danish case, the objective was 'to reduce time spent in a shelter' to no more than three to four months. In the case of the Finnish strategy, this was the one central objective of *Paavo I*, and as progress was made on this, more specific objectives were added (for prevention, women and migrants). The Danish and Irish strategies set out with wider objectives (tackling rough sleeping, youth homelessness, prevention and so on).

In all three countries, and in line with most jurisdictions, dealing with homelessness is the responsibility, in the first place, of local government, so it is not surprising to see all three strategies attempt to work out practical arrangements to ensure that 'national' strategy is carried through into local actions. Only in Ireland do we see a legislative framework which seeks to ensure that every local authority engages in some way with a regional strategy, even where homelessness is rare in their locality. In Denmark and Finland, the concentration is more on engaging the larger population centres where homelessness is prevalent, using some form of financial or contractual arrangement. This balance of central and local authority follows through into the financing of the programmes under the strategy, with 90 per cent of homeless expenditure being covered by central government in Ireland (though, in practice, local government often has to make a higher contribution). A larger contribution is given from municipalities in Denmark, with a significant increase in local funding being a feature of the second and third phases of the programmes as, not entirely successful, efforts are made to incorporate the programmes into mainstream services. In Finland, funding sources are more complex, with significant funding for services and housing being allocated from central funds during each phase.

In Ireland, the 2008 strategy was ambitious in scope; it also coincided with a dramatic reduction in housing output, and, in particular, social housing output. Despite a range of innovative attempts to increase the availability of social housing through tackling voids in the existing stock and the provision of rapid-build housing, the numbers of adults and accompanying child dependants entering homelessness services grew virtually every month from when the new series of statistics were published. Homelessness, often in the form of the death of people sleeping rough, became a major media preoccupation and political issue. This escalation resulted not in a regrouping around the original 2008 consensus approach, but rather in a profusion of different initiatives, strategies and action points. This phase saw, for the first time, the establishment of a range of robust reporting mechanisms that produce monthly data on the number of households in emergency and temporary accommodation, as well as quarterly reports on a range of indicators, including length of time in temporary or emergency accommodation, exits from homelessness, and expenditure on these services. The fact that the escalation in the numbers of adults and child dependants entering homelessness and the sluggish numbers exiting could now be measured with a degree of accuracy and detail than was hitherto the case was of little solace to policymakers, practitioners and the those experiencing homelessness.

While *Paavo I* had not delivered the goals set in terms of ending long-term homelessness, it was evident, from a Finnish perspective, that it was effective enough to make it logical to keep going: while progress was slower than anticipated, the approach was still working. With *Paavo II*, Finland shifted from a homelessness strategy that had been about a specific problem with existing systems being unable to engage effectively with long-term homeless populations, which, in practice, meant building new services for homeless people with high and complex needs. *Paavo II* represented a shift from a targeted strategy about reducing one aspect of homelessness towards a much more ambitious goal that had now become about effectively eradicating homelessness altogether.

In Chapter 4, we will look in more detail at the outcomes of the three strategies through the data on homeless numbers and the evaluations and reviews that were carried out. In Chapters 5 and 6, we will start to see whether it is possible to find explanations for the different outcomes and why things worked out so differently, and, to some extent, ask the question as to whether these were in the control of the policymakers and politicians. Chapter 7 will try to draw lessons from these experiences and insights and explore to what extent such lessons might be usefully applied to future policy and other jurisdictions.

Notes

[1] The date chosen for ending homelessness (2016) was symbolically significant in Ireland as it marked the 100th anniversary of what is commonly known as the Easter Rising, an armed insurrection against British colonial power, which led to

further conflict between 1919 and 1921, ending in British withdrawal from the southern part of the island of Ireland.

2. The terms of reference for the Homeless Interagency Group noted that the work of the group was to be 'informed by the "housing-led"/"Housing-First" policy objectives of the 2013 Homelessness Policy Statement and commitments entered into via the 2016 Government strategy Rebuilding Ireland: Action Plan on Housing and Homelessness'.

4

Trends in homelessness in Denmark, Finland and Ireland

Introduction

This chapter outlines trends in recorded homelessness in the three countries between about 2008 and 2018/19. It first explores in some detail how homelessness is measured in each of the three countries. Each country uses a variety of methodologies to measure homelessness and it is important that the strengths and limitations of these different approaches are understood, particularly in relation to their comparability. In the case of Denmark, data from the national client registration system on homeless hostels are gathered by Statistics Denmark, in addition to a biennial count of adults experiencing homelessness conducted by the Danish Centre for Social Science Research. These two sources provide the basis for the measurement of homelessness in Denmark. Methodologically, the Finnish measurement is based on both administrative data and some estimates, based on a point in time in each year. Such an approach has its limitations, but as it is conducted on a consistent basis, it does allow for the reliable measurement of trends. In Ireland, data on homelessness are primarily based on administrative data via the Pathway Accommodation & Support System (PASS), a national bed-management system for homelessness services, and since April 2014, a monthly report on the number of households in designated homeless accommodation, broken down by gender, age and nature of accommodation, supplemented by a twice yearly survey of rough sleepers in Dublin. Data are also generated from PASS on a quarterly basis on entries to and exits from emergency accommodation, in addition to length of stay.

Of the three methodologies for measuring homelessness, the methodology in Denmark is the most sophisticated and robust, utilising as it does both administrative and survey data. As is well documented, comparative work on the extent of homelessness is beset with definitional issues (Busch-Geertsema et al, 2014; Pleace, 2016a). Having explored the full range of data on homelessness in each country, we then focus on those living rough, in emergency accommodation and in accommodation for the homeless. These are the first three categories in the European Typology of Homelessness and Housing Exclusion (ETHOS), which was described in Chapter 1.

It is important to note that while the comparative figures used in this chapter include only those sleeping rough or in emergency and temporary accommodation, this is a pragmatic, rather than an ideological, decision done only because Ireland does not adequately capture the 'hidden homeless', that is, 'people living in insecure accommodation'. Furthermore, to ensure that we are comparing 'like with like', we are only including ETHOS categories 1–3. In both Finland and Denmark, state measurements of homelessness are inclusive of the 'hidden homeless' population; indeed, they account for the majority of people experiencing homelessness in Finland and about two out of five of the people recorded to be in a homelessness situation in Denmark. Thus, we first present the total number of people experiencing homelessness in these countries, and then, for comparison purposes, present the number in the first three operational categories of homelessness in the ETHOS conceptual framework.

Measuring homelessness and trends in Denmark, 2009–19

In Denmark, there are two main data sources measuring homelessness. Since 1999, administrative data on use of shelters for those experiencing homelessness have been collected nationwide, and national homelessness counts have been conducted every second year since 2007. While the administrative data from homeless shelters are recorded continuously throughout the year, the homelessness count is a point-in-time count based on data collection during a 'count week'. Besides the difference in measurement time, these two data sources have other principal differences as they cover different parts of the ETHOS definition, and also differ in the types of services included in the data collection. While the shelter data only cover shelter users, the measurement of homelessness in the national homelessness count is broader as it includes not only shelter users, but also other ETHOS categories: rough sleepers, people staying temporarily with family or friends, people in short-term transitional housing, people in hotels due to homelessness, and people awaiting discharge from hospitals or treatment facilities, or release from prison, within a month without a housing solution being in place. Accordingly, the data collection for the homelessness count is based on not only data from homeless shelters, but also a wide range of other agencies and services in the welfare system, such as municipal social services, job centres, psychiatric and addiction treatment facilities, and so on.

An important insight from having multiple data sources on homelessness in Denmark is that the different types of data complement each other in understanding the overall pattern of homelessness in terms of both extent and profiles. In the following, we shall examine these differences in more detail, with a focus on trends and patterns over the period from 2009, the onset of the Danish homelessness strategy, to 2019.

Shelter data collected since 1999

Since 1999, data from homeless shelters in Denmark have been recorded through client registration systems and collected nationwide from central data authorities. Initially, from 1999, these data were collected by the Danish Social Appeals Board, but from 2016, the responsibility was transferred to Statistics Denmark, which is generally responsible for collecting administrative data from a wide range of domains of the Danish welfare system.

The shelter data cover all homeless shelters operating under section 110 of the Social Service Act, which requires local authorities to provide temporary accommodation to people who have no place to live or cannot live in the dwelling that they have due to social problems. Thus, besides people in a homelessness situation, homeless shelters can also be used by people who are 'functionally homeless' despite actually having a dwelling, although this latter group only encompasses a small number of the individuals recorded in the data. When enrolling in a homeless shelter, individuals must give their personal number to the shelter, which enables the identification of unique users in the data. Reporting data for the national database is mandatory for the homeless shelters that operate with public funding under the Social Service Act. There are about 70 homeless shelters nationwide operating under this law, which are run either directly by municipalities or by non-governmental organisations (NGOs). Most of these shelters provide emergency accommodation (direct access), as well as temporary accommodation for a longer period. Besides the section 110 shelters, there are also a small number of very basic and low-threshold emergency night shelters, mainly in larger cities, where users can be anonymous and where data for the general database on shelter use are not collected.

Shelter use remained constant over the period of the Danish homelessness strategy and Figure 4.1 shows the annual number of

Figure 4.1: Annual number of homeless shelter users in Denmark, 1999–2018

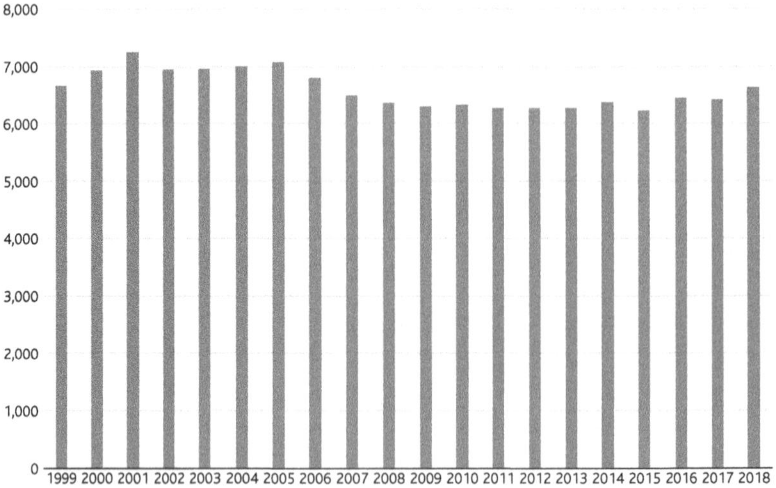

Source: Statistics Denmark, www.statistikbanken.dk, Annual users of Section 110 Accommodation.

shelter users in Denmark from 1999 to 2018, giving information on the number of unique (individual) users each year since the data collection started.

The shelter statistics reveal that the annual number of shelter users in Denmark has been remarkably constant over the entirety of this 18-year period, both in the years after the national strategy was initiated from 2009 and during the decade before. The highest annual figure recorded was in 2001, when 7,286 individuals used a homeless shelter. The lowest figure was recorded in 2015, when 6,223 individuals used a homeless shelter. Although a moderate decrease appears from about 7,000 people using a shelter annually in the early 2000s to about 6,000 shelter users annually from about 2007 onward, this decrease actually took place in the years before the national strategy was initiated as 7,071 shelter users were recorded in 2005 compared to 6,301 in 2009. However, during the years from 2009 onward, the annual number of shelter users remained steady and even moderately increased from 2015 and onwards.

Homelessness counts every second year since 2007

The second major data source on homelessness in Denmark is the national homelessness counts that have been carried out every second year since 2007. These counts are point-in-time counts based on the same methodology as similar counts in Norway and Sweden. The homelessness counts not only encompass the categories of rough sleepers and homeless shelter users, but also aim to include various forms of 'hidden homelessness', most notably, the group of 'sofa surfers', people who stay temporarily with family and friends due to the absence of their own place to live. Moreover, the homelessness counts also include people staying in, for instance, hotels, caravans and garden allotment houses due to homelessness, people in short-term transitional housing, and people about to be discharged from hospitals or other treatment facilities, or released from prisons, without a housing solution in place.

In order to include these broader categories of homelessness, the counts collect data not only from homelessness services, but also from a wide range of other services and agencies in the Danish welfare system, such as municipal social centres, employment offices and addiction and psychiatric treatment facilities. In particular, people in hidden homelessness are often in contact with such services and many of the sofa surfers recorded in the count are reported from these broader types of welfare services outside the homelessness sector. The count is conducted by asking this broad range of services to fill out a two-page questionnaire for each homeless person that they are in contact with, or who are otherwise known by the services to be in a homelessness situation, during the count week. Individual data are collected for each person and a control for double counting (the use of multiple services) is performed using personal numbers, initials, birth dates and so on.

The count takes place in week six of every second year. During this cold winter time in February, a high share of homeless people are assumed to be indoors and in contact with services compared to the warmer summer time. However, as being recorded in the count depends on being in contact with some form of services, there will always be people in a homelessness situation who are not included in the counts. Although there may be people with very complex support needs who have fallen completely through the welfare safety net, in the context of the extensive Danish welfare system, the most likely group to be under-represented in the count are people in hidden homelessness: those who are in precarious and unstable housing arrangements trying to get by without the involvement of social services. Thus, in practice, people in hidden homelessness are counted insofar as they are in contact with some kind of social or health services. As a wide range of services take part in the count, we can be reasonably confident that the count provides a relatively comprehensive and consistent snapshot of the extent and profile of homelessness in Denmark in the count week.

Figure 4.2: Homeless people recorded in the Danish homelessness counts, 2009– 2019

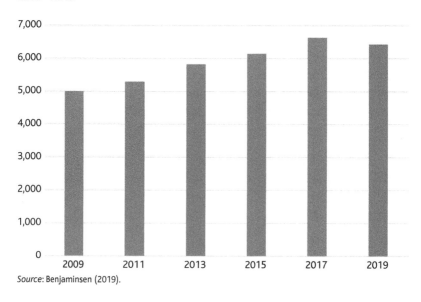

Source: Benjaminsen (2019).

Figure 4.2 shows the number of homeless people recorded in the Danish homelessness counts from 2009 to 2019. As the definition was adapted slightly following the first count in 2007, data from 2009 are used as a baseline. An overall increase in homelessness was observed over the period as 4,998 individuals were recorded as being in a homelessness situation in week six of 2009, increasing to 5,290 in 2011 and to 5,820 in 2013, when the period of the homelessness strategy ended. A further increase was observed to 6,138 homeless people in the count in 2015, and to 6,635 homeless people recorded in 2017. Thus, homelessness in Denmark measured by the point-in-time homelessness counts continued to increase throughout the period covered by the homelessness strategy and the succeeding implementation programme and only in the latest count a slight decrease to 6,431 homeless people was recorded in 2019.

As the data from the homelessness count are a point-in-time measure, these figures cannot be directly compared with the annual shelter statistics that are based on recordings of shelter use throughout the year. In Table 4.1 the results from the homelessness count are delineated by homelessness categories. About one out of ten of the homeless people recorded in the counts were rough sleepers. A homeless person who was recorded as a rough sleeper at any time during the count week was placed in this category, although they might have been recorded in other homelessness situations as well during the count week. The count data also show that during the count week, about 2,000 people

Table 4.1: Individuals by homelessness situation, Danish homelessness counts, 2009–19

	2009	2011	2013	2015	2017	2019
Rough sleeping	506	426	595	609	648	732
Emergency night shelter	355	283	349	345	305	313
Shelter/hostel	1,952	1,874	2,015	2,102	2,217	2,290
Hotel	88	68	70	113	165	191
Family and friends	1,086	1,433	1,653	1,876	2,177	1,630
Short-term transitional	164	227	211	178	169	121
Release from prison	86	88	64	90	68	72
Discharge from hospital	172	173	119	138	149	148
Other or unknown	589	718	744	687	737	934
Total	4,998	5,290	5,820	6,138	6,635	6,431

Source: Benjaminsen (2019).

were recorded in the category 'shelter/hostel', which are the section 110 shelters that are included in the annual shelter statistics compared to the more than 6,000 people that use the shelters on an annual basis. When it is taken into account that some rough sleepers and users of the low-threshold emergency night shelters also used the regular shelters, there were for instance 2,310 people recorded as using the section 110 shelters during the count week in 2017 (Benjaminsen, 2017: 28). This figure widely resembled the number of beds in these shelters, which was about 2,200 beds in 2017. Thus, there were approximately three times as many people using homeless shelters over the year than during the count week. This shows the importance of being precise about the periodisation when comparing homelessness figures and shelter statistics between different countries.

The table shows that the second-largest group recorded in the count, besides shelter users, is the group staying temporarily with family or friends. This is also the category that has shown the largest growth over the period, from 1,086 recorded as sofa surfers in 2009 to 2,177 people in 2017. In 2017, this group was almost the same size as the group of shelter users although it fell considerably in 2019 when the number of young homeless people fell for the first time over the period when the counts have been conducted.

One possible explanation for the significant increase in the number of sofa surfers recorded in the counts might be that the welfare agencies

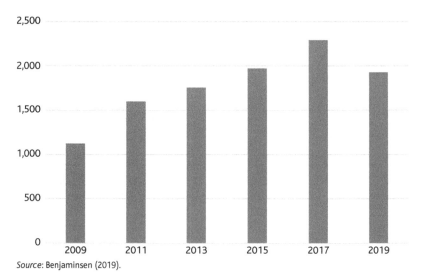

Figure 4.3: Young homeless people, 18–29 years old in the Danish homelessness counts, 2009–2019

Source: Benjaminsen (2019).

and services have become better at counting the hidden homeless over the period since the first counts. However, the data from the Danish counts also reveal that the strong increase in the number of sofa surfers recorded over most of the period was widely attributable to a strong increase in youth homelessness, and sofa surfing is by far the most typical homelessness situation among young homeless people. Figure 4.3 shows how a dramatic increase in homelessness among young people aged 18–29 occurred from 2009 to 2017. While 1,123 individuals aged 18–29 were recorded in the count in 2009, this figure had more than doubled in 2017, when 2,292 young people aged 18–29 were recorded during the count week. Only in the most recent count from 2019 this number decreased to 1,928 young homeless people, which was still considerably higher than in 2009. Thus, by the end of the period almost one in three homeless people in Denmark was a young person under 30 years of age.

While the annual number of shelter users in Denmark has remained widely unchanged since 2009, the figures from the homelessness count imply an upward trend in homelessness in Denmark over the period from 2009 onward with figures stagnating only at the end of the period. Moreover, the discrepancy between rising numbers of people in homelessness and constant numbers of shelter users may also indicate a shelter system running at full capacity or even a lack of beds locally.

It may seem surprising that a comprehensive national homelessness strategy with a relatively large rehousing and support programme did not succeed in reducing the number of people affected by homelessness over the programme period. As we shall explore in greater detail in Chapters 5 and 6, further analysis on Danish homelessness data has shown that the housing and support programmes of the Danish homelessness strategy and its succeeding implementation programme did not encompass more than 5 per cent of the overall number of people that were recorded as homeless in Denmark at some point in time during the period between 2009 to 2015 when shelter data and count data are combined (Benjaminsen and Enemark, 2017). Moreover, the strong increase in youth homelessness over a short time span implies that structural factors impact heavily on homelessness patterns and that young people are likely to have been most exposed to general changes in welfare systems and housing markets as reduced welfare benefits for young people and an increasing shortage of affordable housing affects vulnerable youth the most.

Measuring homelessness and trends in Finland, 2008–18

Data in Finland are less extensive than those collected in Denmark and, as will be seen, in Ireland. Information is centred on an annual survey that has been undertaken since 1987 within the Housing Market Survey conducted by the Housing Finance and Development Centre of Finland (*Asumisen rahoitus-ja kehittämiskeskus* [ARA]).[1] Detailed descriptions of the methodology are not published in English, but the survey collects a set of data on different forms of homelessness in each municipality (local authority) in Finland; counts of the different forms of homelessness in some municipalities are combined with estimates from others in the same reports. The survey is conducted at the same point (15 November) in each year.

Response rates are typically high. On average, 93 per cent of municipalities responded to the survey over the course of 2012–18, with levels never falling below 92 per cent (authors' analysis of ARA data). The range of data collected is narrower than in Ireland or Denmark, being centred on headcounts of specific groups within the homeless population. As at the 2018 count (ARA, 2019), these can be summarised as follows:

- homeless people living outside, in staircases, in larger structures and shelters;
- homeless people in dormitories and boarding houses;
- homeless people in institutional units (including prisons and hospitals);

- homeless people living temporarily with friends or relatives (because they have nowhere else to go);
- lone homeless adults;
- homeless women;
- homeless young people (aged under 25);
- immigrants who are homeless;
- homeless families with children;
- homeless immigrant families; and
- long-term homeless people (homeless for at least one year or several times in the last three years).

During the course of *Paavo I* and *II*, there was an emphasis on recording data on the changes in long-term homelessness and in tracking progress in the cities that were partners in the national integrated homelessness strategy. Partners were considered to be those who had signed the 'letter of intent' that signed them up to *Paavo I/II*.

The Finnish data have been collected in a broadly consistent manner since 1987, which allows for the long-term tracking of trends in homelessness levels due to their more comprehensive, more recently adopted, practices in administrative data collection and survey methodology, which is not possible in either Denmark or Ireland. The annual ARA survey also enabled Finland to understand and record the presence of the long-term homeless population, as well as to develop the Finnish version of a Housing First strategy that was to form the core of *Paavo I* and play a key role in *Paavo II* and the third phase of the Finnish strategy.

Performance has been assessed against a consistently collected, but partially estimated, headcount of different groups of homeless people, lacking the individual detail recorded in some other point-in-time counts but also, as in Denmark, using a broader definition of homelessness, for example, hidden homelessness, than is employed in many other European countries (Busch-Geertsema et al, 2014). There are a number of limitations with this data set that centre on the inability to record the flows within, alongside the flows into and out of, the homeless population.

The Finnish data do not record whether someone has been homeless, exited homelessness and returned to homelessness sometime later. There are data on whether someone has been homeless for a long time, which includes people who have been resident in homelessness services and situations defined as homelessness for a year or more, or on a recurrent basis in the last three years, but the patterns of their

Trends in homelessness in Denmark, Finland and Ireland

service use cannot be tracked in the same way as in Denmark or, to a lesser extent, because data are time limited, in Ireland.

Equally, it is not possible to accurately measure the extent of what the Americans have defined as 'transitional' homelessness (Kuhn and Culhane, 1998): homelessness that begins, is experienced and finishes between one annual count and the next. Finland also lacks detailed data on the needs, characteristics, experiences and trajectories of its homeless population (Pleace, 2017). Further, while response rates are high, not every municipality answers the survey and others provide estimates, which means that groups like hidden homeless people and some people living rough might be missed. There are inherent limits to any point-in-time count. These limitations can be summarised very simply: it is likely that at least some people will be missed (Busch-Geertsema, 2010; Busch-Geertsema et al, 2014).

In comparison to Denmark and Ireland, Finland collects comparatively limited data, but this data collection is in the context of the, again, comparatively simple goals of *Paavo I/II* and the 2016–19 action plan, which included reducing long-term homelessness to the point where it is close to non-existent, preventing homelessness where possible and reducing overall levels of homelessness. While the target for *Paavo I* was an estimate, at around 2,500 long-term homeless people in 2007 (Luomanen, 2010), according to the results of the annual ARA count, long-term homelessness fell markedly under *Paavo I* and *II*, dropping by 31 per cent between 2011 and 2017, as shown in Figure 4.4.

According to the annual ARA surveys, total homelessness fell significantly over the period 2008–18. The two trends were changes

Figure 4.4: Long-term homelessness in Finland, 2011–18

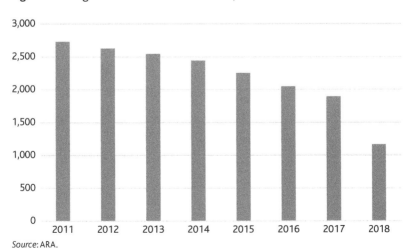

Source: ARA.

in the locations in which homelessness was experienced and in the forms of homelessness being experienced. There was a significant fall in the level of people living in hostels or boarding houses, the reduction reflecting the effective replacement of older models of congregate and communal supported housing with Housing First and housing-led models, as well as the greatly reduced use of emergency accommodation, with levels falling by 58 per cent between 2008 and 2018, as shown in Figure 4.4.

Alongside this, there were marked falls in the number of people defined as homeless in various institutional settings, including prison and long stays in hospitals (see Figures 4.5 and 4.6). While in line with ETHOS, the idea that someone can be 'homeless' while in an institutional setting (on the basis that there is no home available for them to move into when they leave that institution) is contentious, with many other countries only defining someone as homeless at the point at which they leave an institution if they still have no home to go to (Busch-Geertsema et al, 2014). Between 2008 and 2018, there was a 78 per cent fall in the population recorded as homeless in institutional settings.

Levels of people living rough remained fairly constant during the 2008–18 period and the same was true with respect to the level of hidden homelessness recorded by the annual ARA survey. Figures were at their peak in 2008, with 488 rough sleepers recorded, reaching a low point of 332 in 2013, rising to 417 in 2017, but declining to

Figure 4.5: Living rough and in shelters/accommodation for homeless people in Finland, 2008–18

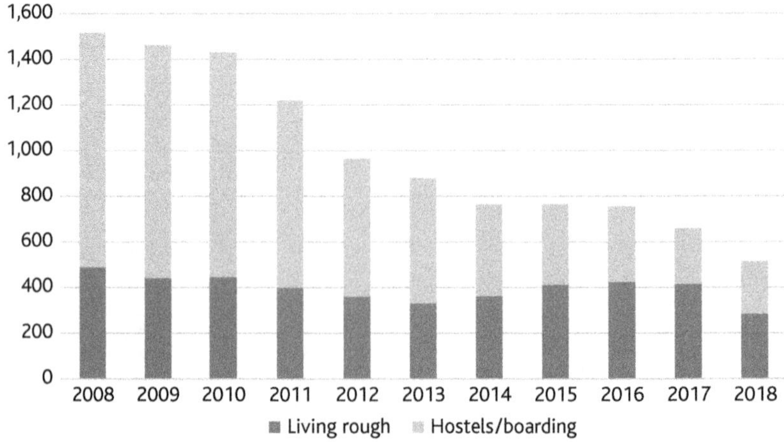

Source: ARA.

Figure 4.6: Homeless people living temporarily in institutions in Finland, 2008–18

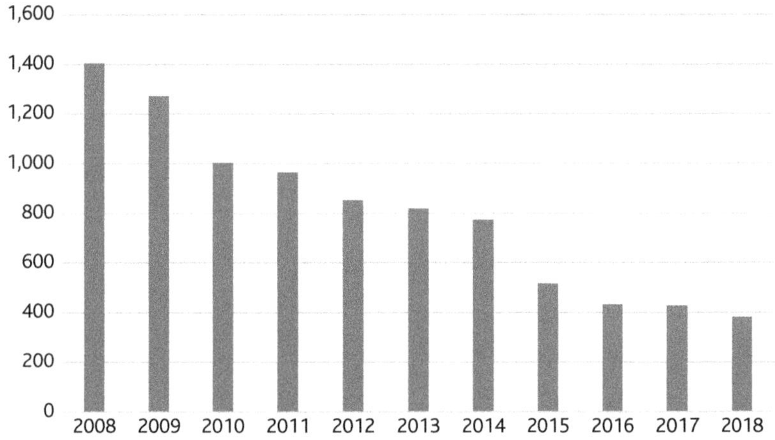

Source: ARA.

283 in 2018. The average across the 2008–18 counts was 397 and the median was 411. As in Denmark, according to the survey data, most of the population recorded as homeless in Finland were experiencing hidden homelessness over the course of 2008–18. Figures here range from a low of 4,795 in 2008 to a peak of 5,795 in 2012; the average across the 2008–18 counts was 5,174 and the median was 5,414.

With the caveats about the Finnish data collection through the annual ARA survey, these figures need to be seen in the context of the total levels of homelessness. During the 2008–18 period, recorded single homelessness peaked at 8,150 in 2009 and dropped to 4,882 by 2018. According to the ARA statistics, single homelessness was 17 per cent less in 2017 than in 2008.

As noted earlier in this book, it is important to see these figures in a wider context of Finland having steadily reduced homelessness to comparatively low levels by the point it began to focus initially on long-term homelessness in *Paavo I*, before moving onto a wider programme to prevent and reduce all forms of homelessness in *Paavo II* and the subsequent 2016–19 programme. As harsh and damaging as homelessness is for the people who experience it, Finland took what was, from a wider European perspective, a residual social problem in terms of scale and reduced that problem still further by 2018. Looking at the ARA data in detail, and considering some of the limitations of those data, the complexities underlying the headline success of Finland in reducing and preventing homelessness become evident. Total levels of lone adult homelessness, long-term homelessness and the use of temporary accommodation were brought down, but rough

Figure 4.7: Homeless families in Finland, 2008–18

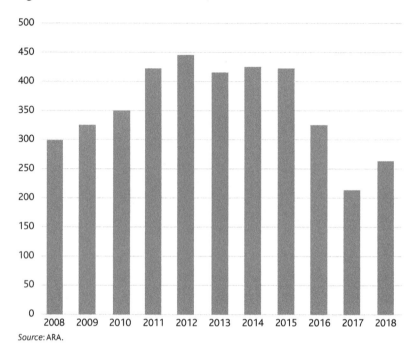

Source: ARA.

sleeping and hidden homelessness, while not occurring at scale relative to the population level and experience elsewhere in Western Europe (Busch-Geertsema et al, 2014; FEANTSA and FAP, 2018), remained at similar levels.

According to the ARA statistics (see Figure 4.7), family homelessness exists at only a small scale in Finland. An increase over the period 2008–12 has been followed by marked falls in reported levels in 2016 and 2017, albeit with a slight increase in 2018. Nonetheless, levels in 2018 were 12 per cent less than in 2008, although there had been a rise in levels over the period 2011–15.

As in Denmark and Ireland, homelessness was concentrated in the capital. Helsinki saw falls from 4,100 homeless people in 2012 to 2,114 in 2018, although the picture was not one of steady reduction, with levels in 2015 having been 3,550 less than the level recorded two years later. While there was an overall reduction, levels had remained broadly constant between the 3,500 to 4,000 level, suggesting that the national-level successes in reducing overall homelessness were not being entirely matched by what was being achieved in Helsinki, albeit that levels had been kept steady and, in overall terms, brought down.

The funding over the 2008–15 period in Finland has been estimated at over €420 million. In summary, this included:

- matched funding of up to 50 per cent from ARA, which has strategic responsibility for housing development, for new-build housing of €84 million;
- a further €87 million from the Finnish Slot Machine Association (*Raha-automaattiyhdistysthe* [RAY]) and the national lottery in grants for buying apartments;
- low-cost loans for social house building of €84 million, and €87 million in loans for buying apartments (approximate figures) from municipalities and NGOs; and
- grants for support services from the central government Ministry of Social Affairs and Health Development of €20 million, and a further €20 million from NGOs and municipalities.

As noted earlier, Finland researched the cost effectiveness of the *Paavo* programmes. This reported very strong results, with an average saving of €15,000 per person per year when someone was transitioned out of support housing into a settled home, including cost offsets for ending homelessness for health and criminal justice systems. Typically, rehousing a homeless person was assessed as (effectively) paying for itself with seven years. Furthermore, according to analysis by the University of Tampere and the Y Foundation, the reduced levels of support needed and the return of some homeless people to the workforce produced potentially greater savings over time.

Measuring homelessness and trends in Ireland, 2008–18

The 2008 strategy identified a number of key performance indicators for monitoring progress in eliminating the 'need to sleep rough' (Department of the Environment, Heritage and Local Government, 2008: 8) and long-term use of emergency shelter beds by 2010. In addition to monitoring expenditure on homeless services, these included the overall number of households experiencing homelessness, the numbers entering and exiting homelessness services, and the numbers sleeping rough and in emergency accommodation for more than six months. The *National Implementation Plan* for the strategy published in 2009 noted the 'importance of data and information on all aspects of homelessness' and that it was essential to be able to identify the 'pathways into and out of homelessness and any barriers that lie therein' (Department of the Environment, Heritage and Local

Government, 2009: 43). However, in practice, no such quantifiable indicators were developed, and it was not until 2014 that these indicators were requested from the local authorities.[2]

Prior to 2014, the only national-level data on the extent of homelessness came from the, at the time, periodic assessments of social housing need as homelessness was one of the categories of need. Data from the 2008, 2011 and 2013 assessments showed an increase in the number of households recorded as homeless, from 1,394 in 2008 to 2,348 in 2011 and increasing further to 2,808 in 2013. Although criticised for its methodological limitations, the fact that the 2013 figure is broadly similar to the more methodologically robust PASS data suggests that the data prior to 2014 provide a reasonably accurate point-in-time count of adult homelessness in Ireland.

In tandem with the publication of the *Homelessness Policy Statement* in February 2013, the Department of Housing identified many of the same indicators that were identified in the 2008 strategy; the purpose of these indicators was to 'give a clearer picture of homelessness in Ireland: the rate of entry, duration and exits, together with the type and nature of accommodation' (Department of Environment, Community and Local Government, 2013: 4). The statement also stressed that the 'extent of homelessness in Ireland must be quantified with confidence so that realistic and practical solutions can be brought forward. It is acknowledged that good data is critical' (Department of Environment, Community and Local Government, 2013: 4). Three key measures were developed: monthly stock or point-in-time data on the number of adults and accompanying child dependants in temporary and emergency accommodation funded by the local authorities; quarterly data on the number of adults/households entering and exiting homelessness, including data on the length of time that adults were in emergency accommodation; and quarterly data on expenditure on homelessness services.

Quarterly performance reports

From January 2014 onward, at the end of each quarter, local authorities were required by the Department of Housing to produce performance reports providing data on a range of indicators, including: the number of new and repeat adult presentations to homelessness services per quarter; the number of adults in emergency accommodation for more than six months; the number of adult individuals exiting homeless services to tenancies in the local authority sector, approved housing bodies or private rented sector (including those in receipt of the Housing

Figure 4.8: New adult presentations to homeless services in Ireland, Q1 2014–Q4 2018

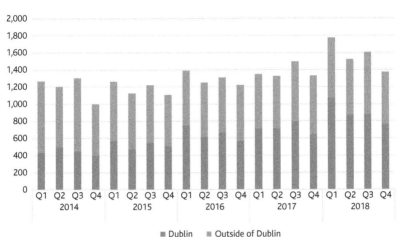

Source: Department of Housing, Planning and Local Government, quarterly performance reports, various years.

Assistance Payment [HAP]), with or without support; and the number of rough sleepers. Since Q1 2014, these reports have provided flow data on the number of adults entering (new and repeat) and exiting emergency and temporary homeless services to local authority housing, approved housing bodies and the private rented sector (including HAP) each quarter, in addition to their length of stay in such accommodation.

As shown in Figure 4.8, between Q1 2014 and Q4 2018, an average of nearly 600 new presentations by adult individuals to homeless services, who were assessed and accepted as homeless, were made per quarter in Dublin, with nearly 700 new presentations outside of Dublin. These are adults who were not previously recorded on the PASS system in the previous two years, and although they may have accessed services previously, they are recorded as new if their episode(s) of accessing homeless services was more than two years prior.[3] In addition to this monthly inflow of new entries to homeless services, there are the numbers of adult individuals accepted as in need of emergency services in a previous quarter but still using emergency services. Thus, at the end of Q4 2018, in addition to the 762 new adult entries to homeless services in Dublin and 610 outside Dublin, there were 4,661 adults in Dublin and 6,647 outside of Dublin who entered homeless services in previous quarters and had either used emergency accommodation services or who had returned to emergency services after previously exiting in the final quarter of 2018. In terms of a daily average, in Q4 2018, just under 15 new presentations and 121 repeat presentations were made.

Figure 4.9: Exits from emergency accommodation to housing (local authority, approved housing body, private rented sector and HAP), Q1 2014–Q4 2018

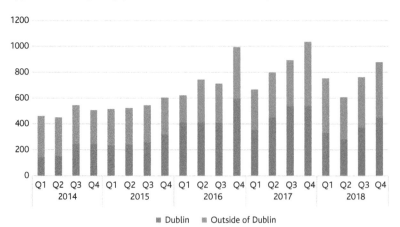

Source: Department of Housing, Planning and Local Government, quarterly performance reports, various years.

Exits from homelessness

This considerable inflow into homelessness is not matched by an equivalent outflow. Although the outflow from homeless services to tenancies in social housing or private renting with subsidies has significantly increased from over 400 adults in Q1 2014 to just nearly 900 in Q4 2018, as shown in Figure 4.9, it is not keeping pace with the rate of inflow into emergency services, hence the ongoing increase in repeat cases quarter on quarter. In Dublin, between 2014 and 2018, 46 per cent of exits to tenancies were to tenancies in the social housing sector (local authority or approved housing body), with the balance receiving social housing support via an income supplement in the private rented sector, usually with the aid of a HAP. Outside of Dublin, 58 per cent of the tenancies secured to exit emergency accommodation were via an income supplement in the private rented sector.

In addition to exits from emergency accommodation to tenancies, there are other less secure exits to family and friends and to health or criminal justice services, as well as relocations to Poland via the Barka Foundation in Dublin. For example, in Dublin in 2018, in addition to the over 1,400 individual adult exits to tenancies, a further nearly 750 adults exited emergency accommodation to family/friends and other services, including 63 relocations to other countries, primarily Poland, and just over 400 exits to health or criminal justice services. With the exception of those relocated, a significant number of the

Figure 4.10: Number of adults in emergency accommodation in Ireland for longer than six months, Q1 2014–Q4 2018

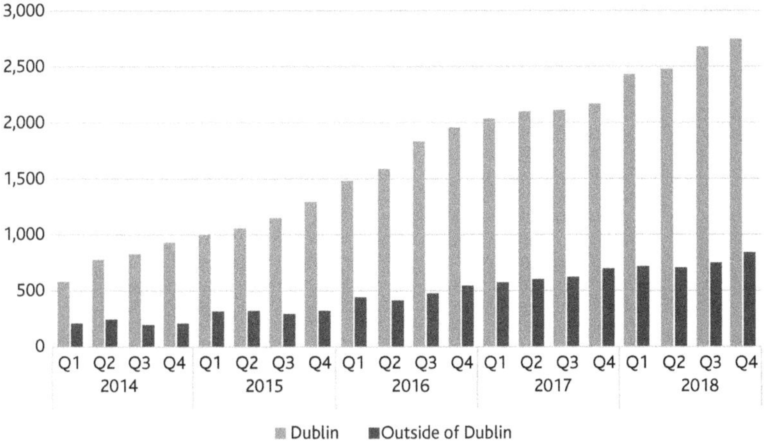

■ Dublin   ■ Outside of Dublin

Source: Department of Housing, Planning and Local Government, quarterly performance reports, various years.

non-tenancy exits return to emergency services. This excess inflow over outflow is also reflected in Figure 4.10, where the number of adults in emergency accommodation for more than six months has risen steadily quarter on quarter since 2014, with nearly a quadrupling of the numbers in Dublin and more than a tripling outside of Dublin. This was a key measure of ending homelessness in the 2013 *Homelessness Policy Statement*: adults would not be in emergency services for more than six months by the end of 2016.

Monthly reports

The publication of monthly reports commenced in April 2014 on a trial basis, and from June 2014, with some modifications, they have been produced on a continuous monthly basis, as shown in Figure 4.11. These data show a 150 per cent increase nationally in the number of adults in emergency and temporary accommodation services in a given week each month between April 2014 and December 2018, and a nearly 400 per cent increase in the number of accompanying child dependants, from 2,477 adults and 727 accompanying child dependants to 6,194 adults and 3,559 accompanying child dependants.

Data are also published on the profile of households in the designated services by household composition, gender, age, nature of accommodation provided for adults and the number of accompanying

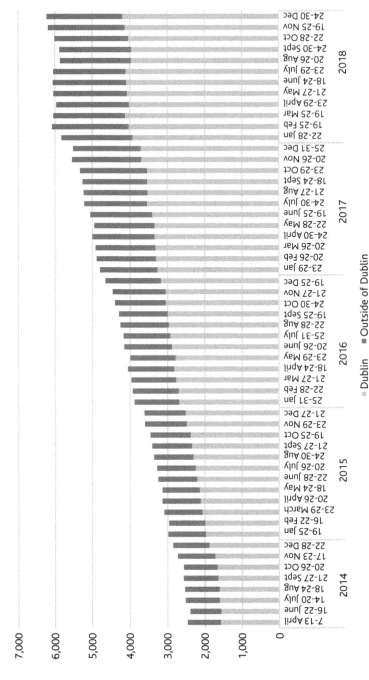

Figure 4.11: Number of adults in section 10 emergency and temporary accommodation in Ireland, April 2014–December 2018

Source: Department of Housing, Planning and Local Government, quarterly performance reports, various years.

child dependants. In comparison with the quarterly performance reports, the monthly reports provide stock data on the number of adults, child dependants and households in a given week each month.

In terms of household composition, at the end of 2018, nearly two thirds were single without accompanying child dependants, 21 per cent were couples with accompanying dependent children and the remaining 15 per cent were single adults with accompanying dependent children. Over 90 per cent of the single adult households with accompanying children were female headed. While the growth in family homelessness (particularly in Dublin, where in December 2018, there were 1,252 families with 2,686 dependants residing in a variety of hotels, Family Hubs and other emergency accommodation, compared to 364 families with 567 dependants in June 2014) has generated considerable policy and media attention, the majority of those utilising homeless services are single. Further, single males account for 46 per cent of all adults who are in emergency accommodation in Ireland.

Despite the relatively short time frame for which detailed data are available – mid-2014 to December 2018 – a growing feminisation of homelessness is evident, particularly in Dublin: by the end of 2018, 44 per cent of all adults in emergency accommodation were female, as compared to 34 per cent in mid-2014. This is largely driven by the increase in adults with accompanying child dependants, who are overwhelmingly female-headed households, as noted earlier. In addition, in December 2018, there were 434 single adult females in emergency accommodation outside of Dublin and 626 in Dublin, a total of 1,060, nearly a doubling of the figure in April 2014 of 524 single females. The distribution of females among those experiencing homelessness is skewed towards the younger age groups: in the case of Dublin in 2016, 57 per cent of those in the age group 18–25 and 55 per cent of those in the age group 26–30 were female, as compared to, for example, only 20 per cent in the 51–60 age group (Reilly and Maphosa, 2018: 31).

At the end of 2018, 51 per cent of adults in emergency services were in what is termed 'supported temporary accommodation', that is, usually purpose-built or re-provisioned congregate shelter-type accommodation, managed exclusively by NGOs, who are funded by local authorities to provide these services. A very small number are accommodated in 'temporary emergency accommodation', also managed by NGOs, but as the number of new presentations to homeless services, particularly among families, grew over the past number of years, they were increasingly placed in what are termed 'private emergency accommodations' (PEAs), usually hotels or 'bed and breakfasts' (B&Bs). Nationally, the numbers in PEAs increased from 33 to 47 per cent of all adults in emergency accommodation between April 2014 and December 2018. While the increase in the number of adults in emergency accommodation at a point in time can be seen across all age groups, those in the age category 25–44 have consistently accounted for 60 per cent of all adults, with nearly 3,500 adults in the age category in emergency accommodation during the week of 24–30 December 2018.

The number of adults in emergency accommodation has increased in both urban and rural areas. Since the commencement of the production of the monthly data in mid-2014, consistently two thirds of adults in emergency accommodation are in Dublin, with between 15 and 16 per cent in the four other major urban areas of Galway, Limerick, Waterford and Cork. Outside of the five urban centres, services for those experiencing homelessness are relatively limited, and this is reflected in growth in the use of private emergency accommodation in the absence of designated homelessness accommodation, which grew from 40 adults in such accommodation in April 2014 to nearly 1,000 adults by the end of 2018.

Limitations of the monthly reports

The monthly reports do not capture a very small number of emergency shelter services, with less than 200 beds nationally, who did not, for various reasons, receive, or indeed seek, section 10 funding, and are therefore not included in the PASS data. Data on rough sleeping are collected via a separate street count twice a year in Dublin (in March and November), but data on rough sleeping are not routinely or systematically collected outside Dublin. The number of people sleeping rough in Dublin,[4] based on consistent point-in-time counts conducted twice a year since 2007, averaged 108 over the past decade, with contact with outreach services ranging from 350 to 450 people sleeping rough per quarter over the past four years. The majority of people sleeping rough also used emergency shelters, with only 20 per cent not accessing emergency shelter services over the period 2012–16. Over the period from 2008 to the end of 2018, the figure for November 2017, at 184, was the highest recorded.

Neither the monthly reports nor the quarterly reports capture the hidden homeless: households in insecure, overcrowded or inadequate accommodation. However, data are collected via the housing needs assessment, which has been carried out by local authorities on an annual basis since 2016. Among the categories of need for social housing support are 'unsuitable accommodation due to particular housing circumstances', 'reasonable requirement for separate accommodation', 'unsuitable accommodation due to exceptional medical or compassionate grounds', 'overcrowded accommodation' and 'unfit accommodation'. In the assessments conducted in 2013, 2016, 2017 and 2018, between 35,000 and 40,000 households were assessed as being in these categories.

From 1 January 2015, accommodation or refuges for those escaping from gender-based violence (ETHOS category 4), funded via section 10 – a total of 21 residential services with a bed capacity of approximately 250, and with annual funding of just over €2.1 million – were transferred to the statutory Child and Family Agency (Tusla), and those accessing these residential services have not been enumerated in the monthly data since that date. This followed from a recommendation of the Homelessness Oversight Group (2013: 23) that:

> such refuges are not homeless emergency accommodation and would prefer to see both a discrete funding stream and separate reporting for the provision of State support to the accommodation needs of persons experiencing domestic violence. This would seem to appropriately reside within the scope of the recently established Child and Family Agency. We recommend therefore that existing funding arrangements for the provision of refuge accommodation and services would be transferred to the Child and Family Agency.

To date, TULSA has not published data on a monthly basis on the number and characteristics of those accessing such residential services.

In March 2018, 253 adults accommodated 'in houses and apartments' who had hitherto been included in the monthly data were excluded, and in April, a further 121 adults were excluded on the same basis that they were not in emergency accommodation, giving a total of 374 adults. Following further investigations by the Department of Housing, 'further cases of houses and apartments being recorded as emergency accommodation' were identified, containing a further 251 adults, and giving an overall total of 625 adults (with 981 accompanying child dependants) excluded in the monthly reports.[5]

Figure 4.12: Expenditure on homelessness services in Ireland, Q1 2013–Q4 2018 (%)

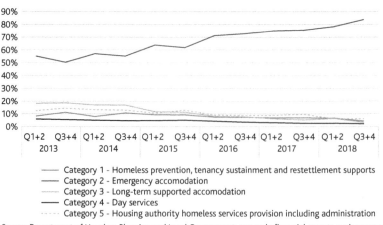

Category 1 - Homeless prevention, tenancy sustainment and resettlement supports
Category 2 - Emergency accomodation
Category 3 - Long-term supported accomodation
Category 4 - Day services
Category 5 - Housing authority homeless services provision including administration

Source: Department of Housing, Planning and Local Government, quarterly financial reports, various years.

Quarterly financial reports

Local authorities were also required to produce detailed quarterly financial reports outlining the distribution of central government and local authority funding[6] on preventive actions, emergency and long-term supported accommodation, and other services for those experiencing homelessness. The reports also provide data on the distribution of this expenditure to NGO and private sector providers of the range of services. These reporting requirements arose from the issuing of a Protocol Governing Delegation of Section 10 (of the Housing Act 1988), Funding for Homeless Services to Local Authorities. The criteria for receiving central government funding was that local authorities adopt a housing-led approach, that is, to provide housing with support as required, rather than the provision of congregate emergency and temporary accommodation, which in 2013, accounted for 50 per cent of all expenditure on services for people experiencing homelessness, and to reorient services towards resettlement and prevention. In practice, these criteria have been largely ignored, and expenditure on emergency and temporary accommodation in the second half of 2018 accounted for 84 per cent of all expenditure (or €79.7 million) on services for those experiencing homelessness. Figure 4.12 provides information on the distribution of funding between Q1 2014 and Q4 2018.

In the case of Ireland, reasonably consistent point-in-time data, albeit with some minor limitations, on adults and accompany child dependants in temporary and emergency accommodation have been available on a monthly basis since April 2014. Validating the data against the Census data on homelessness, and the social housing needs assessments suggest that they are a relatively robust source of information on trends in the extent and composition of those in temporary and emergency accommodation in Ireland, and the recorded increase in the number of households is not an artefact of recording practices.

Flow data on entries and exits from temporary and emergency accommodation, as well as data on the number of households prevented from entering emergency accommodation in the case of Dublin, have also been available on a quarterly basis since 2014. To fully understand the dynamics of homelessness in Ireland and more clearly identify the trajectories into and out of homelessness, rather than simply publishing data on the number of households entering and exiting homeless services, these data need to be disaggregated by household composition, age and length of stay in different types of emergency accommodation. Data on the trajectories of families entering temporary and emergency accommodation are collected on a monthly basis in Dublin, but not outside, and despite the fact that single-person households are most likely to be in emergency accommodation, no data are published on their trajectories into homelessness.

No consistent and reliable source of data exists for those households in overcrowded or inadequate accommodation, such as the hidden homeless in Ireland. The only source is the now annual assessments of social housing need, but they only include 'qualified households', excluding a range of households who do not fulfil certain criteria in relation to income, citizenship status and so on, or who had rent arrears or behavioural issues in relation to a previous social housing tenancy that disqualify them from further social housing supports. It does not mean that they do not have a housing need, but rather means that they do not qualify for social housing support. In addition, changes to the method of assessing net social housing need, where a significant number of households are excluded simply by virtue of their existing tenancy arrangements, for example, in private rented accommodation with an income supplement via the HAP or Rental Accommodation Scheme (RAS), or in local authority or approved housing body tenancies, rather than the condition of the dwelling or numbers in the dwelling, excludes a significant number of households who would be included in Denmark and Finland. Finally, the purpose of the assessment of housing need is not to measure hidden homelessness, and 'does not provide a definitive statement of housing need' (Lewis, 2019: 195).

Conclusion and comparison

While the three countries under consideration deployed strategies that have broad similarities in terms of objectives, analysis and phased deployment, the outcomes are very different. As discussed earlier, at the outset of the strategies in 2008, based on point-in-time data, Finland and Denmark had similar numbers of households in emergency homeless accommodation only, while Ireland had much lower levels. The number of households experiencing homelessness in Ireland grew significantly over the period in question, while falling substantially in Finland. The experience in Denmark is somewhere between the two, with a marginal increase in homelessness (under this measure) occurring over the period.

The explanations for these different experiences are complex and are fully discussed in Chapters 5 and 6. Some explanations are to be found in the content and implementation of the strategies themselves, while others relate to the broader economic and political experiences of the countries during this turbulent period.

For the purpose of comparison, *households rather than individuals are the unit of analysis*. In the case of Denmark and Finland, the difference between the number of households and individuals is relatively slight as the majority of households in temporary and emergency accommodation are single-person households. For example, in Finland in 2018, the 5,482 persons counted as experiencing homelessness in November 2018 comprised 5,146 households; at 95 per cent, the vast majority are single-person households, but when we exclude those households staying with family and friends, all households in emergency and temporary accommodation in Finland are single-person households. This is also widely the case in Denmark as there are only relatively few households with children among shelter users, where they reside in a few designated homeless shelters/hostels for this group. However, in the case of Ireland, the number of individuals experiencing homelessness is significantly higher than the number of households due to the large number of families in emergency accommodation at any point in time. In December 2018, there were 6,194 adult individuals in temporary and emergency accommodation, comprising 5,532 households, of whom 3,915, or just over 70 per cent, were single-person households.

At the end of 2018, the Finnish strategy had largely met its objectives, with 893 households, all single-person households, either sleeping rough or living in emergency accommodation and institutions, down from nearly 3,200 in 2008. Even taking the broader definition, the number of people experiencing broader forms of homelessness, particularly the ETHOS conceptual category of 'insecure housing', declined from 7,715 to just over 4,000 by 2018 (ARA, 2019).

In Denmark, the number of individuals in shelters designated for the homeless or sleeping rough (excluding staying with family and friends) increased gradually over the period, from about 3,000 individuals in 2009 to about 3,500 in 2017 (Benjaminsen, 2017). Using the broader definition of homelessness, the number of individuals experiencing homelessness increased substantially from 5,000 to about 6,500. As there are relatively few families (mainly female lone parents) in Danish shelters, with children only allowed in a few designated shelters, the Danish figures on individual shelter users widely resemble household figures as the vast majority of shelter users are single adults.

In Ireland, the number of households sleeping rough (in Dublin only) and in emergency accommodation (for the entire country) at the end of 2018 was at an all-time high of nearly 5,700 households, double the number of households recorded in December 2014, despite the removal of a significant number of households through re-categorisation in 2018. In the separate assessment of need for social housing conducted in 2018, 33,141 households were identified as living in unsuitable, overcrowded and unfit accommodation, or in a situation where the municipal authority determined that the household had a reasonable requirement for separate accommodation (Housing Agency, 2018). Thus, while not directly comparable with the Finnish or Danish data on 'hidden homelessness', it does indicate the scale of homelessness in Ireland if a definition of homelessness similar to that in Denmark and Finland was used.

By the end of 2018, the political and administrative response had shifted to the containment of the issue through a substantial increase in the provision of various emergency congregate facilities for singles and families, with providers from both the private and NGO sector. The number of shelter beds and beds in Family Hubs doubled from just over 1,500 in 2004 to 3,300 by the end of 2018, with nearly 70 per cent of the beds in Dublin. The number of adults in private emergency accommodation tripled from just over 800 in 2014 to nearly 3,000 by the end of 2018, with just over two thirds in Dublin. Despite this massive increase in shelter beds, Family Hubs and private emergency accommodation, by the end of 2018, the numbers of rough sleepers in Dublin remained stubbornly high, with a minimum of 156 rough sleepers counted in November, from a low of 59 in April 2011.

These outcomes are comparatively highlighted in Figure 4.13, which provides data on the first three operational categories of ETHOS.

Figure 4.13: Households experiencing homelessness and staying in temporary and emergency accommodation in Denmark, Finland and Ireland, 2008–19

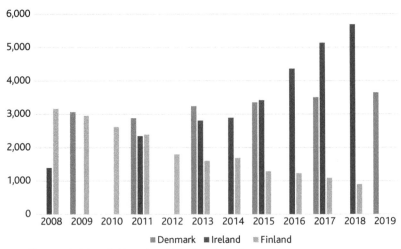

Note: Figures exclude households staying with family and friends.

Figure 4.14 expresses the numbers per 1,000 households, and in all three countries, the numbers experiencing homelessness are strongly concentrated in the capital cities of Helsinki, Dublin and Copenhagen,[7] as shown in Figure 4.15, albeit less so in the case of Copenhagen. The differences between the countries are highlighted in Figures 4.13, 4.14 and 4.15. Danish homelessness, in the sense of households staying in temporary and emergency accommodation, was relatively stable, while the downward trend in Finland and the upward trend in Ireland are both evident in comparison. The relative increases in Ireland, illustrated in Figure 4.14, are perhaps the most striking finding from this analysis, showing the severity of the increases being experienced, while both Denmark and Finland did not show the same pattern. The Finnish data again highlight that while great progress was made with respect to long-term homelessness under *Paavo I* and *II*, Finnish strategy – the mix of political acumen, coordination, service innovation and investment that has made the discussion of the near eradication of homelessness sound like a viable prospect – was directed at what was, proportionately, already something that was close to being a residual social problem in 2008.

Figure 4.15 highlights what appears to be a widespread experience, the relative concentration of homelessness in capital and major cities, which are characterised by higher levels of prosperity and higher rates of economic growth than is the case for many other areas in the same

Figure 4.14: Households experiencing homelessness and staying in temporary and emergency accommodation in Denmark, Finland and Ireland per 1,000 households, 2008–19

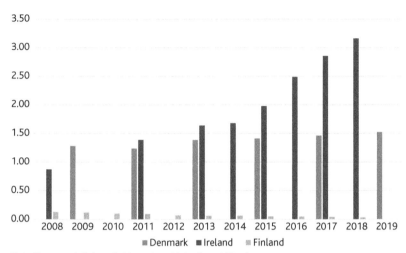

Note: Figures exclude households staying with family and friends.

Figure 4.15: Households experiencing homelessness and staying in temporary and emergency accommodation in Helsinki, Dublin and Copenhagen as a percentage of total households experiencing homelessness, 2008–18

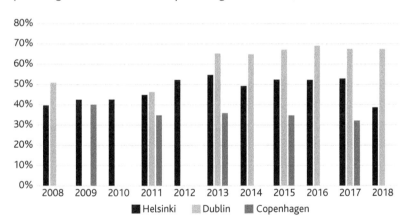

country. In essence, the effects shown here almost certainly reflect a high degree of housing stress, demand and need for adequate, affordable housing outstripping effective supply in all three capitals, just as one would see in Paris, New York or San Francisco. As debates about the nature and causation of homelessness continue, with arguments around the extent to which people who become homeless may be attracted to capital and major cities, the potential associations between simple shortages of affordable housing and homelessness are highlighted by this comparison.

Notes

1. See: www.ara.fi/en-US
2. A survey of people experiencing homelessness in Dublin known as Counted In, commissioned, and later conducted, by the Homeless Agency and later the Dublin Region Homeless Executive in 1999, 2002, 2005 and 2008, was the only reasonably robust data on homelessness in Ireland prior to this period. However, difficulties in verifying the data that led to subsequent delays in publishing the data, cost and personnel constraints led to its discontinuation after the 2008 survey. In any event, with data collection only every three years, it was of limited value for assessing the impact of policy on the extent and nature of homelessness. However, its discontinuation resulted in a significant lacuna in understanding trends in homelessness in the absence of any other robust measure of homelessness.
3. The PASS records on individuals are deleted after two years if there is no activity on their record.
4. At the end of 2018, the majority of local authorities outside of Dublin reported nobody sleeping rough in their functional areas, and those that did, particularly in the south-west, which stated a figure of 165, appear to be recording a flow figure of the number of encounters with rough sleepers, rather than a point-in-time count of unique individuals.
5. Further confusion has arisen as to measuring the number of people experiencing homelessness because different state bodies use different definitions and units of analysis. In addition to the Department of Housing, both the Central Statistics Office (CSO) and the Housing Agency also produce regular data on the numbers experiencing homelessness. It is worth noting that some of this confusion arises simply due to the fact that some report on the number of households, some the number of adults and some the number of adults and accompanying child dependants. For example, in December 2018, based on the monthly report, there were 5,532 households in emergency accommodation, or 6,194 adults or 9,793 adults and children, and these different categories are often used interchangeably.
6. These reports do not include expenditure from other central government departments, in particular, the Departments of Children and Youth Affairs, Health and Employment Affairs, and Social Protection, who in 2017, expended approximately €86.5 million between them on either various services for households experiencing homelessness or on homelessness preventive services (Homelessness Inter-Agency Group, 2018). Neither do they include expenditure on social housing provision and support that has both prevented and ended homelessness for a significant number of households over the same period.
7. Including Frederiksberg, a municipality within Copenhagen.

5

Explanations: housing matters

Introduction

In Chapter 4, we explored in some detail both the construction of homelessness data in Denmark, Finland and Ireland and what these data tell us about trends and the composition of those households experiencing homelessness.

While the construction of homelessness data in the three countries varies significantly in terms of methodology and the definition of who is considered homeless in the official statistics, it was possible to identify a number of common categories of homelessness in all three countries, namely, those in temporary and emergency accommodation and those rough sleeping. Both the Finnish and Danish data also include 'hidden homelessness', but the Irish data do not. As we have shown, whether you explore trends using the country-specific definition or the more restricted comparable definition, similar trends are evident. The numbers of people experiencing homelessness declined consistently in Finland over the past decade and increased slightly in Denmark, while Ireland experienced hyper-homelessness.

The purpose of the remaining chapters is to explore how three countries that started the 21st century with relatively modest and similar numbers of homeless households, and expressed similar levels of ambition to reduce homelessness, ended up with different experiences in the second decade. In this chapter, we first explore the role of Housing First in the three countries, and then go on to contextualise this in the broader housing market, particularly social housing. The impact of welfare policies and political choices will be explored in Chapter 6.

The role of Housing First

The adoption of Housing First as an approach to tackling homelessness features strongly in the story of the three countries. However, as has already been remarked, there are very considerable differences in the practices and broader context of what is referred to as Housing First in the three countries, and also in comparison with the Pathways

Housing First approach pioneered by Sam Tsemberis (2010a) in New York in 1992.

Finland is sometimes portrayed as shifting everything into Housing First in 2008 and, in so doing, 'solving' homelessness, essentially through importing and adapting the model that Sam Tsemberis developed across the Atlantic 15 years earlier. This is not an accurate picture either of the history of policy development or of the nature of the Finnish Housing First approach.

In the next section, we explore in some detail different features of what is referred to as Housing First in each of the countries. In both Finland and Denmark, 'Housing First' features prominently in the description of services from the first phase of the strategies in 2008. In Ireland, while the term 'Housing First' was not used in government strategy until 2013, a broadly 'housing-led' approach was adopted from the start.

However, behind this apparent commonality, the programmes described as Housing First differ significantly in practice and, more fundamentally, in scale and the relation between Housing First and broader homeless and housing policies. We divide the discussion into three elements of Housing First that highlight the differences: Housing First and its relation to social housing; the scale at which Housing First was attempted and delivered; and, finally, criticisms of the programme in each country.

Housing First in Finland

The successes of the Finnish strategy since 2008 are expressed, by the Finns themselves (Y Foundation, 2017), in terms of the development of a Finnish form of Housing First, both as a range of services and as a housing-led philosophy underpinning every aspect of an integrated homelessness strategy (Y Foundation, 2017; Fredriksson, 2018, cited in Ranta, 2019). The most immediate impact of the 2007 *Name on the Door* report was a first-stage strategy centred on building a Housing First model to replace the existing staircase services and emergency shelters.

The circumstances in which Housing First emerged in Finland in 2008 were very different than the circumstance in which it emerged in the US in the early 1990s. At that point in the US, linear residential treatment (LRT) 'Staircase' services predominated, requiring abstinence, treatment compliance, a long list of behavioural changes and completing often multiple steps before being granted access to housing. Everything centred on the individual, their characteristics, their behaviour and the (presumed) need to modify that behaviour.

Access to homelessness services was centred on populations with diagnosed mental illness, and the provision of more basic supports, such as welfare benefits and social housing, was very limited for homeless people with low support needs across much of the country. As has been pointed out elsewhere (Hansen Löfstrand and Juhila, 2012), Housing First was not going to leave that focus on the individual entirely behind, but in replacing the use of congregate and communal accommodation with on-site support with the use of ordinary housing with mobile support, and in emphasising service-user choice and control, alongside harm reduction, Housing First was definitely different (Tsemberis and Asmussen, 1999).

By contrast, in Finland in 2008, harm reduction was already mainstream policy in relation to drugs and alcohol, and it had been integrated into at least part of the homelessness system since the 1990s (Tainio and Fredriksson, 2009). Social housing and social protection systems were extensive. The Y Foundation had been operating since the mid-1980s, providing a dedicated supply of social housing targeted at single homelessness adults. By 2008, homelessness itself was already at levels that would, in relative terms, be seen as negligible in, for example, the US.

Research in Finland (Pleace et al, 2015), alongside reports from those involved in the development of Finnish homelessness strategy during the period 2008–17 (Y Foundation, 2017), shows that Finnish Housing First developed *separately* from the Tsemberis model. Finnish recognition of shared practice led to an engagement with Sam Tsemberis and with other advocates of the Housing First model in Europe, which included bringing Tsemberis and others to Finland in order to explore possibilities around shared learning. A website called Housing First Finland,[1] still available at the time of writing, although not updated since 2016, was built to facilitate these international exchanges, share information and invite comment on the Finnish programme. That site noted the following (www.housingfirst.fi/en/housing_first):

> Understanding housing as a primary need has emerged in different places over the world mainly because of the development work done in the rehabilitating intoxicant and social service fields. In the *Name on the Door* development project the housing first principle is extended not only to serve as a tool for social rehabilitation but also to work as a framework for the theoretical examination of the social service system and to analyse the different housing

operations. The principle is utilised as an analytical method penetrating the whole service system.

This kind of systemic shift towards a housing-led approach to all forms of homelessness echoed Tsemberis's ambitions for Housing First itself (Tsemberis, 2010a; Padgett et al, 2016), however, in the Finnish case, the emphasis was broader, taking in all elements of homelessness, not just those populations with high and complex needs. Finnish Housing First services were part of an integrated, housing-led response to homelessness that followed a broader, strategic idea of – and a philosophical take on – just what a 'housing-first' ethos should mean in responding to homelessness.

In Finland, individual 'Housing First' services were not, in and of themselves, a tactical response to homelessness, but instead part of a strategy in which housing – living in a home of one's own – was the default goal. Housing First, then, in the sense that it is used in Finland, is a *philosophy governing the entirety of homelessness strategy* rather than the model for a particular service. There are, of course, Finnish services that use a service model that can be compared with Tsemberis's Pathways Housing First, but it is not just these services, but *every* service, every aspect of the Finnish strategy, that follow an approach that puts access to housing (rather than treatment) as the first step. The strategic and philosophical reorientation of every aspect of homelessness policy away from 'treatment first 'or 'housing-ready' is at the core of the Finnish concept of what they call 'Housing First' (Y Foundation, 2017). This is echoed in the shift to prevention that occurred from *Paavo II* onwards: keeping people in their existing homes (and so stopping homelessness from being experienced) is as integral to Finnish Housing First strategy as anything that might resemble a Pathways Housing First 'service'. As discussed later, there were also operational differences in the Finnish services that were called Housing First, which looked different to Tsemberis's original in several respects.

Finnish Housing First and public housing

The first and most controversial difference was that Finnish Housing First services could include congregate models: large buildings were turned into Housing First services with on-site staffing, and existing, large, communal emergency shelters for homeless people were converted into blocks of Housing First apartments (Pleace et al, 2015, 2016). This was not unprecedented; the initial wave of federal funding in the US, which was not that strict about defining what

'Housing First' was, saw the emergence of communal and congregate models of Housing First (Pearson et al, 2009), while the Danes and the Canadians have also experimented with congregate forms of Housing First (Benjaminsen, 2013; Somers et al, 2017).

The use of a congregate model reflected the deadlines that Finland set for itself in trying to end long-term homelessness as it was only through the conversion of existing sites that enough housing could be deployed quickly enough to potentially meet the target. However, Finland was also conceptualising and designing its Housing First services in a different way within the broader philosophy that was first expressed in the *Name on the Door* report, more recently defined in terms using a four-principle (Finnish) Housing First philosophy (see Y Foundation, 2017: 15):

- Housing First is used to enable independent living for service users. Both ordinary (scattered) housing and 'supported housing units' can be used, the former being an independent home with support available around the clock, the latter being a reference to congregate models.
- Housing First respects the choices of homeless people; it is not passive as the service follows a harm-reduction approach and tries to help them move away from addiction, but there is respect for the autonomy of individuals and no requirement for abstinence.
- Rehabilitation and empowerment of Housing First service users is centred on the idea of service users rebuilding and empowering their lives on their own terms, emphasising dialogue and interaction, as well as the positive reinforcement of service users. Although the terms are not used, there are elements of co-production and strength-based approaches to service delivery in this aspect of the Finnish approach.
- Integration into the community and society is a goal for Housing First, with settled housing, as with the original model of Housing First, being seen as the core of this process. In the Finnish definition, this involves building community within congregate models of Housing First, as well as social integration for someone living in ordinary housing.

Scale

Finnish Housing First services are extensive. There are a group of congregate services that include larger-scale services; examples include Aurora House (with 125 apartments) and Alppikatu 25 (with 81 apartments), both of which being former emergency accommodation in Helsinki redesigned as Housing First. New-build services include the Väinölä project, with 33 apartments, which became operational in 2014. The reality of Housing First and housing-led services in Finland is a mixture of these larger projects, smaller services and mobile support teams attached to people living in scattered, ordinary apartments. In 2016, Finland had 1,309 units of supported housing (including scattered site and congregate service provision) up from 552 places in 2008. The country has undergone a process of shutting down and replacing the 2,121 hostel/emergency accommodation places that it had in 1985, which, nationally, had been reduced to just 558 by 2008 and then to 52 by 2016. Independent apartments for homeless people, which can receive housing-led services, had reached 2,433 by 2016, up from 2,033 in 2008 (data from the Y Foundation, 2017). Data on Housing First are not centralised, but an estimate in late 2018 was that between 1,000 and 3,000 places were available nationally, based on congregate services and scattered site services (Y Foundation, 2018).

Criticisms of Finnish Housing First

As well as being seen as the exclusive reason for the successes in Finland, the Finnish Housing First approach, as a philosophy, has also been the basis on which criticism has been directed at Finland. Sam Tsemberis gave housing a very specific role in the design of his Housing First service; it was intended to provide an anchor, a sense of ontological security (Padgett, 2007) and, crucially, a mechanism for reintegration. Targeted as it was on homeless people with severe mental illness and addiction, Tsemberis's original model for Housing First sought to begin what is best described as a process of normalisation, which centred on ordinary housing scattered among ordinary people living in ordinary neighbourhoods, facilitated by the Intensive Case Management (ICM) and Assertive Community Treatment (ACT) services and peer support that the Housing First service delivered (Tsemberis, 2010a). As has been noted elsewhere (Johnson et al, 2012), the ways in which ordinary housing facilitates this metamorphic shift to ordinary life and community integration among severely mentally ill drug users with sustained and repeated histories of homelessness is not spelled out very precisely in the evidence base for Housing First; instead, there is a general sense that beneficial osmosis will occur from sustained exposure to ordinary life.

The pursuit of social integration is a widespread goal for homelessness services, and, indeed, the Finnish national homelessness strategy has similar objectives itself (Y Foundation, 2017). While there is, arguably, a fair degree of imprecision with respect to how exactly ordinary housing acts as a catalyst for social integration in the original Pathways model (Johnson et al, 2012; Quilgars and Pleace, 2016), it is nevertheless possible to mount a coherent attack on those Finnish models of 'Housing First' services that use congregate housing from this standpoint.

The first element of this criticism of Finnish congregate services centres on the potential for recovery. This means that when, for example, someone is surrounded by people with problematic drug and alcohol use, as in a congregate Finnish Housing First service, there may be less chance of improvements to health, well-being and social integration than if someone is living in ordinary housing surrounded by ordinary people. The second element centres on the chances for social integration itself, which are arguably reduced because someone living in a congregate Housing First service – albeit in their own apartment with a secure long-term lease – is still living in a 'service', which marks them out as different from the people around them, and that marker may be enough to form a barrier to integration (Busch-Geertsema, 2010).

When Tsemberis himself was invited over to Finland, his reaction to the congregate Finnish versions of 'Housing First' services that then predominated in the model was less than positive. Taking a rather different line to that which might have been expected from other European governments when someone prominent criticised their homelessness strategy, the Finns published his criticisms online at the Housing First Finland website, where they still remain publicly available at the time of writing. Tsemberis did not interpret *Paavo I* as a limited or compromised version of his Pathways Housing First model, but instead took the line that what they were doing was not Housing First and that the programme was, effectively, yet to be implemented in Finland. He suggested that Finland look to the Canadian Housing First programme for guidance (Tsemberis, 2011). This criticism was echoed to a considerable degree when homelessness specialists undertook a European Union (EU)-funded peer review of the Finnish strategy in 2010 (Busch-Geertsema, 2010). A series of reports appeared stating that the Pathways Housing First model, which had proven effective, was not being replicated in Finland, so the strategy could not expect the same results as had been achieved in the US by Housing First. There were also some internally conducted reviews suggesting that management issues were occurring in some of the congregate Finnish Housing First services (Kettunen and Granfelt, 2011).

Beyond the accusations of falling short of Pathways Housing First by 'warehousing' rather than truly rehousing and reintegrating the long-term homeless population, there were also criticisms of the Finnish approach because it was too reflective of problems inherent in the Pathways model. This centred on the logic of Housing First itself and the goals of the Finns in trying to reintegrate long-term homeless people into society. The issue here, as argued by a Swedish and a Finnish academic (Hansen Löfstrand and Juhila, 2012), was that in the pursuit of a recovery orientation, Pathways Housing First and its various, rapidly hybridising, offspring aimed for the same behavioural modification as LRT Staircase services. This critique argued that as the product of an individualistic and individualising free-market culture that interpreted poverty in terms of individual pathology, Pathways Housing First was out of sync with European ideas about social cohesion, and while it was clearly more civilised than an abstinence-based LRT service, Housing First could be seen as ultimately seeking to create quiet, compliant, stable consumers, rather than someone recognisable as an empowered European citizen.

In respect of Finland, this criticism was directed at a strategy that was not yet complete, *Paavo II* having been announced for the period 2012–15 well before the end of *Paavo I*. One defence for Finland was to simply say that the strategy was a work in progress, but it was also possible to counteract this criticism on a number of fronts.

When it came to ending homelessness, there was no doubt that Housing First with high fidelity to the Pathways model was achieving solid results in both the French and Canadian national pilot programmes. It was clear that high-fidelity Housing First worked, at least in terms of ending homelessness (Padgett et al, 2016). The problem in pursuing high fidelity to the Pathways Housing First model as a solution to homelessness in Finland was, on the surface, twofold. One issue was that beyond the clear evidence that Housing First consistently delivered sustainable housing solutions for homeless people with high and complex needs, the evidence base was a lot more uncertain when it came to improvements in physical and mental health, addiction, and, ironically, social integration (Johnson et al, 2012).

The second issue was that it was equally clear that lower-fidelity services that still followed the core philosophy around choice and control for service users, separating housing from support, and pursuing harm reduction but that could be less recovery oriented and were not seeking the behavioural changes that the original model sought were also effective in ending physical homelessness among people with high and complex needs (Pleace and Bretherton, 2013). Housing First

Italia (Lancione et al, 2018) and Housing First England (Bretherton and Pleace, 2015) worked in a different way to the original Tsemberis model, using a lot less resources, and so did the Swedish Housing First services (Knutagård and Kristiansen, 2013), but their housing outcomes were very similar to those for the highly successful, high-fidelity *Un Chez-Soi d'abord* French pilot programme (Pleace, 2016a).

For critics of the Finnish congregate services, some comfort was to be found in the evidence from Denmark, where research showed that scattered site Housing First, using ordinary housing, was outperforming the congregate model of Housing First that was used only to a minor extent in the Danish strategy programme (Benjaminsen, 2013). Canadian research has since cast doubt on the idea that congregate models will necessarily have poorer outcomes than scattered site approaches to Housing First, suggesting that the detail of service design – including factors like the nature and intensity of support – may be an important variable (Somers et al, 2017) and that ICM-only and ACT/ICM may have similar outcomes (Urbanoski et al, 2018).

However, there was a deeper problem with criticisms of Finnish congregate services for lacking fidelity to the Tsemberis model: they were not trying to follow the model in the first place (Y Foundation, 2017; Fredriksson, 2018, cited in Ranta, 2019). The Finns meant something different when they referred to 'Housing First'. As we have seen, in the Finnish homelessness strategy, Housing First meant the housing-led, housing-focused philosophy underpinning an entire homelessness strategy, not reference to a particular American model of service. Yes, the Finns drew criticism by referring to their congregate Housing First projects as 'Housing First', but then they also referred to the whole strategy, the whole ethos of the Finnish strategy, as 'Housing First'.

Again, the Finnish idea of Housing First was a much broader one. It meant a mindset, an approach to all service design that was housing focused and housing led; it was not a reference to the fidelity scale for the Tsemberis model of Housing First – the Finns were not even really talking about the same thing as Tsemberis (Y Foundation, 2017; Fredriksson, 2018, cited in Ranta, 2019). The Finns were not using American Housing First; they were using Finnish Housing First and that meant something quite different. Talking about the fidelity of congregate Housing First services to the Tsemberis model in this context, when the Finns were not actually trying to do the same thing, does not actually make any sense.

There were, and are, arguments to be made that if Finland did follow the Tsemberis model, which Canada and France have at scale, they would see still greater successes, that high-fidelity Housing First will always perform better (Greenwood et al, 2018), and that while the Finns had got most of the way there without reference to Tsemberis (or anyone else, for that matter), more progress could still be made. The problem, of course, is that while high-fidelity Canada and France have reduced their long-term homeless populations, the evidence suggests that what the Finn's refer to as Housing First has taken their response to homelessness much further, rather faster. In Finland, Housing First is not just about long-term homelessness; it has become a wider strategy and philosophy. Moreover, while the Finnish strategy is neither perfect nor an unqualified success (and, as we have noted, there are limitations to the data), it is Finland – and Finland alone – that has brought total homelessness down and kept it down (Pleace, 2017; Y Foundation, 2017).

Housing First in Denmark

At the start of the Danish homelessness strategy in 2008, based on the emerging evidence about the effectiveness of the Pathway's model from the US, it was decided to make Housing First the overall principle of the strategy. Somewhat ironically given the criticisms and debate outlined earlier, the decision to opt for Housing First was also inspired by the turn in policies in Finland, which had initiated its own Housing First programme one year before. Across the Nordic countries, policy was influenced by the growing evidence against the Staircase approach in neighbouring Sweden, as the influential study by Ingrid Sahlin (2005) on the Staircase model in Sweden had shown how it widely hindered access to permanent housing for vulnerable people rather than facilitating it. Recent policy developments in Norway had also swung Danish policymakers away from a Staircase-based approach.

Intensity of support

In Denmark, a key feature of the programme was the implementation and testing of the evidence-based support methods of ICM and ACT in a Danish context. An additional feature, although this method was not part of the American Housing First model, was the use of the Critical Time Intervention (CTI) method.

The ICM programme was by far the largest sub-programme within the Danish homelessness programmes. Actually, only one ACT team was established as part of the Danish programme, namely, an ACT team in the city of Copenhagen. The results and experiences from the ACT were so positive that it was subsequently decided by the municipality of Copenhagen to continue the ACT team after the programme period ended. However, given the high proportion of homeless people with a dual diagnosis in Denmark, a substantial proportion of people affected by homelessness in Denmark belong to the prime target group for the ACT method, with its multidisciplinary support team and high support intensity and flexibility. It is, then, surprising that only one ACT team was established in the field of homelessness services during the period of the strategy programme and succeeding programmes. This is a deviance from the original Housing First model, and the reliance on ICM supports may be one factor in explaining why it has not been possible to bring down homelessness over the period of the national strategy and the succeeding programmes.[2]

Public housing

Another major difference in the Danish programme compared to the original model from the US is the predominant use of public housing, whereas the American programmes widely rely on housing in the private rental sector. This difference arises from the general difference in welfare and housing systems, as well as the widespread lack of public or social housing in the US.

Denmark has a relatively large public housing sector, comprising about 21 per cent of the total housing stock. Public housing is not restricted to low-income or vulnerable groups, but open to everybody regardless of income level and accessible through general waiting lists. However, the public housing law enables municipalities to allocate up to 25 per cent of vacancies in public housing to people in acute housing need according to social criteria set by the municipality. Through this allocation mechanism, municipalities can give access to public housing to specific groups, such as families with children, people with disabilities and homeless people, bypassing ordinary waiting lists.

The possibility to house homeless people in public housing on permanent contracts can generally be seen as a strength of the Danish programme. The availability of public housing for the programme was an important factor in explaining why it was possible to implement a relatively large Housing First programme even in the first Danish programme, whereas Housing First projects in most other European countries have been rather small. Yet, the reliance on access to public housing also comes with some caveats. Although prioritised access to public housing through municipal referral was used in most of the municipalities in the Danish programme, there can still be significant waiting times to be housed. Especially in larger cities, the waiting times for public housing – even through municipal referral – may be six months or even a year, thus compromising the fast access to permanent housing that is a key principle of the Housing First approach.

However, despite the substantial size of the public housing sector in Denmark, the evaluation research pointed to the lack of access to affordable housing as a major barrier for upscaling Housing First at the local level (Rambøll & SFI, 2013; Benjaminsen et al, 2017). These barriers consisted of both general supply shortages and barriers more specifically attached to the local administration of the allocation mechanisms.

The prioritised allocation mechanism for public housing already existed before the homelessness strategy. However, there was a widespread practice of requiring 'housing readiness' before referring homeless people with complex support needs to public housing. In particular, it was quite common for municipalities to set restrictions on access for people with substance abuse problems. Thus, some municipalities did not give priority access to public housing to people with an active substance abuse problem, or they set criteria of adherence to treatment for these people. Thus, the actual practice in local housing allocation systems at that time widely followed principles associated with the treatment-first model by requiring adherence to treatment or even abstinence as a condition for referral to housing. Moreover, the provision of floating support was not systematic, and support was often of a lower intensity than the intensive support required according to the Housing First approach. Thus, the emphasis on Housing First in the homelessness strategy implied a need for a general shift in the principles and practices of providing housing and support for homeless people.

Although some municipalities have negotiated other agreements with local public housing associations and therefore may not need to use this option, there are also municipalities that do not use the allocation mechanism at all or use it only for other groups, such as families with children, rather than homeless shelter users and homeless people with complex support needs. There can be both political and financial reasons behind such local priorities. In some cases, municipalities do not want to impose the allocation rules on local housing associations. At the same time, using the prioritised allocation mechanism has financial implications for municipalities as they are obliged to cover the rent until the person moves in, and to cover eventual damages and repair works on the flat when residents eventually move out again.

Moreover, the use of the allocation mechanism is still no guarantee that homeless people can afford the housing as only public housing units with a rent level low enough to be paid by people on social benefits can, in practice, be used for allocation. Although Danish public housing is entirely non-profit, there is considerable variation in rent levels, with newer housing generally being more expensive. Within the Danish welfare benefit systems, the rent needs to be paid out of ordinary benefits that are not separated between housing and living expenses, with only a minor supplementary housing benefit. In practice, only public housing units with a sufficiently low rent level can be used when homeless people on cash assistance benefits are rehoused. Thus, the Danish version of Housing First takes place within the ordinary system of welfare benefits and with no further special arrangements to meet excessive rent costs.

Systemic integration

In addition to the barriers to providing housing and support, the lessons from the Danish programme also involved organisational aspects. While the Danish version of Housing First does not reflect the all-encompassing philosophical shift seen in the Finnish version, the change of practice from a housing-ready to a Housing First approach involves a mind shift on many levels, involving both organisational and cultural changes of practices and procedures necessary to implement Housing First at the ground level. As previously mentioned, the National Board of Social Services, an agency under the Danish Ministry of Social Affairs, was responsible for the overall implementation of Housing First and has generally played an important role in facilitating and assisting the process in close cooperation with municipalities. However, these organisational and cultural changes were more successful in some municipalities than in others, and were often facilitated by strong and insightful leadership and underpinned by good cooperation by local actors both between different agencies within municipalities and between municipal actors and other local actors, such as civil society organisations.

For instance, differences in approach between employment agencies responsible for people's social benefits – generally marked by a workfare approach – sometimes clashed with the recovery-and-rehabilitation-oriented approach of the municipal social agencies implementing the Housing First approach. A general lesson was that the establishment of formal agreements and procedures on how to cooperate across agencies in cases involving homeless people generally facilitated a more successful implementation of Housing First in daily practice, whereas reliance on ad hoc cooperation and personal contacts could be more fragile (Benjaminsen et al, 2017).

Scale

A Danish study examined the coverage rate of the Housing First programme in comparison to the overall number of people who were recorded as homeless some time during the period from 2009 to 2015 in either data from the homeless counts or in data from the shelter system. The study showed that even in the municipalities that were part of either the strategy programme, the follow-up programme or both, it was only about 5 per cent of all individuals recorded as homeless at some point during this seven-year period who were enrolled in the Housing First programme and received either CTI, ICM or ACT support. Even among long-term shelter users in these municipalities, only 11 per cent were enrolled in the programme (Benjaminsen and Enemark, 2017; Benjaminsen, 2018). Thus, despite the apparently ambitious programme, the overall coverage of the potential target population was relatively low.

Although not all individuals who are homeless are necessarily in need of the intensive support given under the Housing First programme, we may assume that more people would have benefited from access to this intervention, especially given the high share with mental illness or substance abuse problems among the homeless in Denmark, where about four out of five homeless people have either a mental illness or a substance abuse problem, and a third of all homeless people have a dual diagnosis. There may also be homeless people who have been rehoused with support outside of the Housing First programme and are thus not included in the measurement. However, ordinary floating support would often not be as intensive and flexible as the support given under the Housing First programme and may not be associated with the same high housing retention rate.

Thus, despite being one of the largest Housing First programmes in Europe, along with programmes in Finland and France, the relatively low coverage rate of the overall homeless population demonstrates a very fundamental challenge around experimental programmes aimed at developing new interventions. Although very positive outcomes are achieved for the participants in the programme, a major challenge is how to bring the interventions to scale and then mainstreaming them into the service provision of the local welfare system. In the Danish example, such mainstreaming was even a key ambition in the follow-up programme to the homelessness strategy. The evaluation research pointed to structural barriers that made the upscaling of the interventions difficult. In particular, the general lack of affordable housing was given as a primary barrier in practically all municipalities (Benjaminsen et al, 2017).

Housing First in Ireland

In Ireland, Housing First played a much more limited role in the homeless strategies, and while a housing-led approach was evident from 2008, a national-level plan for the provision of 663 Housing First tenancies over a three-year period was only initiated a decade after the 2008 strategy, and Housing First remains a specific programme rather than a philosophy that underpins all homeless services. Awareness of the potential of Housing First to reduce rough sleeping and long-term homelessness was heightened following the European Consensus Conference in December 2010, and the Dublin Region Homeless Executive led Dublin's involvement in the Housing First Europe project (Busch-Geertsema, 2013). In April 2011, a Housing First demonstration project was established in Dublin, managed through the Dublin Region Homeless Executive with staff drawn from a number of statutory organisations and NGOs, with an aim to provide tenancies for 30 adults with a history of sleeping rough (Greenwood, 2015).

This demonstration project operated until September 2014, when the service was put out to contract by Dublin City Council. The contract was won by two non-governmental bodies: Focus Ireland and the Peter McVerry Trust. The service was targeted exclusively at entrenched rough sleepers, with a target to house 100 households by June 2016, with support by ICM.

Public housing

A key constraint was the inability to secure properties in the private rented sector; as a consequence, a significant number of the units were sourced from the local authority and approved housing body stock. The Housing First service in Dublin operated a scattered site approach and mixed economy of provision, with units sourced from local authorities, approved housing bodies and the private rented sector. However, only 18 per cent of tenancies came from the private rented sector, with the remainder coming from existing local authority or approved housing body stock.

As noted earlier in the book, although the 2008 national homelessness strategy implicitly, and the 2013 *Homelessness Policy Statement*

(Department of the Environment, Community and Local Government, 2013) explicitly, endorsed a housing-led approach to ending long-term homelessness, there was no specific funding stream created for Housing First projects; as a result, any initiatives were locally based and somewhat ad hoc in their approach. The aforementioned *Rebuilding Ireland: Action Plan for Housing and Homelessness* aimed to 'strengthen our efforts and resources towards providing homeless people with a home following the housing-led, housing first approach' (Department of Housing, Planning, Community and Local Government, 2016: 37), increased the target for Housing First tenancies in the Dublin region from 100 to 300 and also included long-term shelter users in addition to rough sleepers as the target group. Between October 2014 and August 2018, 214 unique individuals were provided with a Housing First tenancy, of whom 85 per cent were still in their tenancy in August 2018. In early 2018, a national director of Housing First was appointed and in September 2018, a Housing First *National Implementation Plan* (Government of Ireland, 2018) covering 2018–21 was launched.

Scale

The 2018 plan targets rough sleepers and those in emergency accommodation on a long-term basis with high support needs; nationally, 737 such adults were identified, with 543 (74 per cent) located in the Dublin region. Despite identifying 737 adults who met the criteria for Housing First services, the plan proposes to create only 663 tenancies, or 90 per cent of identified need, over its lifetime – approximately 220 tenancies a year – and to create only 273 tenancies in the Dublin region, exactly half the number of units relative to the number of adults identified as homeless on a long-term basis with a high support need. On the other hand, in the West of the Country, 11 adults meeting the criteria for Housing First were identified, but the plan aims to provide 61 Housing First tenancies (Government of Ireland, 2018: 28–30). This regional imbalance between identified need and the provision of Housing First tenancies is not explained in the plan.

The identification of 737 adults who met the criteria of sleeping rough or in emergency accommodation on a long-term basis was at a point in time in December 2017. Over the course of the plan, based on current trends, where there were 6,274 new presentations to homeless services during 2018, as compared to 5,501 in 2017 – an increase of 14 per cent – the Dublin Region Homeless Executive's (2019: 13) *Action Framework* for the period 2019–21 states baldly that 'It is evident that the scale of homelessness will continue to grow' over the next three years. In addition, the number of adults in emergency accommodation for more than six months is increasing each quarter, with 3,587 adults in Q4 2018, as compared to 2,866 in Q4 2017 – an increase of 25 per cent. It is therefore evident that there will be a substantial number of adults who will qualify for Housing First services based on these criteria during the period of the plan. Thus, while the number of tenancies to be created seems ambitious based on a point-in-time analysis of need, it is less so when seen over the lifetime of the plan. Indeed, based on current trends, even if the target of 663 tenancies is achieved, it is likely that the number of adults in long-term emergency accommodation and or sleeping rough will not have decreased at the end of the plan.

Furthermore, no specific stream of housing units is identified in the plan and ring-fenced for Housing First; rather, the majority of units will have to come from existing social housing stock managed by local authorities or approved housing bodies, where demand already substantially exceeds supply, with relatively little coming from the private rented sector. Thus, in the Dublin region, where the promise of Housing First tenancies is considerably less than the identified need, securing 91 tenancies per annum will prove to be challenging, and will make, at best, a helpful, but very modest, contribution to reducing the rate of growth in the numbers in emergency accommodation or sleeping rough over the period of the plan.

Thus, in the Irish case, despite a political and administrative endorsement of the Housing First approach, implicitly in the 2008 homelessness strategy and explicitly in the 2013 *Homelessness Policy Statement*, the potential impact of Housing First in securing tenancies for those sleeping rough or in emergency accommodation on a long-term basis has been limited in terms of both geographical coverage and the very modest initial targets set, albeit increasing at every iteration of adopting Housing First. It took a decade to move from the initial target of 30 Housing First tenancies, in Dublin only, in 2011, to the promise of 663 tenancies nationally by the end of 2021, despite a broad consensus among central government, local government and NGOs on the efficacy of the approach. It is not that funding was lacking; as set out in Chapter 4, revenue expenditure on the provision of accommodation and allied supports for people experiencing homelessness in Ireland tripled from €76 million in 2009 to an estimated €215 million for 2019. The majority of service providers and statutory funders formally endorse a Housing First approach and harm reduction is a generally uncontroversial policy in Ireland, all adding to the puzzle of why Housing First has languished in policy and practice.

Systemic integration

Part of the answer to this puzzle is that unlike Finland and Denmark, in practice, Housing First is generally seen as a specific programme for particular individuals, rather than a philosophy underpinning policy responses to homelessness in Ireland. The majority of service providers have, at least rhetorically, endorsed a Housing First approach but, in practice, massively expanded their emergency and temporary shelter services, with a much more modest provision of secure housing. For example, the number of emergency shelter beds in Dublin more than doubled from approximately 800 in 2014 to over 2,000 by 2018, in stark contrast to the number of Housing First tenancies created, at just over 200.

This increase in emergency beds results, at least in part, from the political imperative to claim that sufficient emergency beds exist in order to render the need to sleep rough unnecessary and hence a 'choice' (for further details, see Chapter 6). Hence, much of the energy and expenditure on services for people experiencing homelessness has been focused on the management and containment of homelessness, rather than developing Housing First at scale or as a philosophical approach.

The broader role of affordable and social housing

From the preceding discussion, we can see that public housing is an influential factor in the effectiveness of Housing First, but the broader provision of social and affordable housing also has important roles to play in both preventing and responding to homelessness. The manner in which social housing is provided, whether through the direct provision of tenancies by public authorities or through cash subsidies to support tenancies in the private rented sector, is also significant.

Social and affordable housing in Finland

In Finland, the long-standing commitment to procure, redevelop and build housing in response in homelessness is integral to success in reducing homelessness. Here, the role of the Y Foundation, which has been acting as a dedicated source of social housing targeted at lone adult homelessness for decades, is important. There is less homelessness in Finland because this supply of affordable and supported housing has been in place. Figure 5.1 shows the ways in which increasing the supply of Y Foundation homes has been associated with reductions in lone adult homelessness. More recently, Finnish strategy has become

Figure 5.1: Single adult homelessness and Y Foundation apartment procurement and building in Finland, 1987–2016

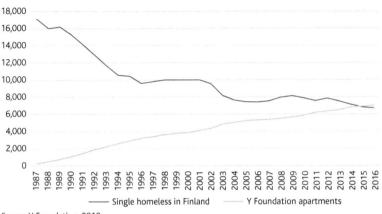

Source: Y Foundation, 2018.

focused on increasing the general accessibility of the social rented sector to homeless people, alongside the building of new homes that was integral to the current action plan, as well as *Paavo I* and *II*, at the time of writing.

Finland has its pressures around affordable housing supply, particularly in Helsinki, and the extent and continued presence of homeless people, including long-term homeless people living with friends and relatives, who now form the bulk of homelessness, shows ongoing housing supply problems. Young people can also find it difficult to meet housing costs. However, Finland does not have very high levels of housing stress relative to many other European countries; its housing markets are still relatively affordable and housing standards are generally good (FEANTSA and FAP, 2018).

There has been an upward trend in living in apartments in towers and blocks, reflecting increasing land prices in metropolitan areas, but space standards for the Finnish population have improved over recent decades (Statistics Finland, 2018). The contrast with some other countries is marked. The UK, for example, which had largely broken the association between relative poverty and poor housing conditions at the end of the last century, through the use of interventions to improve the general standard of housing and a substantial social housing building programme, has since seen the association between low income and poor space standards start to reassert itself as it ceased large-scale interventions to improve housing conditions and stopped building social housing at any scale (Tunstall, 2015).

In common with most European countries with sizeable social housing sectors, Finland is building less social housing than it once did. Social housing is around 12 per cent of total Finnish housing stock, although there are reports of pressures on the system, which is based on the regulation of housing developed with state loans but that ceases to be regulated as social housing once the loans are paid off (this is usually several decades). The scale of involvement by the state has fallen since the 1970s, an exception being dedicated building and development programmes and the Y Foundation. Levels of state funding in the 1970s were sufficient for 300,000 homes to be built, but there were closer to 50,000 completions during the period 2001–10 (Ruonavaara, 2017).

While the relative scale of Finnish social housing investment has fallen, some 1 million units have been built with government loans and interest-subsidy loans since 1949 (ARA, 2019), and it is still a significant element of total housing stock. The quality of social housing developments is high and rental costs are low, being between 20 and 50 per cent under the level in the private rented sector.

Finland has nevertheless responded to homelessness by building housing and this policy, *Paavo I* and *II*, and the 2016–18 action plan should, in themselves, deliver more than 5,000 homes specifically targeted at homelessness. The Y Foundation had some 16,650 homes by 2018 targeted at homelessness; there is some overlap between these figures, but the scale of building relative to the levels of homelessness is evident. The current homelessness strategy has seen an upsurge in social housing building, some 8,500 new units were started in 2017 by city housing companies and non-profit NGOs (data from the Y Foundation, 2017).

Issues with housing affordability do exist in Finland, particularly within Helsinki, but the strong associations between inadequate affordable housing supply and a highly pressured housing market do not exist in the same way as in Ireland, nor are spikes in homelessness associated with increased housing demand in specific cities, as is the case in Denmark. Eviction has also been targeted by preventive services that have increased significantly in scale since the shift towards prevention within *Paavo II*.

One area where Finland differs is in the use of specific programmes to increase housing supply for lone adults. This is led by the Y Foundation, and while building levels are not as high as they were, the continued development of social housing has been associated with the overall reductions in homelessness that have been achieved (see Figure 5.1).

Paavo II saw a shift in emphasis towards prevention in Finland as the strategy moved on from the initial focus on ending long-term homelessness and towards a broader approach to reducing all the remaining forms of homelessness. The primary focus is on what can be (loosely) translated as housing social work services, a mix of information, advice, practical support and case management. Joint working systems enabling the cooperation of housing advice services, debt counsellors and municipal social workers have been seen as effective in reducing the risk of unplanned moves and eviction from the private and social rented sectors. In 2012/13 in Helsinki, there were over 16,000 housing advice clients and 280 evictions were prevented thanks to housing advice work. During the years 2001–08, housing advice services were reported to have decreased evictions by 32 per cent in Helsinki (Pleace et al, 2015). The most recent Finnish strategy has placed further emphasis on increasing preventive activity. In 2017, 80 housing advisors prevented 2,871 evictions in Finland (data from the Y Foundation, 2017).

There are specific services in place to reduce the risk that homelessness will occur when leaving prison, residential care and hospitals, again employing the 'social work' model that focuses on the coordination of support services and arranging access to housing prior to discharge from an institution. Associations between migration and the threat of eviction have also been noted, with services being developed to assist people at risk of losing their homes who have Finnish as a second language.

Affordable housing supply is not an issue in the same way as in Ireland and Denmark, but is nevertheless an important factor in how effectively Finland is able to prevent homelessness and reduce the levels of hidden homelessness. The review of the first two phases of the Finnish homelessness strategy found that while service coordination within an integrated strategy had made a significant difference to homelessness in Finland, success would ultimately be determined by whether there was sufficient adequate and affordable housing supply (Pleace et al, 2015).

Social and affordable housing in Denmark

Denmark has a relatively large public housing sector as there are about 570,000 dwellings in public housing, comprising about one fifth of the entire housing stock in Denmark. Public housing associations provide rented housing for no profit that can be applied for by everybody, regardless of income level, and accessed through ordinary waiting lists. The public housing associations are regulated by the Law on Public Housing and democratically governed by tenants. Moreover, municipalities have to approve of the new construction of public housing locally as they provide part of the funding capital for new public housing units.

As previously mentioned, municipalities have a right to allocate up to 25 per cent of vacancies in public housing to people in acute housing need, based on social criteria set locally by each municipality. Most larger cities and suburban municipalities make full use of this possibility for social allocation, and in most cities, this mechanism plays an important role in providing housing for homeless people and other vulnerable groups. However, a number of mainly smaller and medium-sized municipalities do not make use of this option, either because the need for housing even for vulnerable groups could widely be met through ordinary waiting lists, or because they have chosen not to use this option for political (ideological) or financial reasons as there are also costs attached for municipalities when they use this option.

Even though the overall stock of public housing in Denmark is large, the construction of new units has been quite modest. Figure 5.2 shows annual completions of new public housing units, compared to overall housing completions (private and public). Over the period from 2007 to 2018, a total of approximately 27,000 new dwellings in public housing were completed out of a total of about 240,000 new dwellings of all types. When the lowest level of completions in public housing were recorded at only 760 dwellings in 2010, this should not be seen as a consequence of the financial crisis from 2008/09, but rather as a consequence of years of strong economic growth before the crisis (2006/07), when very high construction costs in the building sector

Figure 5.2: Dwellings completed in Denmark, 2007–18

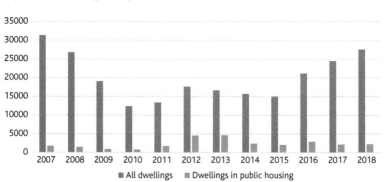

were a barrier to the new construction of public housing. By contrast, the high levels of annual completions, at about 4,600 public housing dwellings, in both 2012 and 2013 widely reflect that the financial crisis paradoxically led to an increase in the building of new units due to falling overall construction costs in the building sector due to the crisis. Moreover, one of the countermeasures against the financial crisis was to speed up the renovation queue in the existing public housing stock. Thus, a certain element of a countercyclical trend in the investment in public housing can be observed over the period. Towards the end of the period, overall housing construction in Denmark has again been growing strongly, along with rising economic growth. In 2018, more than 27,500 dwellings were completed nationwide, with about 2,200 of them being in public housing.

Despite the large-scale public housing sector, housing markets in larger cities are generally characterised by strong demand, rising property prices in the private market and increasing challenges of housing affordability. Yet, there are also considerable local differences. Danish cities and towns have experienced somewhat different local trends in homelessness, and these are probably associated with differences in demography (population growth) and variations in local housing markets, as well as the extent to which a strategic focus on providing housing and support has been mainstreamed into local housing and welfare policies.

More than half of all homeless people in Denmark are recorded in the two largest urban areas, Copenhagen and Aarhus, when including also the suburban areas around these cities. The number of homeless people recorded in the city municipality of Copenhagen remained quite constant over the period at a relatively high level of 1,494 in 2009 and 1,442 in 2019, whereas in Aarhus, figures increased from 466 in 2009 to 750 in 2019. Both Copenhagen and Aarhus are affected by a general tendency of re-urbanisation in Denmark, with strong population growth in these two cities and increasingly tight housing markets as a consequence. Although the homelessness counts do not provide evidence on the underlying causes of the observed trends, the increasing shortage of affordable housing is an important factor in explaining the increase in homelessness as it becomes increasingly difficult for vulnerable individuals to find housing that they can afford.

In contrast, a decrease in homelessness was recorded in Denmark's third-largest city, Odense, where homelessness fell from 208 homeless people recorded in 2009 to only 125 homeless people recorded in the count in 2019. Odense did not experience the same strong population growth over the period as Copenhagen and Aarhus. Moreover, besides a more relaxed housing market, the municipality of Odense has mainstreamed the Housing First approach into its local social welfare system, with a strong emphasis on providing housing and support for homeless people with complex support needs.

However, over the period, there were also increases in homelessness in a number of medium-sized towns, mainly those that were near to major urban growth centres, such as towns in Eastern Jutland near Aarhus, or towns on the island of Zealand in commuting distance from Copenhagen. These are generally towns that either experienced considerable population growth or are otherwise affected by the tightening housing markets in nearby urban areas. Some of these towns do not make use of the possibility for prioritised allocation of homeless or otherwise vulnerable people to public housing, although a substantial stock of public housing generally exists in most of these towns. In some municipalities, it was previously not necessary to make use of this option as the need for housing could widely be covered by access through ordinary waiting lists. However, with increased pressure on local housing markets, these towns are experiencing increased difficulties in providing housing for homeless people and may need to make use of municipal referral to public housing if they want to curb the local increase in homelessness.

Social and affordable housing in Ireland

As noted in the introduction to this book, one of the consequences of the economic downturn in Ireland was the virtual cessation of the building of social housing units by local authorities and a much-reduced output from approved housing bodies, which had long-term implications for the outcome of the strategies.[3] By 2015, only 75 units of social housing were built by local authorities – the lowest number in the history of the state – down from nearly 5,000 in 2008. Similarly, due largely to changes in the funding regime, the new build output from approved housing bodies declined from nearly 2,000 units in 2008 to 401 in 2015, giving a total of 476 new units of social housing completed nationally. Other schemes to secure social housing from the private market provided a further 1,500 units for letting to qualified households.

The year 2015 was the low point in the supply of new social housing, and completions have increased each year since then, with nearly 3,400 units completed in 2018, and a further nearly 2,600 units acquired or leased by local authorities and approved housing bodies for social letting. However, despite the increase in supply, there were 71,858 households assessed as qualified for housing support but on the waiting list for housing as of June 2018. Of these, 5,663 (8 per cent) were literally homeless, including those in temporary or emergency accommodation.

As the homeless strategy was published in 2008, the social housing landscape was already in the process of changing in a number of ways, resulting in a much altered landscape for social housing. It is important to note, as Norris and Byrne (2017) convincingly argue, that while this process of transformation accelerated during the global financial crisis, it actually had its origins in the late 1980s, when the model of funding social housing switched from borrowing by local authorities to capital funding from the exchequer. This made social housing output vulnerable during times of austerity as capital cuts are politically more palatable than revenue cuts. This was exactly what happened between 2008 and 2014, when capital funding for social housing was cut by 88 per cent.

There were three key features that explain the transformed landscape of social housing over this period. First, there was a much greater mixed economy of social housing providers, with local authorities joined by over 500 approved housing bodies – albeit the majority being small-scale providers – constructing, acquiring and leasing dwellings for allocation to qualified households. By the end of 2017, approved housing bodies were managing a stock of about 30,000 units of social housing (Library and Oireachtas Research Service, 2018), as compared to less than 1,000 in 1988, with local authorities managing 144,000 units.

The second key feature that explains the transformed landscape of social housing over this period was the introduction of housing benefit or demand-side subsidies by local authorities. Two slightly different schemes were introduced: initially the Rental Accommodation Scheme (RAS) in 2004; then the Housing Assistance Payment (HAP) in 2014. The growth in these schemes, in which households are accommodated in private rented accommodation but with the majority of their rent being paid by the local authority, resulted in a drift from providing social housing directly to 'social housing supports'. Unlike the older Rent Supplement Scheme, both RAS and HAP are seen as 'long-term social housing supports'; hence, recipients of these payments are deemed to have had their housing needs met (Corrigan and Watson, 2018). The impact of having a large proportion of private rented accommodation taken up to provide 'social housing supports' will be discussed later.

The third key feature that explains the transformed landscape of social housing over this period is the decline in the construction of social

Figure 5.3: Social housing provision in Ireland, 2008–18

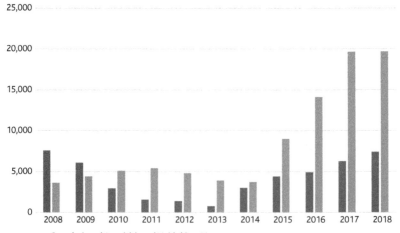

- Completions / Acquisitions / Voids/ Part V
- Social Housing Supports (Rental Accommodation Scheme / Housing Assistance Payment / Social Housing Current Expenditure Programme)

Source: Department of Housing, Planning and Local Government.

housing. Although the construction of social housing has increased since the historic lows of 2014/15, it is striking how dependent local authorities are on either acquiring or leasing existing housing stock, providing income supports to qualified households to meet the costs of renting in the private sector, and using private hotels and 'bed and breakfasts' (B&Bs) in the case of homeless families. In 2008, 60 per cent of social housing output was in the form of new construction; this declined to a low of 3.4 per cent in 2016 but had risen to 12.6 per cent in 2018.

Figure 5.3 highlights the decline in social housing output, both from construction/acquisition/leasing and from social housing supports, from 2008 to 2013, and while overall output has increased significantly since 2014, just over 70 per cent of provision is now in the form of 'social housing supports' rather than provision arising from completions or acquisitions. This compares to just over 30 per cent in 2008.

Somewhat paradoxically, the number of households in social housing tenancies or receiving a social housing support increased substantially over the period, rising from 145,000 households in 2008 to just over 250,000 in 2018, or from 9 per cent to 15 per cent of all households[4] (see Figure 5.4).

This is accounted for by: (1) the virtual cessation of the tenant purchase scheme between 2014 and 2016; (2) the return to nearly 10,000 units of local authority stock for rental that was previously void; and (3) the transfer of households from the welfare-based rent

Figure 5.4: Stock of social housing in Ireland, 2008–18

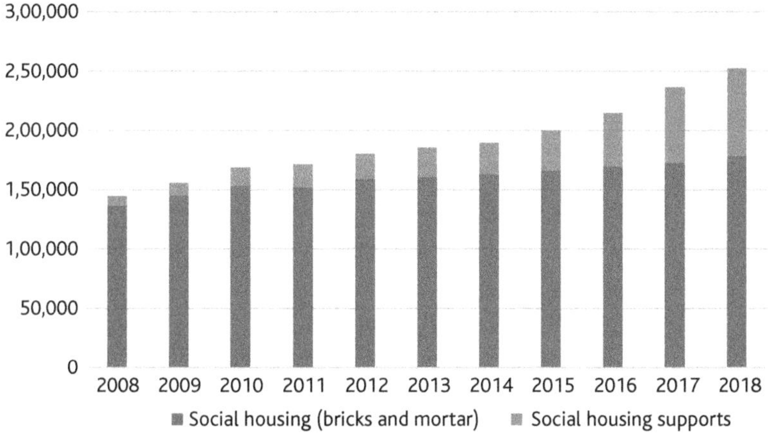

■ Social housing (bricks and mortar)   ■ Social housing supports

Source: Department of Housing, Planning and Local Government.

supplement, where they were not counted as receiving social housing support, to the HAP payment, where they are. The question remains as to how this increase in available social housing tenancies coincided with a rapid increase in homelessness.

Social housing allocations

The allocation of social housing tenancies and approval for social housing supports are functions of each local authority,[5] which, as in Denmark, have discretion to prioritise the allocation of dwellings both to their own and to approved housing body-owned stock. While there is no standardisation across local authorities, in general, they prioritise the people in a number of categories, including homelessness, unfit accommodation, disability, care leavers and so on. In practice, most allocations are based on how long a household has been on the list, with some opaque element of medical/welfare priority. An increasing number of local authorities use choice-based letting schemes.

In response to the very low supply of new social housing, there was increased interest in ensuring that the available supply of new social housing tenancies had the maximum impact on reducing homelessness, as well as a reliance on the reintroduction of properties that had become void due to dilapidation back into the housing stock, as noted in Chapter 3. Following the publication of the *Implementation Plan on the State's Response to Homelessness*, the Department of the Environment, Community and Local Government noted in a Circular to all Local Authorities issued in 2014 that only 4.1 per cent of all social housing allocations (including voids) by local authorities were made to homeless households. The circular warned local authorities that the minister had the power to instruct them on how to allocate their housing units and was considering whether to do so. In January 2015, the minister issued a directive to the four Dublin local authorities to the effect that 50 per cent of dwellings available for allocation for the period 27 January to 26 July 2015 should be allocated to homeless and other vulnerable households, and that 30 per cent should be allocated in the other urban centres of Galway, Cork, Waterford and Limerick.[6] The directive was later extended twice to apply until the end of April 2016, but it was not renewed thereafter.

This instruction was not welcomed by local authorities. On 22 April 2016, the chief executives of the four Dublin councils wrote to the minister to request that the directive not be extended. They argued that '[i]t is our view that this requirement is now having the effect of encouraging some households who are in housing need and who are awaiting social housing to enter the "homeless" system in the mistaken belief that this will hasten the allocation to them of a social housing unit' (Keegan, 2016). In February, the Housing Agency, at the request of the Department of the Environment, Community and Local Government, conducted a review of the impact of the directive. The Housing Agency's review, a relatively short document, concluded blandly that there was 'emerging evidence that the extent to which homeless households have been prioritised on the waiting list for housing has contributed to the expectation that a household presenting as homeless will receive secure tenure housing from the State after a very short period of waiting' (Housing Agency, 2016: 17).

Despite not elucidating what the 'emerging evidence' was, the review recommended that the ministerial directive should lapse in April 2016. As noted earlier, the *Report of the Committee on Housing and Homelessness* (Houses of the Oireachtas, 2016) recommended reintroducing the directive. However, *Rebuilding Ireland: Action Plan for Housing and Homelessness* did not specifically address or debate this recommendation; rather, it claimed that the expanded supply of social housing that the plan aimed to deliver would address the issue (Department of Housing, Planning, Community and Local Government, 2016: 107).

The issue was also raised specifically in relation to the allocation policy of Dublin City Council, the largest social housing landlord in the county and the authority with the highest number of households in emergency accommodation. In early 2018, it decided that they would no longer prioritise homeless families ahead of other households who had been on the housing waiting list for a longer period of time. The primary rationale for the change in allocation was that:

> We are concerned that families may endure a prolonged period in emergency accommodation (particularly in commercial facilities) and not consider alternatives, in order to secure what they believe to be the most sustainable option for their family i.e. permanent social housing. This is completely understandable but DCC [Dublin City Council] does not have adequate housing stock and families may not realise that waiting for a permanent social housing offer given the current numbers in homeless services is likely to take some years.

The alternatives that the council refers to are primarily the HAP.

While a HAP social housing support tenancy is, in theory, substantially quicker to access than a social housing unit provided by a local authority or approved housing body, it is, in effect, a private rented sector tenancy. As Finnerty and O'Connell (2014: 178) argue, 'these offers are manifestly not equivalent'; rather, there is a hierarchy of offers. For Finnerty et al (2016: 256):

> Households in stock directly provided by local authorities occupy the top rung of the ladder in terms of secure settled accommodation and all of the tangible and symbolic attributes that accompany it. They are joined on the top rung by direct provision tenants of housing associations. In contrast, households in stock supplied under lease and RAS/HAP are vulnerable to a range of factors outside their control which will influence how secure and settled their accommodation is, principally because at the end of the lease or rental agreement, the property reverts to the private supplier.

The role of private rented housing in Ireland

In contrast to the situation in Finland and Denmark, developments in the private rental sector in Ireland had a significant impact on the homeless situation – both through the eviction of tenants into homelessness and by providing a subsidised route out of homelessness. At the end of 2018, just under 87,000 households (approximately 25 per cent of all households living in the private rented sector) were collectively in receipt of a housing benefit (HAP, RAS or Rent Supplement) to support their tenancy, amounting to €600 million. The number of households receiving these supports to live in private rented accommodation is slightly higher than was the case in 2008, but the majority of tenants are now in receipt of a HAP or RAS payment rather than Rent Supplement. This is significant because it signals that the state sees the private rented sector as a long-term solution to meeting the needs of households who qualify for social housing, rather than only providing a short-term income supplement via the social protection system. Given the importance of the sector in meeting the needs of households who would otherwise enter homeless services and as a means of exiting homelessness, considerable energy and expenditure has been devoted to protecting existing tenancies, preventing households entering homeless services by providing enhanced payments to landlords and providing enhanced supports to those currently in emergency accommodation to exit to the private rented sector. The state has also attempted to moderate rent inflation by introducing rent control zones.

Protecting tenancies

Commencing in June 2014, initially in Dublin but rolled out to some other urban centres and the counties adjacent to Dublin at a later stage, a Tenancy Protection Service was established, provided by the NGO Threshold but funded via section 10 of the Housing Act 1988. Between June 2014 and the end of 2018, just over 10,500 households deemed at risk of homelessness contacted the service in Dublin alone, and nearly 5,500 were protected from entering emergency services for those experiencing homelessness, with less than 100 households entering emergency accommodation. Initially, the majority of households, some 85 per cent, were protected from entering emergency services *via* having their Rent Supplement (housing income support) payment increased to cover increases in the rent demanded by their landlord, or to clear rent arrears brought about by increases in rent. However, with the introduction of rent control zones in early 2016 (see later), this dropped to 17 per cent in 2018, with 79 per cent having their tenancies maintained through advocacy work on behalf of Threshold, who negotiated with landlords and the state regulator, the Residential Tenancies Board, compared to only 11 per cent in the first 18 months of the operation of the service.

Preventing homelessness

In addition to protecting tenancies in the first instance, an increasing emphasis is on rapidly rehousing, or maintaining in their existing housing, households who present to local authorities as requiring access to emergency accommodation in the near future as their tenancy will legally terminate, thus preventing them from entering emergency accommodation. Data are only available in Dublin, but from Q1 2017 to Q4 2018, of the nearly 6,500 households who newly presented as needing access to emergency accommodation to homeless services in the four Dublin authorities and were deemed to qualify for social housing supports, more than half or nearly 3,500 households were provided immediately with either a social housing support, primarily in the form an enhanced HAP, or, in small number of cases, a social housing tenancy.

Providing tenancies

In early 2015, a Homeless HAP Place Finder Service was established in Dublin, which was extended to Cork in 2017 and across the rest of the county from January 2018. The purpose of the service was to provide assistance to households in emergency accommodation to access the private rented sector and receive support via the HAP scheme. The services include liaising with landlords on behalf of homeless households and providing one month's rent as a deposit and two month's rent in advance in order to secure the property. By the end of Q3 2018, more than 4,300 households had received assistance from these services.

Rent Pressure Zones

With rapid rent inflation from 2013 in Dublin, after a period of decline and stability, measures to regulate rent increases were announced by the Minister for the Environment, Community and Local Government in February 2015. Following protracted negotiations between the Minister for Finance and the Minister for the Environment on increasing rent stability and security of tenure in the private rented housing market, legislation amending the Residential Tenancies Act 2004 was signed into law in December 2015. These amendments came into effect on 9 May 2016 and included the following provisions: that rent cannot be reviewed upwards more than once in any 24-month period (it had been once every 12 months); an extension of notice periods for both landlords and tenants in respect of the termination of longer-term

Figure 5.5: Rent indices, Ireland, Q3 2007–Q4 2018

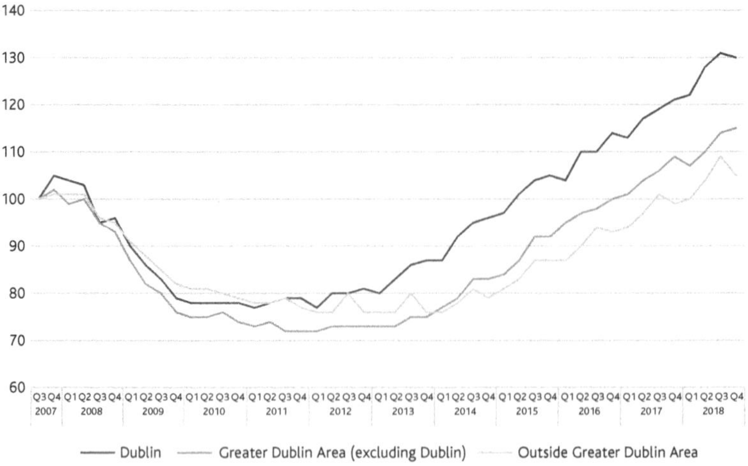

―― Dublin ―― Greater Dublin Area (excluding Dublin) ―― Outside Greater Dublin Area

Source: Economic and Social Research Institute and Residential Tenancies Board (2019) *The RTB Rent Index*.

tenancies (up to 224 days for landlords and 112 days for tenants); and verification procedures where the landlord intends to sell or refurbish a property and therefore terminate the tenancy. On 23 December 2016, the Planning and Development (Housing) and Residential Tenancies Act 2016 provided for the introduction of 4 per cent rental growth limits in designated Rent Pressure Zones (RPZs) and the extension of standard tenancies from four to six years. However, as Figure 5.5 shows, despite these measures, rents have continued to grow.

Analyses of the trajectories of a significant number of homeless families suggest that upward rent reviews in the private rented sector contributed to their initial homelessness, and the subsequent inability to access alternative private rented housing was because the rate of rent subsidy was not keeping pace with market rents, or because landlords were refusing to accept tenants in receipt of a rent subsidy. After a number of years in which rent allowance levels were stagnant, in July 2016, significant increases in the level of the rent subsidies were announced. In most areas of Dublin, for example, the rent subsidy limit for a single person increased by 20 per cent and for a couple or one person with one child by just over 30 per cent. In addition, under the HAP housing benefit scheme, discretion is given to increase the basic payment by up to 20 per cent, and for those at risk of homelessness by up to 50 per cent. In practice, in urban areas, and especially so in Dublin, this discretionary payment is now the norm rather than the exception. In the Greater Dublin area, of the just over 10,500 HAP tenancies at the end of 2018, 36 per cent were in receipt of a discretionary payment of up to 50 per cent and 55 per cent were in receipt of a discretionary payment of up to 20 per cent; less than 10 per cent of households were not in receipt of a discretionary payment. Similarly, under the Rent Supplement scheme, tenants can be provided with a supplement in excess of the proscribed amount on a case-by-case basis, and between 2015 and 2018, some 13,000 households received the excess payments. Thus, although the base rate for rent subsidies has remained unchanged since 2016, a significant number of tenants, and the majority in urban areas, are in receipt of a discretionary excess payment in order to keep pace with rent inflation.

With further declines in the availability of properties to rent predicted, particularly in Dublin, increasing rent allowances will have only a marginal effect in assisting households to exit homelessness. Furthermore, it would appear that over the past number of years, a key reason for the ending of a tenancy in the private rented sector leading to homelessness was not rent increases, but the repossession of dwellings by the banks or landlords. Between Q3 2012 and Q4 2018, 5,330 buy-to-let (BTL) residential properties were repossessed with vacant possession following an order or voluntarily surrendered or abandoned. With 11,240 BTL properties in arrears for over 720 days in Q4 2018 (Central Bank of Ireland, various years), the repossessions of these dwellings will continue. That the number of registered private rented dwellings with the Residential Tenancies Board declined by nearly 4 per cent, from 319,311 to 307,348 dwellings, between Q2 2017 and Q4 2018 suggests that in addition to repossessions by banks, landlords are validly terminating tenancies in order to use the dwellings for their own use or to sell the dwelling.

Despite the relative success of the various schemes in protecting nearly 5,000 private rented sector tenancies, preventing a further 3,000 households from entering emergency accommodation in Dublin alone by providing them with enhanced payments to remain in or access the private rented sector, and assisting over 4,000 households to exit emergency accommodation and secure private rented tenancies, as we saw in Chapter 3, the number of households in emergency accommodation nonetheless rose each month. Utilising the stock of the private rented sector to meet social housing need is critical in preventing and responding to homelessness given the sluggishness of output from local authority of approved housing body providers. One quarter of those residing in this sector are receiving some form of state income support to allow them to maintain their tenancy. Despite enhanced payment schemes to prevent households entering emergency services, and enhanced payments and supports to assist households to exit emergency accommodation, the number of households entering emergency accommodation continues to increase and the number of households exiting continues to decrease.

Conclusion

Housing clearly matters in both preventing homelessness and reducing the number of households in temporary and emergency accommodation. However, as we draw out in greater detail in the conclusion to this book, both the scale of secure affordable housing and the targeting of those experiencing homelessness are crucial. The Irish do worse in this regard despite expending considerable amounts of public funding on the provision of social housing. This is because it largely relies on private providers to provide housing, with the gap between ability to pay and market rents made up by a housing benefit payment. However, while this approach meets the affordability criteria, it does not meet the security criteria as terminations of tenancy in the private rented sector are also key drivers of homelessness in Ireland. Given the very limited supply of social housing becoming available, any preferential allocation to homeless households is politically contested. In addition, Housing First services are not the norm; rather, Housing First is seen as a limited programme for a limited number of people.

Denmark retains a considerable stock of public housing, with allocation mechanisms that can be used to allocate housing for rehousing homeless people if municipalities decide to do so, and with the private rented sector playing a smaller role. It has a targeted housing and relatively ambitious Housing First programme but is facing tight housing markets in its major urban areas, particularly Copenhagen, where homelessness in concentrated. The tight housing markets and the extent of housing need in the larger cities clearly creates barriers of access to affordable housing despite the existence of a large public housing sector.

In Finland, the steady provision of secure affordable housing, targeting and the embeddedness of a distinct 'Housing First' philosophy centred on a housing-led/focused response to homelessness have allowed for the provision of a significant number of secure tenancies for households. The fact that there is a stream of social housing specifically designated for households moving out of homelessness, where they are not seen as being in conflict with 'ordinary households' on a social housing waiting list, emerges as one of the key differences in the housing/homelessness systems in the three countries.

Notes

1. See: www.housingfirst.fi/en/housing_first
2. Although there is Canadian evidence suggesting comparable effectiveness between ICM and ACT (Urbanoski et al, 2018), and the Dutch, Finnish and UK experience with ICM with people with complex needs has suggested that it can engage with higher-need individuals.
3. Private housing completions also declined dramatically during this period, with only 4,575 units of housing completed in 2013 (included social housing). Due to methodological issues that exaggerated the extent of new construction, it is problematic in comparing housing completions prior to 2011, but the figures published by the Department of Housing in the five years prior to the global financial crisis (2004–08) were that that were 351,696 private housing completions during that period, an average of just 70,000 per annum. Notwithstanding that these data exaggerate new construction, the decline in new construction is remarkable. Output has increased since 2013, with just over 18,000 new dwellings (including social housing) completed in 2018.
4. At the end of 2018, there were a further 24,303 households in receipt of a rent allowance.
5. In accordance with section 22 of the Housing (Miscellaneous Provisions) Act 2009 and Social Housing Allocation Regulation 2011 (S.I. 198 of 2011).
6. The scheme was restricted to those who were residing in designated homelessness accommodation on 1 December 2014 or had resided in designated homelessness accommodation in the preceding six months. A couple or one person with one child who qualified could obtain rent support of up to nearly €1,900 in most parts of Dublin (Statutory Instrument No. 575 of 2014, Housing Assistance Payment [Section 50] [No.3] Regulations 2014).

6

Explanations: welfare and politics matter

Introduction

Having explored the role of housing in explaining the variable outcomes in the three countries under review, in this chapter, we turn to assessing the role of welfare provision in shaping trends in homelessness. Finland and Denmark are unambiguously part of the social-democratic welfare family, having high levels of decommodification for health and welfare services, with Ireland fitting somewhat uneasily, particularly in relation to housing, into the liberal cluster of welfare regimes (Esping-Anderson, 1990). In addition to housing-related factors, systemic factors related to welfare reforms have likely affected current trends in homelessness. Welfare benefits have generally been under reform in many countries following trends towards labour market activation for unemployed people and both the containment and the reduction of spending on social protection. This combination of growing shortages of affordable housing and reductions in welfare benefits has contributed to the housing exclusion of vulnerable groups.

The welfare state and homelessness in Denmark

Denmark has one of the most extensive welfare systems in the world, with a high level of income redistribution, universal health care, extensive social services and the provision of social housing. Wider social and housing policy probably helps explain why homelessness levels in Denmark are relatively low in international comparisons, with Denmark also possessing a significant and comparatively well-funded homelessness services sector. It also explains why homelessness is widely concentrated in people with complex support needs who fall through this otherwise extensive welfare safety net (Benjaminsen and Andrade, 2015). In particular, the scale of the public housing sector, in combination with relatively generous welfare benefits for families with dependent children, probably explains why family homelessness has remained at very modest levels in Denmark compared to many other countries, and to Ireland in particular (Baptista et al, 2017).

Although Denmark has largely avoided the austerity measures experienced by many other countries after the financial crisis, welfare reforms aimed at strengthening the financial sustainability of the system have been pursued, including 'workfare'/labour market activation-oriented reforms, mirroring wider trends in the economically developed world. The need to 'motivate' young people to take up education and work was a major policy concern of successive reforms, including social benefits being generally set at a lower level for young people from the 1980s onwards. In particular, a reform from 2003 set most social assistance benefits for young people at a considerably lower level than for older benefit receivers and successive reforms and reductions in benefits have continued since then (Hansen and Schultz-Nielsen, 2015).

As we saw in Chapter 4, one of the most significant developments in Danish homelessness was the spike in youth homelessness during the last decade, with homelessness among young adults more than doubling over the period from 2009 to 2017, before decreasing somewhat in 2019. While a direct causal link cannot be established from existing data, the lower welfare benefits for young people probably played an important role in explaining the overall increase over the period. Another factor perhaps explaining the rise in youth homelessness is the increasing shortage of affordable housing in Denmark's larger cities from the early 2000s onwards. It is very likely that the interaction of these adverse structural trends – lower social assistance benefits for young people and barriers of access to affordable housing – created the cocktail that, in recent years, has driven growing numbers of vulnerable young people into homelessness, as well as creating barriers to finding exits from youth homelessness. Danish municipalities have highlighted the barriers of finding housing for homeless young people due to their lower ability to meet the costs of rent when they are reliant on the welfare system (Rambøll and SFI, 2013; Benjaminsen et al, 2017).

Neither the homelessness strategy programme nor the follow-up programme addressed such wider structural factors and changes to housing and welfare systems that may have affected the overall upward trend in homelessness. The emphasis on providing housing and support following the Housing First approach was, as we have seen, not accompanied by more general initiatives to alleviate the growing shortage of affordable housing in larger cities and towns, nor was there a systematic attempt to address the increased difficulties for marginalised youth to find housing that they could afford.

Despite the existence of a generally comprehensive welfare system and large public housing sector, a disconnect can be observed between homelessness policies and general housing and welfare policies in Denmark. As a result, the impact of structural and systemic factors on homelessness patterns in Denmark is largely unrecognised in policy terms and the housing affordability crisis in larger cities remains largely unmet by national initiatives.

The welfare state and homelessness in Finland

Welfare systems in Finland are extensive. There are systems of unemployment benefit that are contribution based, which can be combined with a general housing allowance to cover rental costs when levels of unemployment benefit are not very high, alongside social assistance payments to ensure that basic living costs are met. This universally accessible safety net means that homelessness is unlikely to occur for solely financial reasons, although a small level of hidden homelessness, thought to be associated with insufficient affordable housing supply, is still present (Pleace et al, 2015). In July 2018, 355,937 households were receiving an average of €320 a month in rental support; there are approximately 2.6 million households in total, meaning that just under 14 per cent of all Finnish households receive some support with their housing costs (KELA, 2018).

Where children are present, welfare payments for the parents as carers and for each child are available, in addition to social assistance and the general housing allowance (and potentially unemployment benefit if someone is eligible). The Finnish benefits system allows small amounts of money from part-time or temporary work to be earned without any welfare benefits being reduced or taken away, enabling people reliant on welfare benefits to top up their income to some degree.

The Finnish welfare state was an archetype of the social-democratic model of welfare, centred on universal access to welfare for all citizens, an all-encompassing system promoting social cohesion and solidarity. This ethos of welfare provision started to shift in the late 1980s as economic challenges presented themselves and attitudes towards the sustainability of a heavily funded welfare system began to change. Attitudes towards people reliant on welfare benefits also began to harden (Hellman et al, 2017).

Finland has not been immune from the changes to welfare systems that have occurred across much of North-Western Europe and in other parts of Scandinavia. Changes began in the mid-1990s that saw welfare policy shift towards labour market activation, with eligibility and conditionalities for unemployment benefit becoming tighter. The insurance-based principle for unemployment benefit in Finland was weakened, with eligibility ceasing after set time periods, making those experiencing longer-term worklessness increasingly reliant on lower, means-tested benefits. Finland also introduced benefit sanctions at an earlier point than some other countries, with reforms between 1995 and 2001 making it possible to withdraw benefit if someone refused a job offer or declined to take part in labour market activation programmes. Unlike some other countries, Finland employs sanctions that reduce welfare benefits for a set period if behaviour that is seen as blocking labour market activation is deemed to have occurred. Sanctions are also time limited. Finns retain a right to at least some social assistance, but the reductions in benefits can be scaled up if refusal to participate in labour market activation is defined as deliberate and persistent. The trend towards the use of labour market activation and sanctions has not abated, with sanctions being extended from those aged over 25 to those aged under 25 in 2010 (Kananen, 2012).

In part, these welfare reforms have been driven by the sustained series of economic shocks that have put public spending under pressure. In the 1990s, Finland experienced economic problems following the collapse of the Soviet Union, which had been a major trading partner. Later, having dominated the mobile/cellular phone market, Nokia fell into steep decline following its purchase by Microsoft, with the wider economy dropping into recession from 2012. This created the kinds of pressures on public expenditure experienced in other post-industrial economies, with public health systems coming under pressure. A new concern with the level of taxation in relation to attracting foreign investment began to permeate debates around health and social policy. What had been a resource-intensive strategy for public health started to be modified, with an attempt being made to curtail expenditure through restructuring but with potentially adverse impacts on the quality and availability of health services (Saltman and Teperi, 2016; Kokkinen et al, 2017). Finland has experienced the cuts and restructuring of welfare programmes that have been experienced in other countries. However, although the nature of the welfare system has changed, it remains extensive and generous when compared to many other European countries (Y Foundation, 2017).

The experience of migrant populations without residency rights who become homeless in Finland appears to be different because they cannot access welfare systems available to citizens. The issue here is the same as in all other North-Western European countries that receive higher rates of application for asylum and experience higher rates of illegal, economic migration: migrants without the right of residence in Finland cannot access welfare and other systems, which means that homelessness can be associated with destitution for some migrants. This is a complex issue as the intersection between what is essentially immigration policy and how a country treats people who are not citizens or have not been granted rights of residence and homelessness policy is somewhat blurred. Clearly, an illegal migrant can become homeless and should be assisted. However, if they have no right to live in a country, housing them, particularly in a context where citizens of that country require housing, may not be a politically or socially viable option. Equally, there cannot be a system that removes illegal migrants who are housed but houses illegal migrants who are homeless. Attempts to arrive at a balanced policy around illegal migrant homelessness combine humanitarian responses with repatriation, sometimes referred to as a reconnection process, but are responses to illegal migrant homelessness that centre on removing the illegal migrant and returning them to the country that they left or fled (Pleace, 2011). More generally, illegal migrant homelessness in Finland is an illustration of the role that welfare systems play in preventing homelessness through the provision of a basic safety net (Pleace et al, 2015).

The welfare state and homelessness in Ireland

In comparative terms, the Irish welfare state appears to fit, albeit sometimes somewhat uncomfortably, within the liberal cluster of countries, where levels of decommodification are low and the role of the market is significant in the delivery of welfare. However, housing policy in Ireland was historically strongly decommodifying (Norris, 2016) and is currently an unusual hybrid, providing high levels of decommodification, security and poverty-proofing in local authority and approved housing body tenancies, in addition to providing income support and poverty-proofing for qualified tenants in the private rented sector, though with considerably less security of tenure. Considerable discretion can be applied to increase housing-related payments to up to 50 per cent above the standard rate for households at risk of and/or exiting homelessness.

The launch of the strategy to end homelessness in 2008 coincided 'with the sharpest and deepest recession in the history of the state' (Watson et al, 2018: 554), but by the time of the publication of the *Homelessness Policy Statement* in 2013, economic recovery was tentative, but evident, and unemployment was starting to decline. The seasonally adjusted employment rate was under 6 per cent in 2008, but with the impact of the global financial crisis, it rose rapidly, peaking at 16 per cent by mid-2012. However, the rate has fallen continuously since and was at 5.3 per cent at the end of 2018. The unemployment rate for those under 25 was considerably higher at 12.2 per cent at the end of 2018, down from over 30 per cent in mid-2012, and a staggering 39 per cent for males aged 15–24. However, as we saw in Chapter 4, those most likely to be in temporary or emergency accommodation are those aged 25–44, rather than those aged 18–25. The 18 per cent unemployment rate for males in mid-2012 was considerably higher than the 12.5 per cent rate for females; by the end of 2018, the rates for males and females were 5.3 per cent and 5.4 per cent, respectively. Thus, the period from 2014 to 2018, where the numbers entering and remaining in emergency and temporary accommodation increased each quarter, was also a period of rapidly declining unemployment for both males and females and across all age groups.

Whelan and Nolan (2017: 112) have persuasively argued that despite the perception that the impact of 'austerity' measures taken by the Irish government was felt disproportionally by the most vulnerable, in fact, 'the level of income inequality in Ireland was rather stable through the crisis and the income losses associated with discretionary budgetary measures were broadly proportionate across the income distribution'. However, in reviewing housing affordability between 2005 and 2015, Corrigan et al (2018) demonstrate the variable impact of the recession in Ireland: while there was only a very slight increase in the amount that households were spending on average on housing between 2005 and 2015, households in the private rented sector, in Dublin and on low incomes faced significantly higher housing costs. However, for those households in the private rented sector and on low incomes, this was the case throughout the period under review, leading Corrigan et al (2018: 37) to conclude that these 'affordability issues are structural rather than cyclical in nature'.

This short analysis suggests that the austerity measures taken in Ireland during the global economic crisis were, as Whelan and Nolan (2017: 113) argue, 'progressive in the immediate response to the crisis and broadly proportional overall'. If this is the case, the rise in homelessness cannot simply be attributed to a general deterioration in the circumstances of the vulnerable during the crisis. Furthermore, the rate of unemployment has plummeted during the same time that the numbers of households in temporary and emergency accommodation substantially increased. Escalating costs in the private rented sector have contributed to the increase, but the fact that the housing costs associated with living in the private rented sector and being poor were always high suggests that that is only a partial explanation.

A large number of Irish households live in private rented accommodation while in receipt of different kinds of state rental subsidy. As rents began to accelerate in 2014, the Department of Social Welfare (Social Protection) was reluctant to increase the maximum level of Rent Supplement available, partly to contain costs but also out of concerns that such increases would further inflate rent levels. Between 2014 and 2016, rent arrears were the single largest reason given by families in Dublin for being homeless. As noted in Chapter 4, a Tenancy Protection Service (TPS) commenced in 2014 whereby households could obtain higher rent subsidies on a case-by-case basis; rent arrears in subsidy-dependent households declined as a cause of homelessness, being replaced by terminations of tenancies arising from landlords either selling their property voluntarily or under pressure from the banks. Tenancies could be legally terminated if landlords wished to use the property for their own use or for other family members or if a landlord had to sell the property.

In addition, in 2016, 24 per cent of homeless adults in Dublin were non-Irish nationals (data are unavailable for outside of Dublin) and 9 per cent nationally were Irish Travellers, figures that are likely to have increased in 2017 and 2018. Thus, roughly a third of adults in emergency and temporary accommodation were from minority ethnic groups or non-Irish nationals with fewer protective factors, such as social networks and capital, to withstand adverse events such as termination of tenancy. This issue is not related to illegal immigration, most of the non-Irish nationals in homeless services had lived in Ireland in the private rented sector for a number of years prior to becoming homeless. The 2016 Census recorded that, with the exception of UK nationals, the majority of non-Irish nationals were renting their dwelling, almost exclusively in the private rented sector, with rates of renting in excess of 80 per cent for Latvians, Brazilians, Romanians, Poles and Lithuanians, compared to 18 per cent in the general population. Given that terminations of tenancies in the private rented sector are such a significant route into homelessness, these elevated rates of living in relatively precarious tenancies have contributed to the disproportionate numbers of non-Irish nationals in homelessness services. Non-Irish nationals do not have an unqualified right to emergency and temporary accommodation; rather, depending on the situation, most are provided with such accommodation on an ad hoc night-by-night basis.

Furthermore, Irish Travellers have larger-than-average families, with nearly one third of Traveller women aged 40–49 in 2016 having six or more children compared to 1.3 in the general population. There is considerable evidence of prejudice against Travellers as an ethnic group, which extends to landlords being reluctant to offer them tenancies, but large family size may increase the difficulties that they face in accessing rented property, accentuate the risk of entering homelessness and reduce the ability to exit, particularly to private rented dwellings.

Furthermore, the number of lone-parent households in temporary and emergency accommodation increased from just under 250 households in mid-2014 to nearly 1,000 by the end of 2018. As noted earlier, the general observation that, on average, the impact of austerity was proportionate for all households may not hold true for specific groups. As Doorley et al (2018: 37) explain:

> Lone parents, however, present a particular case. Most lone parents are women, and lone parents lost proportionally more than singles without children during the austerity period. This higher loss can be attributed to reductions to Child Benefit during the austerity period. Additionally, when singles without children were making budgetary gains during the recovery period, lone parents continued to see a fall in their disposable income due to policy reforms, mainly due to changes to other welfare payments such as the One Parent Family Payment.

The level of social welfare payments available to young people was significantly cut in a number of stages over the period from 2010, with 18- and 19-year-old claimants receiving half the full adult welfare payment from 2014 onwards. As in Denmark, the policy rationale was to incentivise employment, but expenditure savings during a period of substantial government retrenchment were also a factor. In recognition of the disproportionate effect that these measures would have on those without family networks to fall back on, these welfare cuts did not apply to young adults with a history of being in state care. While homeless services report cases of young people experiencing homelessness as a result of these cuts, and youth homelessness rose substantially over the period, it is notable that youth homelessness did not rise faster than any other age cohort. Thus, these particular youth-focused welfare cuts cannot be directly linked to an increased rate of homelessness.

Political and administrative decision-making structures

Denmark

To understand the driving forces behind the development of homelessness policies and programmes in Denmark, it is important to understand the widely decentralised political system in which there is a high degree of autonomy for municipalities to organise and provide welfare services. Thus, the development of the Danish homelessness strategy and its implementation at the local level were shaped by the interplay of central government agencies responsible for homelessness policies and the municipalities that participated in the strategy and succeeding programmes. The development of the Danish programmes cannot be attributed to single individuals, but is rather the result of committed work by civil servants at both the central and local levels, as well as a widespread consensus across the political spectrum.

However, the government decision to conduct the first national homelessness count in 2007 was widely attributable to the advocacy of the prominent psychiatrist Preben Brandt, at that time chairman of the Danish Council for Socially Marginalised People, and chairman of Project Outside (*Projekt Udenfor*), a non-governmental organisation (NGO) providing street outreach work for the most marginalised rough sleepers in Copenhagen. Preben Brandt used his long-standing influence to argue that Denmark should conduct a nationwide homelessness count similar to those that had been conducted in both Sweden and Norway. In 2006, the Minister of Social Affairs, at that time Eva Kjer Hansen from the centre-right Liberal Party (Venstre), agreed to conduct the first homelessness count, which took place in February 2007. When the results of the first count were published in August 2007, this also marked the launch of the homelessness strategy that was to be developed and implemented over the following years. At the onset, there was already a focus on 'giving homeless people a home', which marked the key focus on housing and support that was integral to the programme. The homelessness strategy was accompanied by a substantial amount of funding as DKK500 million (approximately €65 million) was set aside for the programme from a general central government programme ('*Satspuljen*') aimed at initiatives towards vulnerable people and backed by a broad spectrum of parties in Parliament.

Administratively, the programme and its implementation were the responsibility of the Ministry for Social Affairs and its policy implementation agency, the National Board of Social Services, which has a key role in developing evidence-based policies and supporting their implementation at the local level in municipal welfare services. The strong focus of this agency on using evidence-based methods was probably a key reason why Denmark opted for a Housing First-oriented policy given the emerging evidence from North America for this approach, evidence that was also being shared by the European

Federation of National Organisations Working with the Homeless at European conferences. As previously mentioned, this led to the strong focus on rehousing and support that were the key elements of the programme.

Moreover, to understand the implementation process of such programmes, the interplay between central and local government agencies is crucial. While the central government sets the key focus and principles (for example, the premise of using the Housing First approach), the participating services are anchored in municipalities that, besides the overall regulations, have widespread autonomy in the organisation and provision of services. The implementation of the new services is thus carried out through cooperation between central and local government agencies. In the case of the homelessness strategy and succeeding programmes, this took place in the form of meetings, seminars, workshops and training, as well as through continuous monitoring and evaluation.

As we have already shown, despite this comprehensive focus on the implementation of evidence-based policies and methods, the Danish homelessness strategy and succeeding programmes did not achieve an overall reduction in homelessness in Denmark. Over the period of the strategy, there was a moderate increase in overall homelessness and a marked increase in youth homelessness. Although relatively ambitious in both scale and focus, the intervention-oriented programme did not manage to address the more general structural forces that were likely to be the primary drivers of this rising trend in homelessness, namely, a growing shortage of affordable housing in most larger Danish cities and towns and welfare reforms putting a further squeeze on the ability of vulnerable people and, especially, marginalised youth to find housing that they could afford.

Finland

The Finnish successes in preventing and reducing homelessness are, in large part, a story of a highly orchestrated political strategy. Two individuals, Juha Kaakinen (Y Foundation) and Pieter Fredrickson (*Ympäristöministeriö* [Ministry of the Environment]), led the development of the Finnish strategy. Drawing on fieldwork conducted for the 2014 review of the Finnish homelessness strategy (Pleace, 2014), it is possible to outline the ways in which political support was built up to end homelessness. The starting point was the definition of a clear, very simple goal to halve long-term homelessness by 2011 under *Paavo I* (2008–11), although it is important to understand the context in which this objective was set. Finland had been bringing down homelessness for years, to the point where it was – while still a concern and a visible problem – at almost residual levels.

As noted earlier in the book, there were 17,110 lone homeless adults reported in the annual count in 1987. A programme of investment in homelessness services, in a context of relatively high levels of social housing (though levels of building had declined markedly since the 1970s (Ruonavaara, 2017) and still extensive welfare benefits (though there had been cuts here too), had seen that level drop to 7,530 in the 2007 count (data from the Housing Finance and Development Centre of Finland [ARA] and the Ministry of the Environment). Politically, what was important was that after falling steadily, the levels had plateaued at around the 7,500 mark in 2004 and then not fallen further, and when investigated, it was found that around 45 per cent of this population were 'long-term' homeless people.

From a policy perspective, this narrow goal – that progress in reducing homelessness had stalled because of long-term homelessness and that stopping that long-term homelessness would largely remove this social problem – meant that *Paavo I* could be expressed in a very straightforward way and assessed against a single, simple outcome measure. There was also a strong degree of confidence about what to do about long-term homelessness, which was to employ the Housing First models that had been home-grown in Finland within a broader strategy that was focused on using housing-led approaches and that effectively dropped 'housing-ready' approaches to service design (Y Foundation, 2017). Finnish approaches to long-term homelessness bore some resemblance to Tsemberis's Housing First approach that governments all over the economically developed world were looking at because it not only looked effective, but also appeared to be a way to reduce spending on homelessness (Pleace, 2011). However, the Finnish 'Housing First' responses were their own, and as has been noted elsewhere, Finland neither imported the Tsemberis model nor built an exclusively 'Housing First' strategy; instead, it integrated Finnish Housing First services into a comprehensive and coordinated strategy. Alongside having a clearly defined, simple goal, the strategy could also point to the international evidence that everyone else was starting to listen to and say, in effect, 'this is what we're going to do, and the international evidence is that similar services are working'.

Another factor was an apparently minor ruling by the ombudsperson with responsibility for constitutional law in Finland that had been taken in 2002 (Pleace, 2014). There is no absolute right to housing in Finland, but there is a right to a home, and in this 2002 ruling, the ombudsperson had concluded that accommodation was not a home if two or more unrelated people were being forced to live together. This created a context in which dormitory/communal homelessness services that had shared sleeping spaces were potentially illegal. It is important to stress that quite a lot of the homelessness services in Finland had a clear trajectory towards harm reduction, choice-based approaches and independent living in ordinary housing prior to this ruling, and that the direction of policy had been away from traditional emergency accommodation (Y Foundation, 2017). Nevertheless, from a political perspective, this helped in establishing a clear, easily measured goal and a direction of travel, reinforced by law, away from using emergency accommodation to warehouse rough sleepers and other homeless people, and towards providing sustainable exits from homelessness.

The simple goal for *Paavo I* was used as the building block for a snowball strategy that built up political support across a range of actors. Lobbying within the Ministry of the Environment, coupled with support from the Y Foundation, whose entire mission centred on reducing lone adult homelessness, got the key central government department and politicians onboard. The Ministry of Social Affairs, the Criminal Sanctions Agency, ARA and Finland's slot machine association (*Raha-automaattiyhdisty* [RAY]), which helps finance social housing, were all signed up. Alongside this, a standardised 'letter of intent' that committed elected local authorities (municipalities) to *Paavo I*, both in the sense of pursuing its objectives and financially, was devised and the ten major urban areas, including Helsinki, were asked to sign up. Partnerships were also secured with major homelessness service providers, including the Salvation Army, which committed to turning an existing emergency shelter into Housing First, meaning that *Paavo I* began life with all the key administrative and political players on board (Pleace et al, 2015).

Paavo I did not meet its goal of a 50 per cent reduction in long-term homelessness, but it had made enough of a dent in the social problem – a 28 per cent reduction between 2008 and 2011, with 1,519 housing units, more than the original target, being delivered – to mean that renewal was almost inevitable as it was clearly working, even if not as quickly as had been hoped. Upping the objectives in *Paavo II* – to eliminate long-term homelessness and to begin the process of putting an end to homelessness more generally – was ambitious but looked feasible and, from a political perspective, highly dynamic and effective. Government had made a serious difference to homelessness already and now it was going to end it. This momentum was kept going after *Paavo II* because long-term homelessness kept falling and total homelessness, unlike just about everywhere else in Europe (except Norway), had also been brought down, by 16 per cent between 2012 and 2016 (data from ARA).

Opposition existed, particularly to the development of larger-scale congregate Housing First services, including from residents' groups and some of the less compassionate elements of the Finnish media. At one point, Housing First was described as 'bottle first' (a reference to the lack of any requirement for abstinence before someone was given access to a settled home), but in the face of falling numbers of homeless people and the very careful management of community relationships, these attacks failed to have a lasting impact. Resources were used to minimise risks, including teams sweeping the area around the larger congregate Housing First services to ensure that there was nothing happening that would alarm or distress neighbouring households and businesses, although the people using Housing First were more likely to be characterised by vulnerability than anything else, including criminality (Pleace, 2014).

The final, vital component was money; there were serious resources behind *Paavo I* and *II*, which meant that elected municipalities, government departments and the homelessness sector were prepared to sign up, even where some of the financial commitment had to come from them. Total spending on housing was close to €382 million over the period 2008–15, with another €40 million funding for support services (data from the Y Foundation).

Finland ran research on the cost effectiveness of the *Paavo* programmes. This reported very strong results, with an average saving of €15,000 per person per year when someone was transitioned out of supported housing into a settled home, as well as cost offsets for ending homelessness for health and criminal justice systems. Typically, rehousing a homeless person was assessed as (effectively) paying for itself within seven years. In addition, the reduced levels of support needed and the return of some homeless people to the workforce produced potentially greater savings over time (data from the University of Tampere and the Y Foundation).

There were shared ideas but the Finnish strategy was not – and never intended to be – a low-fidelity implementation of a North American service model. The Finnish 'Housing First' philosophy was wider and distinct, and had systemic, indeed cultural and structural, goals to reorient responses to every aspect of homelessness at the societal level. *Paavo I* was designed, in part, to clear the way for *Paavo II*, which, in turn, cleared the way for the current strategy at the time of writing.

The goals were never restricted to using a version of Housing First to end long-term homelessness; the goal was to end homelessness altogether (Pleace et al, 2016; Y Foundation, 2017; Fredriksson, 2018, cited in Ranta, 2019).

Ireland

In the Irish case, the continuity of personnel evident in the Finnish case was not present over the period in question. Between 2008 and 2018, six ministers and five principal officers (civil servants) held national political and administrative responsibility for people experiencing homelessness. Prior to the appointment of the Labour Party's Alan Kelly in July 2014, ministerial responsibility for homelessness was at junior, rather than senior, ministerial level, and subsequent senior ministers to Kelly have taken responsibility for the homelessness portfolio. The ministers responsible straddled the social democratic–Christian democratic divide and all publicly resolved to end homelessness. Yet, the political focus on homelessness has not translated into a reduction, despite a massive increase in statutory funding of services for people experiencing homelessness.

As noted in Chapter 4, in 2008, expenditure on services for people experiencing homelessness by central and local government was €76.6 million, rising to over €191 million in 2018, a cumulative spend of just over €1 billion between 2008 and 2018. Nationally, expenditure on emergency accommodation consumed just over half of total expenditure in 2013, rising to nearly 81 per cent of all expenditure nationally, and 84 per cent in Dublin in 2018. As noted earlier, as designated emergency accommodation reached capacity, families and individuals were increasingly placed in hostels and 'bed and breakfast' (B&B) accommodation, otherwise known as private emergency accommodation. Nationally, the cost of placing families and individuals in such accommodation increased from €11 million in 2013 to just over €83 million in 2018, or nearly 40 per cent of total expenditure on homelessness services.

Between central/local government funding and fundraising by the primary providers of homeless services in Ireland, NGOs, close to €300 million was spent providing emergency and allied services to those experiencing homelessness in 2018. This does not include the expenditure on preventing families entering homelessness via enhanced Housing Assistance Payments or through having their tenancies protected via increases in their Rent Supplement payment, as discussed in Chapter 5.

The rapid rise in expenditure on homelessness services reflects the demand-led nature of homelessness, and the nature and structure of homelessness services largely reflects the mission of individual non-governmental agencies and the availability of beds in commercial hotels and B&Bs. No local or municipal authority in Ireland operates homelessness accommodation services directly. Historically, most local authorities made provision for homeless men in the casual wards of county homes (former workhouses), but they began to be phased out from the mid-1960s (Doherty, 1982). Dublin City Council was unique in that it provided hostel accommodation for homeless men and women, but these services were contracted out to an NGO in 2014.

Thus, the nature and type of homelessness service in Ireland is determined, in part, by the origins and ethos of various NGOs, and, more recently, by their funding arrangements with local authorities. Being dependent on a disparate range of providers, often with little in common with one another, and seeking to develop services via funding protocols limits the ability of policymakers to develop coherent strategies. It has also led to a relatively small number of agencies providing most services – for example, in Dublin in 2018, just over 45 per cent of expenditure went to a myriad of private accommodation providers whose primary business is not providing for the needs of those experiencing homelessness; nearly 40 per cent went to 29 NGOs, but nearly three quarters of that expenditure went to just five NGOs. Thus, in Dublin, the primary providers of services for those households experiencing homelessness in 2017 were hoteliers/B&B providers and five NGOs with diverse origins, each with their own particular ethos and model of service delivery. Planning a coherent response to those experiencing or at risk of homelessness in such a context poses considerable challenges to policymakers, irrespective of the political will of the minister. As has been noted earlier, a similar context of multiple players and the lack of central control also applies in the area of the building of social housing.

At one level, the massive increase in expenditure on temporary and emergency accommodation is puzzling given that, as noted earlier, expenditure on the provision of Housing First was modest, and yet outcomes from Housing First are vastly superior to outcomes from placements in emergency congregate facilities. The doubling in the number of beds in emergency congregate accommodation nationally, and nearly tripling in Dublin, is partly explained by a political imperative to claim that a shelter bed is available to any person experiencing homelessness and therefore anybody sleeping rough is doing so 'voluntarily' rather than out of necessity. This followed the political fallout when a man who was sleeping rough died in the vicinity of the Irish Parliament in early December 2014. The Minister for Housing at that time, Alan Kelly, quickly organised a forum of all key stakeholders to address the issue and issued the following statement: 'Our ambition is that there will be no need for anyone to have to sleep rough in Dublin this Christmas unless they make that choice themselves, for whatever reason'. This statement has been reiterated, in essence, by each successive minister. Thus, if a rough sleeper was to die, particularly around Christmas time, the provision of ineffective emergency congregate accommodation serves to avoid any blame on the part of ministers as the claim can be made that a bed was available to him/her but they choose not to avail of it.

Furthermore, initially, the 2008 strategy was broadly the product of a consensus between the government and NGO service providers that homelessness could be ended, albeit that, as noted in Chapter 3, not all NGO providers felt adequately consulted on the strategy. The National Homelessness Consultative Committee (NHCC), which was established in April 2007, chaired by the Assistant Secretary for Housing in the Department of Housing, with membership comprised of central and local government representatives and NGO providers, was an important forum for the discussion and sharing of information on homelessness. This committee was merged with a pre-existing committee, the Cross Departmental Team, comprising only public servants in 2009. Between 2007 and 2013, the NHCC met on 19 occasions but was particularly active between 2007 and 2010 and again between 2013 and 2014, coinciding with the publication of the homelessness strategy and *Homelessness Policy Statement* (Department of the Environment, Community and Local Government, 2013), respectively.

However, since the relentless increase in the numbers experiencing homelessness, the NHCC has rarely been convened: only once in 2016, once in March 2017 and not at all 2018. Thus, what can be argued to have been a crucial forum for deliberative discussion, consensus building, the resolution of disagreements and the sharing of information and knowledge between service providers across the country, and with local and central government, was effectively disregarded as the number of households entering emergency and temporary accommodation was remorselessly increasing. On the other hand, the Regional Homelessness Consultative Forums, established under section 38 of the Housing (Miscellaneous Provisions) Act 2009, meet on a regular basis, providing a forum for the sharing of information.

Two additional institutional structures were put in place to guide policy on homelessness. The first was a Homelessness Oversight Group, established in conjunction with the *Homelessness Policy Statement* in 2013, but as noted in chapter 3, it was effectively made redundant by a change in the minister with responsibility for homelessness within a year of its establishment. The second was the Homelessness Inter-Agency Group, established in September 2017 following a housing summit chaired by the minister. The aim of the group is to 'to deliver homeless services in a coherent and joined-up way between the relevant departments and agencies', but it is comprised of only statutory bodies, with none of the NGOs that are delivering the majority of services as members. It published its first report in June 2018, which consisted of a general commentary on the extent and nature of homelessness in Ireland, with 36 recommendations, including one that the Department of Housing, Planning and Local Government should convene meetings of the NHCC on a biannual basis. However, no timeline for the implementation of the recommendations was published, and at the end of 2018, none of the recommendations had been implemented.

Thus, over the period in question, policymaking moved at a national level from a relatively inclusive process via the NHCC to a more closed process, where the service providers were increasingly consulted at the local, but not at the national, level. Of course, in the absence of housing, partnership and consensus building in itself will not end homelessness, but it can lead to a focus of energy on ending homelessness, as in the case of Finland, rather than increasingly on the interpretation of data on homelessness, levels of funding and the introduction of non-evidenced policy decisions, such as Family Hubs.

Conclusion

Comprehensive and generous welfare systems that encompass housing, health and other social services, as well as income supports, provide important buffers that lessen the likelihood that people will experience homelessness. The evidence from Denmark is that those who do experience homelessness despite such developed welfare systems tend to have a higher rate of psychosocial difficulties compared to the general population, and this is also likely to be the case in Finland. It was traditionally the case in Ireland, but has become less so in recent years. The high rates of poverty-related homelessness that are evident in liberal welfare regimes are largely prevented by these generous and comprehensive welfare systems, and those that do experience homelessness are small in number and largely single, and have various disabilities and often substance addiction problems.

In the case of Finland, its generous and comprehensive welfare system, when linked to a dedicated stream of housing for those who did experience homelessness, ensured that the experience of homelessness was relatively short-lived. This allowed them to close the bulk of their emergency congregate accommodation, which, in addition to being prohibitively expensive, had poor outcomes in terms of ending homelessness. Having a clear philosophy on how to end homelessness, supported by key individuals in the public service and an administrative structure to deliver a dedicated supply of housing, was central to the Finnish experience.

In the case of Denmark, the welfare system also protects the majority of citizens from the likelihood of entering homelessness. However, certain citizens, particularly those under 25, did experience benefit cuts and this may, in part, explain the increase in young people experiencing homelessness over the period in question. Despite their success in broadly stabilising the numbers experiencing homelessness, exiting homelessness to the comparatively large public housing sector remains a competitive process, with a range of other citizens experiencing social exclusion also seeking such housing.

In the Irish case, over the period in question, while income support services were broadly maintained, the service side of welfare, particularly health and housing, saw very substantial cuts. In respect of housing, there was an intensification of a longer-term trend to shift the provision of social housing to the private rented sector, with rent supplements, rather than the provision of direct-build social housing units for letting by local authorities or approved housing bodies. For those experiencing homelessness, the primary mechanism of exit is increasingly via the private rented sector (with an enhanced Rent Supplement), although their entry into homelessness in the first place arose from the termination of a tenancy or unsustainable rent increases in that sector. In the absence of a dedicated supply of housing as is the case in Finland, or a large public housing sector as is the case in Denmark, Irish authorities are dependent on the private market to address homelessness, a market that is not primarily concerned with addressing social exclusion, except at a considerable price. In the absence of a supply of secure tenancies, the numbers experiencing homelessness have grown dramatically, and a substantial infrastructure of hugely expensive congregate accommodation has been put in place to prevent their literal homelessness.

7

Conclusion

Introduction

At the outset of this book, we described a context in the early years of this century in which a 'fundamental shift in expectations' was generating a degree of optimism that homelessness could be ended in many countries. In the three countries under consideration, there was a high level of evidence-based optimism. Recent innovations in practice, combined with international research evidence, suggested that housing-led models, approaches that provided housing and support as the first step for people experiencing homelessness, would prove more successful than traditional approaches that largely focused on 'treatment' first. There was also the realisation that the number of those experiencing homelessness with high and complex needs was much smaller than had been previously understood. This, coupled with the emergence of effective Housing First, created an atmosphere, initially in the US and later in other jurisdictions, that homelessness was, in fact, solvable. If these practices could be delivered at the necessary scale, it would be possible to effectively reduce homelessness to 'functional zero' – in which homelessness would be rare, short-lived and non-recurrent. There was also a new political willingness in many advanced industrial economies not only to articulate ending homelessness as a realistic political commitment, but also to set out ambitious broad strategic frameworks. This political commitment and strategic framework established a context in which the scaling up of effective practice could occur, delivering real change.

This optimism and political commitment existed in a wide range of countries, and we have been able to look in detail at the experiences of three in this book. The three countries were selected for largely pragmatic reasons: they have published detailed data on the numbers experiencing homelessness that, to a large degree, are comparable. The similarity in population size and shared membership of the European Union (EU) provide a backdrop for useful comparison. On the other hand, historical differences in social, housing and welfare systems, as well as differences in political complexion over the period, provide useful areas for debate about the reasons behind the very different outcomes.

After documenting the policies, practices and outcomes over the intervening years in the three countries, we are forcibly reminded that homelessness is a complex issue not just at the personal level, but also within our economic and social systems. One of the three countries, Finland, made remarkable progress towards bringing homelessness to an end, and while there is still more to be done, it can reasonably be seen as achieving the aspirations set out at the start. At the other extreme stands Ireland, where overall homelessness has increased substantially and is still rising; furthermore, family homelessness, which was a marginal issue at the start of the strategy, has grown to levels that have been referred to as a 'national crisis' by the Ministers for Housing since 2016. Denmark falls somewhere in between, with significant progress being made in some areas but with this progress substantially undermined by increases in homelessness among young adults, over the decade under study.

While the outcomes are starkly different as assessed by 2018/2019 data, all three stories have positive lessons as well as warnings to offer. In each narrative, there is an extremely complex range of factors at play, feeding into progress or undermining it. Some factors that play a central role in some countries hardly deserve a mention in others. For instance, the private rented sector plays a pivotal role in the Irish story, raising complex questions of regulation, investment and public subsidy, but the entire private rented sector merits little mention in the stories of Denmark or Finland. Despite the comparable data and the other similarities, such differences in housing systems, welfare regimes and political choices are very difficult to disentangle when we come to draw useful conclusions. A few key themes emerge from the three studies that provide, if not clear-cut lessons, then at least food for thought for policymakers in countries continuing to struggle with increases in homelessness.

The global financial crisis

Perhaps the obvious explanation for things working out so much worse than planned is the scale of the global financial crisis (GFC), which hit just as the strategies were being signed off. While this crisis undoubtedly had major implications for the countries involved and impacted on the housing and homeless programmes deployed over the decade, it is not sufficient in itself to explain the differences in each country.

The crisis in Ireland attracted more international headlines, and Ireland was the only one of the three to require a 'bailout' from the European institutions and International Monetary Fund. During the three years from 2008 to 2010, Irish gross domestic product (GDP) contracted the most severely (–7.5 per cent),[1] and it is tempting to look no further than Ireland's financial crisis of the late 2000s to explain its homeless crisis in the mid-2010s. However, although they received less international attention, both the Finnish and Danish economies were also hit by global events, shrinking by 4.6 per cent and 3.5 per cent, respectively, over the same three years. More significantly, in subsequent years, the Irish economy has recovered and grown faster than either of the other two. In the three years 2012–14, where the data on homelessness start to diverge most strongly, Irish GDP grew by 10.3 per cent while the Danish economy grew by 2.5 per cent. Over the same period, the Finnish economy experienced a further three years of recession and contracted by –2.8 per cent. Overall, during the 11-year period from 2007 until 2017, the Irish economy averaged 4.1 per cent growth and the Danish economy 0.6 per cent, while the average yearly growth in Finland over those crucial years was zero.

Of course, there are other factors at play in understanding the impact of the GFC, including the health of the lending institutions, the fiscal position of the economies and the consequent requirement for government expenditure cuts. Ireland's 'bailout' resulted in a significant number of major decisions being made by (or at least negotiated with) the 'Troika' of the EU, International Monetary Fund and European Central Bank.[2] Nevertheless, it is clear that the choices and priorities set by the different countries – and, at least in the Irish case, by EU and international institutions – as they dealt with the economic crisis determined the impact on homelessness more than the fact of the crisis itself. For instance, as we have seen, in Ireland, as part of the crisis response, capital funding for social housing was cut by 88 per cent between 2008 and 2014. Meanwhile, although it had seen significant cuts to social housing in earlier years, Finland continued to build social housing, even enhancing the existing Y Foundation strategy to build more social housing units specifically for homeless people, and Denmark continued to build, albeit at lower levels than in earlier periods.

One crucial factor in understanding policy responses here is the time lag between the immediate impact of the economic crisis and the impact on the level of homelessness, which is particularly the case in Ireland. The delay is partly caused by the strengths of the social systems in each of the countries – most people who became unemployed due to the GFC were not immediately at risk of homelessness as a consequence because of the safety net provided by the welfare systems. In these developed welfare states, most people are not 'just three pay cheques' away from homelessness. Even in the limited number of cases where the GFC has longer-term social and economic consequences, it may take several years for these to result in an increased risk of relying on emergency homeless services.

In addition, and perhaps more significantly, because of the time involved in the planning, procurement and building processes, any decision to reduce housing investment does not impact on housing supply for several years. This lag creates challenges for policymakers in understanding and balancing the immediate and urgent needs emerging during the crisis (For example, in the Irish case, would the banking system survive?) with the medium-term effect of more people having to rely on emergency shelters or sleeping rough in several years' time.

At the most dramatic period of the crisis in Ireland, when the country entered the 'bailout' in 2011, the number of people experiencing homelessness (on our limited, comparable basis) was the lowest of the three countries. The problem or risk of homelessness was not mentioned in any of the reports related to the crisis at the time, and housing only featured in the international documents as a source of employment for construction workers.

The decision in Ireland to prioritise the immediate demands of the financial crisis by cutting investment in public housing can be understood in a number of ways: a decision forced on policymakers by the harsh financial realities; or a decision forced on Irish policymakers by international institutions; or a failure to consider, or understand, the longer-term consequences on the housing system. It is beyond the scope of this book to take a view on how this decision was arrived at, but it is this decision, rather than the GFC itself, that shaped the different pattern of social housing construction in the different countries.

Was the money made available?

A second ready explanation for the differences in outcome would be that while the strategy was good, there was a failure to provide the necessary resources to deliver it. Again, even in the less successful case of Ireland, there was very considerable expenditure of public and charitable funds. As in so many of the dimensions of this exploration, it is impossible to put a definitive comparable total cost on the programmes in each of the countries – the public announcements of different costs include and exclude different elements, and make different assumptions about 'existing' and 'new' spending, as well as the attribution of costs to different stages of the programmes. With this caveat, there is no evidence to support the hypothesis that, for instance, the different outcomes can be explained by any difference in willingness to fund what was promised in the strategic plans. All three countries invested heavily in their homeless services as part of the strategies. Indeed, expenditure on homelessness increased most rapidly in Ireland, the least successful case.

The crucial issue is, of course, what the money was spent on and whether the government kept strategic control of the expenditure or whether it was wrested from their control by short-term political and media demands. The issue is not about how much money the Finns spent on the homeless strategy, but that they decided to invest it in a different way. Finnish policy was a well-thought-through 'Housing First' strategy, which is better viewed as a long-term housing-led/housing-focused strategic programme, rather than 'Housing First' in the North American sense. Finland avoided fire-fighting homelessness through building more shelters and using more temporary accommodation, and there was also recognition that existing Staircase model services had limited effectiveness. Spending was redirected into more effective – and, in the long term, more cost-efficient – Housing First, housing-led and preventive services. Crucially, the Finns always saw that sufficient affordable housing supply had to be the core of any effective homelessness strategy. The Y Foundation developed social homes that were specifically to house homeless people at a sufficient scale and with sufficient speed to have a significant effect on overall levels of homelessness. Within a highly coordinated strategy, the Housing Finance and Development Centre of Finland (ARA) and the municipalities supported Y Foundation efforts by making more social housing stock available. In Ireland, recent increases in expenditure on homeless services appear to be more of a penalty for failure than an investment in success. The question of different levels of investment in housing – as opposed to homeless services and the homeless strategy – is a different matter and will be discussed more fully later.

If these factors do not explain the different outcomes, what does emerge?

The role (and meaning of) Housing First

A large part of the optimism at the start of the book comes from the growing evidence base that interventions that start with providing housing, simultaneously linked to appropriate levels of support, are more successful than those that try to alter behaviour and meet treatment needs prior to providing housing. Nothing that has emerged in the intervening period, even in the least successful of the three case studies, provides any reason to question that insight.

The most obvious difference between the approaches in the three countries is the question of scale. In Denmark, a commitment to Housing First featured strongly in their revised approach to homelessness. Given the level of policy commitment and apparent financial investment in this approach, it was a surprise when subsequent analysis showed that Housing First was only made available to a relatively small proportion (5 per cent) of the total homeless population, of whom many more could have benefited from it. Even though the Housing First programme was relatively large, it did not make up for the fact that, in total, many times more people were affected by homelessness over the years covered by the strategy. The Irish case is somewhat different, with a significantly slower adoption of Housing First in policy documents and a long run into seeing any significant structured funding for programmes. Ireland had to wait until late 2018 for a national implementation plan on Housing First, and until 2019 for any investment in Housing First outside the capital. Even then, as we have seen, the significantly increased rhetoric about Housing First is not matched with the ambition to provide it to everyone who could benefit from it in Dublin. By contrast, Finland's *Paavo I* strategy devoted significant resources specifically at the aspect of homelessness that previous strategy and policy had not addressed: those people with high and complex needs who were long-term homeless.

Linked to the question of scale is the challenge of ensuring that Housing First programmes efficiently target those who are most likely to benefit from them. The Finnish system appears to have been most effective at achieving this, reflecting what *Paavo I* was designed to do. One obvious reason around the first wave of projects was that they were sometimes physically converting the sites where long-term homeless people were being temporarily housed. The first phase of the Irish Housing First programme, while on a much smaller scale, was highly targeted at people with long histories of rough sleeping.

The Finnish use of intensive, housing-led services was not on a huge scale, but within their 'Housing First' (housing-led) strategy, Finnish Housing First was highly coordinated, fitting alongside the preventive, lower-intensity and other services in a multi-agency response to homelessness. *Paavo II* reinforced the response to long-term homelessness but also began to build up prevention; the interventions around long-term homelessness worked because they had a clear role within a highly integrated strategic response to all homelessness. Finland transformed the approach of the entire homeless system by ensuring that part of the housing system is directed towards addressing homelessness, and began to successfully reduce and prevent homelessness in a coordinated, holistic way. There is no doubt that Finnish Housing First is successful at achieving long-term secure tenancies for homeless people with complex needs. The question has been raised about whether it is, in fact, Housing First, as understood and evaluated elsewhere, particularly in North America. However, it has become apparent that the Finns have developed their own services, with some close operational similarities to the Tsemberis model, but neither derived from it, nor seeking to emulate it; Finnish 'Housing First' was home-grown and distinct, not imported (Y Foundation, 2017; Ranta, 2019). Much of the most heated debate on this issue has concerned the role and appropriateness of 'congregate housing' but, as we have seen, this form of housing was developed because it was the quickest and most cost-effective way to meet the targets set by *Paavo I* and is only a small part of the overall Finnish housing provision for people moving out of homelessness. These larger congregate Finnish Housing First services always existed alongside a larger provision of fixed-site supported housing and scattered site supported housing using mobile support.

The greater question raised by Finland's relative success (and the relative failure of the others) is whether when we talk of 'Housing First', we are referring to 'one programme among many' or to a transformation of the entire system of responding to those experiencing homelessness, as well as its relationship to the provision of housing. The experience of these three countries strongly supports the idea that when we say that 'Housing First' is the key element of Finland's relative success, we are referring to a *broad 'Housing First' philosophy* rather than a *particular programme* that can be bolted onto an existing housing and homelessness system. At the heart of that philosophy is the view that housing is a human right and people experiencing homelessness should have their agency and preferences respected, and that the response to homelessness should *start* with a house. These values are, of course, at the heart of the Housing First programme as first defined by Sam Tsemberis too. However, within the Finnish version of 'Housing First', actual Housing First services have a necessary but clearly defined role – they are there to support long-term homeless people with complex needs – the other aspects of homelessness and prevention are handled by other services.

The idea that Finns were showing low 'fidelity' to Housing First is problematic because they meant something different from the North

American model. Finnish strategy was not about one programme model for one aspect of homelessness – as Housing First in the North American sense is designed for one thing and one thing alone, homeless people with high and complex needs – it was a holistic, housing-led strategy that was aimed at all levels of homelessness. From a Finnish perspective, everything was 'Housing First', whether it was housing-led low-intensity mobile support, services that were close to the North American Housing First or the array of preventive services expanded from *Paavo II* onwards; the strategy was also 'Housing First' because it focused considerable resources on building more affordable homes. Terminology and jargon can blur a picture, particularly across different languages, but where North American Housing First meant a type of homelessness service, Finnish Housing First meant a housing-led/housing-focused philosophy expressed in a succession of comprehensive, integrated strategies.

More generally, in the North American sense, Housing First cannot function as an effective homelessness strategy in and of itself. Within an integrated strategy, it can play an important role in reducing long-term and recurrent homelessness among people with high and complex needs, but when needs are neither high nor complex, it has no role. Housing First is not an effective response to most family homelessness as many families just need secure, affordable, adequate homes, nor is it an effective response when a lone adult with low support needs is at risk of or experiencing homelessness because it is designed for a high-need population. In Denmark and Finland, evidence suggests that because homelessness being triggered for purely or largely economic reasons is unusual, largely due to relatively extensive welfare systems, Housing First (in the North American sense) has a potentially much greater role in relation to total homelessness because people who are homeless are much more likely to have high support needs. The Finnish 2008 estimate of 45 per cent of the homeless population being long-term homeless is in stark contrast to the 10–15 per cent estimate for the US homeless population (Tainio and Fredriksson, 2009; Culhane, 2018).

In Denmark, a comprehensive effort was made by central government agencies to facilitate the implementation of Housing First in local, municipal welfare systems, and like in Finland, the Danish approach goes beyond the small-scale local Housing First projects found in most other European countries. Yet, the lack of a systematic approach to increasing the general availability of affordable housing remained a barrier throughout the Danish strategy and succeeding programmes. Although implementation efforts aimed at making municipalities use existing housing allocation mechanisms more systematically towards homeless people, the strategy did not include any measures to increase the general supply of affordable housing, and, as such, the strategy was detached from overall housing policies. The absence of a clear focus on housing supply and targeted housing provision in the Danish case is a major difference compared to the lessons from Finland but clearly resonates with Irish experience flowing from the decision to radically cut investment in new social housing supply.

In Ireland, Housing First was adopted (on different timescales) as a number of localised programmes; these programmes are successful in themselves, as expected on previous evidence, and there are individual beneficiaries, but there is no systemic change. The lesson may be that only the resources and political will of the state can operate on a sufficient scale and with sufficient force to develop and deliver an effective, integrated homelessness strategy. This is not to say that the non-governmental organisation (NGO) sector should not be involved and receive resources to do so – cooperation and collaboration from the homelessness sector was integral to strategic success – but the Finnish strategy was driven at the national level and had very clear, very simple targets, and success was very much around political acumen, building consensus, being able to promise to deliver against realistic targets and each stage of the strategy being able to present enough success to attract more funding.

Welfare policy

There has been considerable research exploring the links between particular forms of welfare regime and the extent and nature of homelessness (Benjaminsen and Andrade, 2015; Stephens and Fitzpatrick, 2007). However, one question for this book is whether particular changes in welfare policy can explain the differences in the level of homelessness over the period. The potential link between the rise of youth homelessness in Denmark over the period and the lower rates of welfare payment for young people was discussed in Chapter 6. Although the reduced welfare payment for young people widely preceded the strategy period and was only reinforced over the following years, the lower income for young welfare-dependent adults will inevitably have resulted in more vulnerable young people (particularly those without recourse to support from wider family) being vulnerable to homelessness, especially since the shortage of affordable housing in larger cities grew worse. The absence of mitigating measures within the 2008 strategy to recognise this developing problem most certainly contributed to the failure to prevent rises in youth homelessness.

While there were changes in the Finnish welfare model over the period, with a shift towards a greater level of conditionality (Kananen, 2012), these were by no means as far-reaching as those in the US or UK and they do not appear to have featured as either a contributory factor or a barrier to the relative success of the homelessness strategy. Given the scale of cutbacks in government spending in Ireland during the 2010–14 period, welfare cuts would perhaps be expected to feature as one of the underlying causes of the Irish homelessness problem. However, as has been noted, while the 'austerity' policies of the Irish governments during this period were extensive, the Irish welfare system was relatively unscathed, except in the case of lone parents. Limitations on the level of private rent that could be subsidised through the housing benefit system played a role in increased homelessness, particularly in the early stages of the crisis, but these policies were dictated by concerns about the impact of subsidies on overall rent levels rather than by austerity, albeit that the consequences may be the same. Furthermore, as noted previously, while the base rate for housing benefit has not increased since 2016, the majority of households in urban areas are in receipt of discretionary payments of up to 50 per cent of the base rate, and households at risk of homelessness or exiting emergency accommodation are entitled to this discretionary payment.

Given the link between poverty and homelessness (Bramley and Fitzpatrick, 2018), there is little doubt that the nature and extent of the different welfare regimes in each of the countries influence the nature and extent of homelessness, but there is little evidence that changes in welfare policy over the period, even under the pressure of the GFC and austerity policies, can explain the different outcomes across the three countries. Relatively speaking, they all had and retained highly developed and extensive welfare systems, despite the cuts.

If there is no overarching impact of welfare on the outcomes of the homeless strategies, there are certainly examples of welfare changes that would have had potential impacts on specific groups where the existence of a homeless strategy helped in the implementation of mitigating policies. For example, in Ireland, young adults leaving care were specifically excluded from the reduction in welfare rates for other young people in a systematic recognition of their vulnerability in the housing market.

The importance of a stable policy context

One of the most intangible factors that is frequently deployed to explain the delivery of – or failure to deliver – effective responses to homelessness is the presence or absence of 'political will'. At the most simplistic level, this is understood to mean the commitment of the individual government minister to drive through the reforms and actions that are needed to deliver change. While all three countries had the same number of governments during the period, it is striking that the most successful country has been characterised by the continuous engagement of a small number of influential public service and voluntary sector actors, with a shared understanding of housing and homelessness, over a long number of years – preceding the period covered in this study. On the other hand, the least successful country has had six government ministers and similar number of senior civil servants in each of the key roles involved in deciding and delivering policy. Denmark, whose outcomes fell between the two extremes, had a similar level of change of social ministers and governments, but the change in both ministers and governments did not appear to have a major impact on the direction of homelessness policies as the political support for a Housing First-oriented approach remained high throughout the period. Yet, the lack of connection between homelessness policies and more general housing policies also remained unchanged over changing governments and ministers.

Despite this rather crude backdrop, it is impossible to be certain of the links between such political/administrative stability and success. The Finnish success can be ascribed to effective control being handed to senior public servants who were skilled enough to deliver and so keep ministers believing in the agreed approach and providing the funding. 'Political will' for the purposes of understanding Finland was the will and focus of senior public servants who secured and sustained political cooperation that was one remove from implementation. Would Finland's story be different if, for instance, Peter Frederickson had retired a decade earlier or Juha Kaakinen had not been running the Y Foundation? Or, would the system have brought forward someone else who understood the plan and implemented it?

Furthermore, of course, such stability would be marked down as one of the causes of failure if the people in place had the wrong plan or lacked the motivation to deliver it. No amount of political will can make a badly conceived or limited idea work. Something that was perhaps also important was that the Finnish programme was not spending enough to attract much government attention, largely achieved its objectives and was unproblematic. A public programme characterised by unproductive expenditure and noisy failures, or simply by relatively high expenditure, is less likely to enjoy a long and peaceful life.

It is important to note that the turnover in politicians and public servants involved in the programme in Ireland was only marginally caused by the wider economic crisis, and while not unique to the housing/homeless domain, was more extreme there than in other areas. For instance, there were only two Ministers for Finance over the two governments from 2011, while there were five Ministers for Housing over the same period. It is difficult to disentangle the extent to which this short political lifespan was the cause or the effect of the gathering housing crisis.

Delivery of the Finnish strategy was not without its challenges. Some early problems with planning permission and local objections to congregate Housing First being developed resulted in negative publicity and the pejorative label of 'bottle first' in the popular press, which might have been enough to bring an end to the policy in some countries. This capacity to maintain strategic direction in the face of negative public opinion can be contrasted with the policy shift towards building emergency shelters in Ireland that followed the tragic death of a male rough sleeper in the vicinity of the Irish Parliament.

The case studies reinforce the view that success builds the foundations for further success, while failure creates the conditions for further failure. In the Finnish case, the progress achieved under the first strategy led on to greater ambition in the second, within what was a long-term plan to bring homelessness to an end. In Ireland, as we have seen, the rising number of people who were homeless led to significant public attention on the problem of rough sleeping, creating political pressure to build more and yet more emergency shelters.

This conclusion draws attention to a significant limitation in the current study. While the three countries found themselves in apparently similar circumstances with apparently similar objectives in 2008, their previous experience over the previous century and certainly since the Second World War constrained and determined many of the choices that they were able to make. As we have seen, the story of Finland's relative success pre-dates 2008 and, to some extent, the higher levels of homelessness in Finland in the late 1980s created a more robust platform for long-term change than the relatively low level found in Denmark, and markedly lower level in Ireland, at the time. The scale of the Finnish problem resulted in changes in policy thinking and practice that laid the foundations of the homeless strategies and the relative success that we are trying to account for now. This might suggest that an even more daunting 25-year-long policy span is needed to achieve the success that Finland is now seeing.

However, Finnish policy is not a continuous line stretching back over 30 years or more. The 1987 pledge to end homelessness was followed by a plunge into very serious recession (Kärkkäinen, 1996). While enough spending was still in place to keep homelessness low, the impetus for systemic change came from the realisation in the mid-2000s that levels had plateaued, that a large part of the reason for that was the presence of long-term homeless people and that by drawing on Finnish experience and ideas about an integrated 'Housing First' strategy, homelessness could be further reduced. Having a set of working instruments, a simply defined problem of long-term homelessness and the ability to intervene and be confident that results would be positive and not involve major spikes in expenditure all created the political space and the opportunities needed for *Paavo I*. *Paavo I* enabled *Paavo II*, paving the way for further intervention because a short, focused strategy had clearly already shown significant effectiveness and could be built upon. Arguably, the elements of image creation – here is a clearly defined problem that can be solved and is being solved – and being able to build positive narratives around the success of policy responses were almost as important to the success of *Paavo I* and subsequent strategies as getting more houses and apartments built (Pleace et al, 2016).

When embarking on the scale of transformation envisaged by all three countries, it would appear that there is a need to establish a deep and robust consensus at the start of the process so that it can survive the personnel changes and external economic/political shocks that will inevitably come along over the years needed to deliver transformative change. This is particularly important in relation to homelessness – not only because it involves such a wide range of potential policy elements (from mental health to building construction), but also because the 'new paradigm' for ending homelessness is complex and not yet fully worked out. It is certainly not yet the dominant paradigm, and in the absence of dedicated leadership, policy quickly reverts to the default setting of emergency shelters and responding to homelessness like it is 1920, not 2020.

One potential conclusion from this is the importance of moving away from a public discussion of homelessness that emphasises a 'crisis' that has complex causes and is difficult to solve, and promoting a wider public understanding of the 'new paradigm' which shows that there are workable, affordable and effective solutions to homelessness. This would make the next round of strategies and plans, as they emerge, less dependent upon the inevitable vagaries of public service appointments and the economic cycle.

The importance of housing policy

While there is more to homelessness than housing, homelessness cannot be resolved in the absence of housing, and the housing histories of the three countries over the period closely follow the overall narrative. While all three countries saw a slowdown in housing construction during the period, housing construction continued in both Finland and Denmark, while it had come to an almost complete stop in Ireland by 2014. Both Finland and Denmark used the construction or renovation of public housing stock as a countercyclical measure, while taking advantage of reduced construction costs. In addition, the 'slot machine' funding to the Y Foundation in Finland gives it access to funding that, as it is not public expenditure, is relatively insulated from the economic cycle and the distributional conflict of political decision making. A combination of better forward planning and greater autonomy for local government and quasi-governmental actors in Finland (the municipalities and the Y-foundation) meant that foundations were being built (literally and figuratively) even in the year when the economy contracted by 8.3 per cent (in 2009).

In Ireland, maintaining social housing spending was seen as impossible due to the overwhelming scale of national indebtedness and the fiscal policies imposed by the Troika and later by the Fiscal Stability Treaty. However, as has been noted, there was little discussion of the need for such building or the long-term housing consequences of deconstructing the construction sector.

While overall housing supply is important, the key component is affordable and secure housing for lower-income households, in particular, access to social housing. All three countries report pressure on their social housing systems over the period, particularly in large urban areas and for young people.

However, the overall supply of social housing does not appear to be the most determining factor – Finland has only marginally more social housing (12 per cent of total housing, though, as noted earlier, this supply is not static) than Ireland (9 per cent), with Denmark having the highest proportion at around 20 per cent. The question of how an appropriate proportion of social housing is allocated to people who are homeless (or would otherwise become homeless) appears to be crucial.

In Ireland, ministerial efforts to ring-fence a certain proportion of social housing for homeless households were ultimately defeated by administrative and political resistance to what was essentially a question of perceived distributional unfairness. In Denmark, a similar prioritisation of public housing supply for rehousing homeless people by local municipalities was a factor that facilitated the implementation of Housing First programmes in cities such as Odense, which were successful in reducing homelessness. Yet, in both Denmark and Ireland, the lack of affordable housing presented a major barrier to the delivery of Housing First.

The Finnish solution is different: a distinct and autonomous stream of social housing, funded in a way that was secure and predictable, dedicated to people who are homeless being provided via the Y Foundation, alongside the support given to the strategy by other social landlords. This approach side-steps the distributional conflicts that arise when the same stream of social housing must be rationed between those who are homeless and those who have a low income. It also provides a solution to the widespread resistance of general social landlords, in both the statutory and not-for-profit sectors, giving tenancies to people moving out of homelessness. The risk that this approach will result in a lack of social mix (that is, formerly homeless people being concentrated into specific neighbourhoods or housing blocks) is overcome by the Y Foundation purchasing individual housing units. Where they build an apartment block themselves, there are also approximate rules for what proportion of the given block can be used for people moving out of homelessness. The Finns are also still developing some smaller-scale congregate supported housing schemes; some of the second wave of (insofar as the term applies) 'Housing First' was smaller-scale congregate schemes, a lot smaller, like 20 units instead of 90, as well as scattered housing to which mobile support can be delivered.

In both the Danish and Irish strategies, the delivery of the actual houses into which people will move is largely assumed, that is, the strategies are designed almost as if the necessary housing is already there or will soon be available, albeit that this is very clearly not the case. There are some attempts to take a different approach. In the Irish strategy of 2013, one component of the approach to end long-term homelessness was to bring back into use a large number of social housing units that had become void for various reasons and ring-fencing them for allocations to the long-term homeless. In the event, while many of the units were brought back into use, they were largely allocated to households on the general housing waiting list. The 2016 Irish strategy has homelessness and housing as 'pillars' within the same strategy, but the assumption is that the general greater availability of housing will naturally partly flow towards those experiencing homelessness. A few streams of housing ring-fenced for those experiencing homelessness either did not materialise or went to general allocations because of the political decisions discussed earlier.

In Denmark, with public housing accounting for 20 per cent of dwellings, policy is designed to address a wide range of social needs. Local authorities have the power to allocate up to 25 per cent of available public housing to vulnerable people in acute housing need. This allocation can be used when rehousing homeless people but can also be used to assist other groups in need of housing. Despite efforts to make municipalities use these allocation mechanisms more systematically towards homeless people, some cities and towns still decline to use this discretion, and priorities in other cities change over time, making access variable across the country. In Copenhagen, where available allocation mechanisms are already used extensively, the pressure on the available social housing stock is acute, mirroring the pressures in Dublin and, to a lesser extent, although the issue is still present, in Helsinki.

The distinctive features of the Finnish strategy are not just that it started with clearer objectives, but that the Y Foundation also held the resources needed to deliver those objectives, and drafted in support from ARA and the municipalities, accessing social housing on top of what they were building (and getting ARA and municipalities to develop). It also helped that (relatively speaking) they did not need huge amounts of housing; the Finns knew that 1,000 units would make a very serious dent in overall homelessness in the Finnish context. In both Denmark and Ireland, no matter how effective the homeless services might be in delivering services to support people out of homelessness, they ultimately found themselves in competition for any available housing. For those allocating the housing (local governments), providing homes for the homeless was, at best, only one of a number of competing priorities – with very compelling reasons why the competing groups (lone parents, people with disabilities and the vulnerable elderly) should get precedence. In Ireland, a few homeless NGOs are also approved housing bodies and build or buy housing, but their housing stock is relatively small and allocations to it remain under the control of the local authority.

Summary

It is important to acknowledge that the form of homelessness that the Finnish homeless strategy was designed to tackle happens to be the form of homelessness that it was possible to compare in this study. As we noted in Chapter 1, Denmark, Finland and Ireland were selected for comparison not only because of similarities in size, location and adoption of homeless strategies, but also because they publish homelessness data that are, within some limitations, comparable. These comparable data primarily relate the number of people being provided with emergency accommodation in homeless shelters of some type. The result of this pragmatic approach is that our analysis concentrates on outcomes in relation to this fairly extreme form of homelessness.

It is worth emphasising again that this focus does not reflect a view that this form of homelessness is more important or a better guide to public policy than wider definitions of homelessness, such as the numbers of people sofa surfing or living in unsuitable conditions. Both Finland and Denmark publish data on other forms of homelessness as defined under the European Typology of Homelessness and Housing Exclusion (ETHOS) definition, such as sofa surfers, people about to be released from prison with no home to go to and so on. However, since definitions of these situations differ and Ireland does not collect comparable data, it has not been possible to provide comparisons on these closely related issues.

Beyond this, it is arguable that the effectiveness on the bulk of what Finland defines as homelessness, that is, people living with friends and family, has been much lower than on long-term homelessness. Most homeless Finns are experiencing what Finland regards as a form of homelessness but that would not be recorded as homelessness in many other countries, they are 'doubled up' to use North American terminology, or overcrowded because there is more than one household in housing designed for one household. In 2008, 4,795 Finns were reported as experiencing this form of homelessness, by 2017, the figure was 5,528 and had averaged around 5,300 across the counts conducted between 2008 and 2017 (the median was 5,435). Recalculations and methodological changes in the 2018 count in relation to Helsinki suggested that this had been a partial miscount and overestimate, with levels of 3,167, but as the basis for this number was different, it could not be directly compared with the results of earlier years (ARA, 2019). From this perspective, the bulk of Finnish homelessness – defined by the Finns as people living with friends and family – remained at very similar levels throughout *Paavo I* and *II* and was still at similar levels as the third phase of the strategy came to an end. On this measure, the Finns regard themselves as having a lot more work to do before homelessness is really ended (Pleace et al, 2015, 2016).

Denmark and Ireland share these problems – as does most of the more economically developed world. Equally, as social housing remains a limited resource in all countries, a decision to dedicate a stream of housing specifically to marginalised homeless people means that some other non-homeless groups are less well catered for than would otherwise be the case, unless there is some sort of return to the mass building programmes of the last century. This fact, however, is ultimately a statement of what is means to have a strategy in the first place. To prepare and publish a national strategy must be understood as a decision to give greater importance to the objectives within the strategy than to other issues that may exist or come into existence during its lifetime. The Finnish strategy had the autonomy to retain its original focus, which now gives Finland the rare opportunity to move on to wider and more ambitious objectives taking account of less severe forms of homelessness.

One of the challenges presented by homelessness is that it is simultaneously extremely complex and very simple. It is simple to solve because all it needs is access to affordable housing and a recognition that people who are homeless are fellow human beings who need to be given the choices, dignity and support that they need. It is complex because these do not turn out to be easy things for us to do.

In its simple manifestation, homelessness is a serial victim of big and simplistic solutions. There is some danger that if not properly understood, Housing First may become just the latest of these total solutions. Housing First as a programme has much to offer in solving homelessness for people who have complex mental health and addiction issues. If this were the only form of homelessness that existed, it might be the only programme that was necessary, but in most places, homelessness comes in a wider range of forms, so that other responses and programmes are likely to have a role. Housing First as a system (or philosophy), as developed in Finland, provides us with a wider context to understand the range of responses that are needed. Both approaches share an understanding that all effective responses to homelessness must start with the offer of an affordable home, but the Finnish approach addresses the fundamental question raised by the Housing First programme: where are the homes to come from? The Finnish model itself has many challenges still to address and there is much in the Finnish approach that is not readily transferable to other political and social contexts. Perhaps the biggest challenge is the realisation that the success of the Finnish approach cannot be replicated by even the most determined NGO, but requires the dedication and commitment of the state, both central and local. For state policymakers, perhaps the greatest challenge is presented by the need to set the goals, dedicate the resources, ensure organisational capacity and then allow sufficient autonomy to carry out the job.

Notes

1. See Eurostat, available at: https://ec.europa.eu/eurostat/statistics-explained/images/5/53/Real_GDP_growth%2C_2007-2017_%28%25_change_compared_with_the_previous_year%3B_%25_per_annum%29_FP18.png (accessed 12 March 2019).
2. See the 2011 'Economic adjustment programme for Ireland', available at: http://ec.europa.eu/economy_finance/publications/occasional_paper/2011/pdf/ocp76_en.pdf

References

ARA (Housing Finance and Development Centre of Finland) (2017) *Homelessness in Finland 2016*, Helsinki: ARA.

ARA (2019) *Homelessness 2018*, Helsinki: ARA.

Aubry, T., Farrell, S., Hwang, S.W. and Calhoun, M. (2013) 'Identifying the patterns of emergency shelter stays of single individuals in Canadian cities of different sizes', *Housing Studies*, 28(6): 910–27.

Aubry, T., Cherner, R., Ecker, J., Jetté, J., Rae, J., Yamin, S., Sylvestre, J., Bourque, J. and McWilliams, N. (2015) 'Perceptions of private market landlords who rent to tenants of a Housing First program', *American Journal of Community Psychology*, 55(3/4): 292–303.

Aubry, T., Bernard, R. and Greenwood, R. (2018) 'A multi-country study of the fidelity of Housing First programmes: Introduction to a special edition of the *European Journal of Homelessness*', *European Journal of Homelessness*, 13(3): 11–27.

Australian Bureau of Statistics (2018) *Census of Population and Housing: Estimating Homelessness, 2016*, Canberra: Australian Bureau of Statistics.

Avramov, D. (1995) *Homelessness in the European Union: Social and Legal Context of Housing Exclusion in the 1990s*, Brussels: FEANTSA.

Bahr, H.M. (1973) *Skid Row: An Introduction to Disaffiliation*, NY: Oxford University Press.

Baker, T. and Evans, J. (2016) '"Housing First" and the changing terrains of homeless governance', *Geography Compass*, 10(1): 25–41.

Baptista, I., Benjaminsen, L., Busch-Geertsema, V. and Pleace, N. (2017) *Family Homelessness in Europe*, Brussels: FEANTSA.

Benjaminsen, L. (2013) 'Policy review up-date: Results from the Housing First based Danish homelessness strategy', *European Journal of Homelessness*, 7(2): 109–31.

Benjaminsen, L. (2016) 'Homelessness in a Scandinavian welfare state: The risk of shelter use in the Danish adult population', *Urban Studies*, 53(10): 2041–63.

Benjaminsen, L. (2017) *Hjemløshed i Danmark 2017. National kortlægning* [*Homelessness in Denmark 2017. National Census*], Copenhagen: SFI (Danish National Centre for Social Research).

Benjaminsen, L. (2018) 'Housing First in Denmark: An analysis of the coverage rate among homeless people and types of shelter users, *Social Inclusion*, 6(3): 327–36

Benjaminsen, L. (2019) *Hjemløshed i Danmark 2019. National kortlægning* [*Homelessness in Denmark 2019. National Census*], Copenhagen: VIVE (The Danish Center for Social Science Research).

Benjaminsen, L. and Christensen, I. (2007) *Hjemløshed i Danmark, 2007. National kortlægning.* [*Homelessness in Denmark, 2007. National Census*], København: SFI – Det Nationale Forskningscenter for Velfærd.

Benjaminsen, L. and Dyb, E. (2008) 'The effectiveness of homeless policies: Variations among the Scandinavian countries', *European Journal of Homelessness*, 2(1): 45-67.

Benjaminsen, L. and Andrade, S.B. (2015) 'Testing a typology of homelessness across welfare regimes: Shelter use in Denmark and the USA', *Housing Studies*, 30(6): 858–76.

Benjaminsen, L. and Knutagård, M. (2016) 'Homelessness research and policy development: Examples from the Nordic countries', *European Journal of Homelessness*, 10(3): 45–66.

Benjaminsen, L., and Enemark, M. H. (2017) *Veje ind og ud af hjemløshed. En undersøgelse af hjemløshedens forløb og dynamik* [*Pathways in and out of homelessness. A study of the sequences and dynamics of homelessness*], Copenhagen: VIVE.

Benjaminsen L., Dyrby, T.M., Enemark, M.H., Thomsen, M.T., Dalum H.Sl. and Vinther, U.L. (2017) *Housing First i Danmark. Evaluering af Implementerings- og forankringsprojektet i 24 kommuner.* [*Housing First in Denmark. Evaluation of the Implementation Project in 24 municipalities*], København: SFI – Det Nationale Forskningscenter for Velfærd & Rambøll.

Bittner, E. (1967) 'The police on skid-row: A study of peace keeping', *American Sociological Review*, 32(5): 699–715.

Borner Stax, T. (1999) 'Denmark', in C.O. Helvie and W. Kunstmann (eds) *Homelessness in the United States, Europe and Russia*, Westport, CT; London: Bergin and Garvey, pp 87–114.

Bramley, G. and Fitzpatrick, S. (2018) 'Homelessness in the UK: Who is most at risk?', *Housing Studies*, 33(1): 96–116.

Bretherton, J. (2017) 'Reconsidering gender in homelessness', *European Journal of Homelessness*, 11(1): 1–21.

Bretherton, J. and Pleace, N. (2015) *Housing First in England: An Evaluation of Nine Services*, York: University of York.

Brownlee, A. (2008) 'Paradise lost or found? The changing homeless policy landscape in Ireland', in D. Downey (ed) *Perspectives on Irish Homelessness: Past, Present and Future*, Dublin: Homeless Agency, pp 34–43.

Burt, M.R. (2001) 'Homeless families, singles and others: Findings from the 1996 national survey of homeless assistance providers and clients', *Housing Policy Debate*, 12(4): 737–80.

Busch-Geertsema, V. (2001) 'Homelessness in Germany: Housing poverty in a wealthy country', in V. Polakow and C. Guillean (eds) *International Perspectives on Homelessness*, Westport, CT: Greenwood Press, pp 85–117.

Busch-Geertsema, V. (2010) *Finland 2010. The Finnish National Programme to Reduce Long-Term Homelessness*, Synthesis Report for European Peer Review, Vienna: OESB.

Busch-Geertsema, V. (2013) *Housing First Europe, Final Report*, Brussels: EU.

Busch-Geertsema, V. and Sahlin, I. (2007) 'The role of hostels and temporary accommodation', *European Journal of Homelessness*, 1: 67–93.

Busch-Geertsema, V., Benjaminsen, L., Filipovič Hrast, M. and Pleace, N. (2014) *Extent and Profile of Homelessness in European Member States*, Brussels: European Observatory on Homelessness.

Central Bank of Ireland (various years) *Residential Mortgage Arrears and Repossession Statistics*, Dublin: Central Bank of Ireland.

Corrigan, E. and Watson, D. (2018) *Social Housing in the Irish Housing Market*, Working Paper No. 594, Dublin: Economic and Social Research Institute/Department of Housing Planning and Local Government.

Corrigan, E., Foley, D., McQuinn, K., O'Toole, C. and Slaymaker, R. (2018) *Exploring Affordability in the Irish Housing Market*, Working Paper No. 593, Dublin: Economic and Social Research Institute/Department of Housing, Planning and Local Government.

CSO (Central Statistics Office) (2008) 'Construction and housing in Ireland', www.cso.ie/en/media/csoie/releasespublications/documents/construction/current/constructhousing.pdf

CSO (2019) 'New dwelling completions', quarter 1, https://pdf.cso.ie/www/pdf/20190516083148_New_Dwelling_Completions_Q1_2019_full.pdf

Culhane, D.P. (1992) 'The quandaries of shelter reform: An appraisal of efforts to "manage" homelessness', *Social Service Review*, 63(3): 428–40.

Culhane, D.P. (2008) 'The cost of homelessness: A perspective from the United States', *European Journal of Homelessness*, 2(1): 97–114.

Culhane, D.P. (2016) 'The potential of linked administrative data for advancing homelessness research and policy', *European Journal of Homelessness*, 10(3): 109–26.

Culhane, D.P. (2018) 'Chronic homelessness', Center for Evidence-Based Solutions to Homelessness, www.evidenceonhomelessness.com/wp-content/uploads/2018/04/evidence-page-chronic-homelessness-April-2018.pdf

Culhane, D.P. and Metraux, S. (2008) 'Rearranging the deck chairs or reallocating the lifeboats? Homelessness assistance and its alternatives', *Journal of the American Planning Association*, 74(1): 111–21.

Culhane, D.P., Metraux, S., Byrne, T., Steno, M., Bainbridge, J. (2013) 'The age structure of contemporary homelessness: Evidence and implications for public policy, *Analyses of Social Issues and Public Policy* 13(1): 228-44.

Culhane, D.P., Park, J.M. and Metraux, S. (2011) 'The patterns and costs of services use among homeless families', *Journal of Community Psychology*, 39(7): 815–25.

Daly, M. (1992) *Homeless People in Europe – The Rising Tide*, summary report of the European Observatory on Homelessness, Brussels: FEANTSA.

Daly, M. (2019) 'Ireland: The welfare state and the crisis', in S. Ólafsson, M. Daly, O. Kangas and J. Palme (eds) *Welfare and the Great Recession*, Oxford: Oxford University Press, pp 115–131.

Della Porta, D. (2013) 'Comparative analysis: Case-oriented versus variable-oriented research', in D. Della Porta and M. Keating (eds) *Approaches and Methodologies in the Social Sciences: A Pluralist Perspective*, Cambridge: Cambridge University Press, pp 198–222.

Department of the Environment and Local Government (2000) *Homelessness – An Integrated Strategy*, Dublin: Department of the Environment and Local Government.

Department of Housing and Urban Development (2018) *The 2018 Annual Homeless Assessment Report to Congress*, Washington, DC: Department of Housing and Urban Development.

Department of Housing, Planning, Community and Local Government (2016) *Rebuilding Ireland: Action Plan for Housing and Homelessness*, Dublin: Department of the Environment, Community and Local Government.

Department of Housing, Planning, Community and Local Government (2017) *Review of Rebuilding Ireland: Action Plan for Housing and Homelessness*, Dublin: Department of Housing, Planning, Community and Local Government.

Department of the Environment, Heritage and Local Government (2008) *The Way Home: A Strategy to Address Adult Homelessness in Ireland 2008–2013*, Dublin: Department of the Environment, Heritage and Local Government.

Department of the Environment, Heritage and Local Government (2009) *Homeless Strategy National Implementation Plan*, Dublin: Department of the Environment, Heritage and Local Government.

Department of the Environment, Community and Local Government (2013) *Homelessness Policy Statement*, Dublin: Department of the Environment, Community and Local Government.

Department of the Environment, Community and Local Government (2014) *Implementation Plan on the State's Response to Homelessness*, Dublin: Department of the Environment, Community and Local Government.

Dillon, B., Murphy-Lawless, J. and Redmond, D. (1990) *Homelessness in County Louth*, Dublin: SUS Research.

Doherty, V. (1982) *Closing Down the County Homes*, Dublin: Simon Community – National Office.

Doorley, K., Bercholz, M., Callan, T., Keane, C. and J.R. Walsh (2018) *The Gender Impact of Irish Budgetary Policy 2008–2018*, Dublin: Economic and Social Research Institute/Parliamentary Budget Office.

Dublin Region Homeless Executive (2019) *The Homeless Action Framework for Dublin, 2019–2021*, Dublin: Dublin Region Homeless Executive.

Economic and Social Research Institute/Residential Tenancies Board (2019) *Rent Index 2018*, Dublin: Residential Tenancies Board.

Edwards, G., Hawker, A., Williamson, V. and Hensman, C. (1966) 'London's skid row', *The Lancet*, 287(7431): 249-52.

Esping-Andersen, G. (1990) *The Three Worlds of Welfare Capitalism*, Princeton, NJ: Princeton University Press.

Fahey, T. and Watson, D. (1995) *An Analysis of Social Housing Need*, Dublin: Economic and Social Research Institute.

FEANTSA (European Federation of National Organisations Working with the Homeless) and FAP [Fondation Abbe Pierre] (2018) *Third Overview of Housing Exclusion in Europe*, Brussels: FEANTSA.

Finnerty, J. and O'Connell, C. (2014) 'Fifty years of the social housing "offer" in Ireland: The casualisation thesis examined', in L. Sirr (ed) *Renting in Ireland: The Social, Voluntary and Private Sectors*, Dublin: Institute of Public Administration, pp 170–81.

Fitzpatrick Associates (2006) *Review of Implementation of Homeless Strategies*, Dublin: Department of the Environment, Heritage and Local Government.

Finnerty, J., O'Connell, C. and O'Sullivan, S. (2016) 'Social housing policy and provision: A changing regime?', in M. Murphy and F. Dukelow (eds) *The Irish Welfare State in the Twenty-First Century: Challenges and Change*, London: Palgrave Macmillan, pp 237–59.

Garland, D. (2016) *The Welfare State: A Very Short Introduction*, Oxford: Oxford University Press.

Garret, G.R. (1989) 'Alcohol problems and homelessness: History and research', *Contemporary Drug Problems*, 16(3): 301–32.

Gerstal, N., Bogard, C.J., McConnell, J.J. and Schwartz, M. (1996) 'The therapeutic incarceration of homeless families', *Social Services Review*, 70(4): 543–72.

Gladwell, M. (2006) Million-dollar Murray: Why problems like homelessness may be easier to solve than to manage, *The New Yorker*, February, 13 and 20.

Goul Andersen, J. (2019) Denmark: The welfare state as victim of neoliberal economic failure?', in S. Ólafsson, M. Daly, O. Kangas and J. Palme (eds) *Welfare and the Great Recession*, Oxford: Oxford University Press, pp 237–59.

Gounis, K. (1992) 'The manufacture of dependency: Shelterization revisited', *New England Journal of Public Policy*, 8(1): 685–93.

Government of Ireland (2016) *A Programme for Partnership Government*, Dublin: Government of Ireland.

Government of Ireland (2018) *National Housing First Implementation Plan 2018-2020*, Dublin: Government of Ireland.

Greenwood, R.M. (2015) *Evaluation of Dublin Housing First Demonstration Project: Summary of Findings*, Dublin: Dublin Region Homeless Executive.

Greenwood, R.M., Stefancic, A. and Tsemberis, S. (2013a) 'Pathways Housing First for homeless persons with psychiatric disabilities: Program innovation, research, and advocacy', *Journal of Social Issues*, 69(4): 645–63.

Greenwood, R.M., Stefancic, A., Tsemberis, S. and Busch-Geertsema, V. (2013b) 'Implementations of Housing First in Europe: Successes and challenges in maintaining model fidelity', *American Journal of Psychiatric Rehabilitation*, 16(4): 290–312.

Greenwood, R.M., Bernad, R., Aubry, T. and Agha, A. (2018) 'A study of programme fidelity in European and North American Housing First programmes: Findings, adaptations, and future directions', *European Journal of Homelessness*, 13(3): 275–98.

Hall, G., Walters, S., Gould, H. and Lim, S. (2018) 'Housing versus treatment first for supportive housing participants with substance use disorders: A comparison of housing and public service use outcomes', *Addiction*, DOI: 10.1080/08897077.2018.144904.

Hansen, H. and Schultz-Nielsen, M.L. (2015) *Kontanthjælpen gennem 25 år – modtagere, regler, incitamenter og levevilkår fra 1987 til 2012* [*Social assistance benefits throughout 25 years. Receivers, rules, incentives and living conditions from 1987 to 2012*], Copenhagen: Gyldendal.

Hansen Löfstrand, C. (2015) 'The policing of a homeless shelter: Private security patrolling the border of eligibility', *European Journal of Homelessness*, 9(2): 17–38.

Hansen Löfstrand, C. and Juhila, K. (2012) 'The discourse of consumer choice in the pathways Housing First model', *European Journal of Homelessness*, 6(2): 47–68.

Hearne, R. and Murphy, M. (2018) 'An absence of rights: Homeless families and social housing marketisation in Ireland', *Administration*, 66(2): 9–31.

Hellman, C.M.E., Monni, M. and Alanko, A.M. (2017) 'Declaring, shepherding, managing: The welfare state ethos in Finnish government programmes, 1950–2015', *Research on Finnish Society*, 10(1): 9–22.

Hennessy, T. (1993) *The Homeless: Who Cares? A Study of the Living Conditions of Homeless People in Dublin's Night Shelters*, Dublin: National Campaign for the Homeless.

Henwood, B.F., Wenzel, S.L., Mangano, P.F., Hombs, M., Padgett, D.K., Byrne, T., Rice, E., Butts, D. and Uretsky, M.C. (2015) *The Grand Challenge of Ending Homelessness*, Working Paper No. 9, Cleveland, OH, American Academy of Social Work and Social Welfare.

Hoch, C. (2010) 'Sheltering the homeless in the US: Social improvement and the continuum of care', *Housing Studies*, 15(5): 865–76.

Homelessness Inter-Agency Group (2018) *Report to the Minister for Housing, Planning and Local Government*, Dublin: Homelessness Inter-Agency Group.

Homelessness Oversight Group (2013) *First Report*, Dublin: Homelessness Oversight Group.

Honohan, P., Donovan, D., Gorecki, P. and Mottiar, R. (2010) 'The Irish banking crisis: Regulatory and financial stability policy', a report to the Minister for Finance by the Governor of the Central Bank.

Hopper, K. (1988) 'More than passing strange: Homelessness and mental illness in New York City', *American Ethnologist*, 15(1): 155–67.

Hopper, K. (1989) 'Deviance and dwelling space: Notes on the resettlement of homeless persons with drug and alcohol problems', *Contemporary Drug Problems*, 16(3): 391–414.

Hopper, K. (1990a) 'The ordeal of shelter: Continuities and discontinuities in the public response to homelessness', *Notre Dame Journal of Law, Ethics and Public Policy*, 4: 301–23.

Hopper, K. (1990b) 'Homeless men in historical perspective', *Journal of Social Issues*, 46(4): 13–29.

Hopper, K., Jost, J., Hay, T., Welber, S. and Haugland, G. (1997) 'Homelessness, severe mental illness, and the institutional circuit', *Psychiatric Services*, 48(5): 659–64.

Houghton, F.T. and Hickey, C. (2000) *Focusing on B&Bs: The Unacceptable Growth of Emergency B&B Placement in Dublin*, Dublin: Focus Ireland.

Housing Agency (2016) *Review of Ministerial Direction on Housing Allocations for Homeless and Other Vulnerable Households*, Dublin: Housing Agency.

Housing Agency (2018) *Summary of Social Housing Assessments 2018: Key Findings*, Dublin: Housing Agency.

Housing Centre (1986) *National Directory of Hostels, Night Shelters, Temporary Accommodation and other Services for Homeless People*, Dublin: The Housing Centre.

Houses of the Oireachtas (2016) *Report of the Committee on Housing and Homelessness*, Dublin: Houses of the Oireachtas.

Johnson, G., Parkinson, S. and Parsell, C. (2012) *Policy Shift or Program Drift? Implementing Housing First in Australia*, Melbourne: AHURI (Australian Housing and Urban Research Institute).

Johnson, G., Scutella, R., Tseng, Y.P. and Wood, G. (2015) *Entries and Exits from Homelessness: A Dynamic Analysis of the Relationship between Structural Conditions and Individual Characteristics*, Melbourne: Australian Housing and Urban Research Institute.

Kananen, J. (2012) 'Nordic paths from welfare to workfare: Danish, Swedish and Finnish labour market reforms in comparison', *Local Economy*, 27(5/6): 558–76.

Kangas, O. (2019) 'Finland: From the deep crisis of the 1990s to the Great Recession', in S. Ólafsson, M. Daly, O. Kangas and J. Palme (eds) *Welfare and the Great Recession*, Oxford: Oxford University Press, pp 154–74.

Kärkkäinen, S.L. (1996) *Homelessness in Finland*, Helsinki: STAKES.

Kearns, K.C. (1984) 'Homelessness in Dublin: An Irish urban disorder', *American Journal of Economics and Sociology*, 43(2): 217–33.

Keegan, O.P. (2016) 'Letter to Minister Alan Kelly re: Ministerial directive regarding housing allocations', 22 April.

References

KELA (Social Insurance Institution) (2018) www.kela.fi/web/en

Kelleher, P. (1990) *Caught in the Act: Housing and Settling Homeless People in Dublin City – the Implementation of the Housing Act, 1988*, Dublin: Focus Point.

Kelleher, C., Kelleher, P. and McCarthy, P. (1992) *Patterns of Hostel Use in Dublin*, Dublin: Focus Point.

Kertesz, S.G., Crouch, K., Milby, J.B., Cusimano, R.E. and Schumacher, J.E. (2009) 'Housing First for homeless persons with active addiction: Are we overreaching?', *Milbank Quarterly*, 87(2): 495–534.

Kettunen, M. and Granfelt, R. (2011) 'Observations from the first year of the Finnish name on the door project: Recommendations for the long-term homelessness reduction programme for years 2012–2015', www.housingfirst.fi/en/

Knutagård, M. and Kristiansen, A. (2013) 'Not by the book: The emergence and translation of Housing First in Sweden', *European Journal of Homelessness*, 7(1): 93–115.

Koegel, P. (1992) 'Understanding homelessness: An ethnographic approach', in R.I. Jahiel (ed) *Homelessness: A Prevention Orientated Approach*, Baltimore, MD: The Johns Hopkins Press, pp 127–38.

Kokkinen, L., Muntaner, C., O'Campo, P., Freiler, A., Oneka, G. and Shankardass, K. (2017) 'Implementation of health 2015 public health program in Finland: A welfare state in transition', *Health Promotion International*, 34(2): 258–68.

Kolstrup, S. (2014) *Den danske velfærdsmodel 1891–2011 – Sporskifter, motiver, drivkræfter* [*The Danish Welfare Model 1891–2011 – Changes, Motives, Drivers*], Frederiksberg: Frydenlund.

Kuhn, R. and Culhane, D.P. (1998) 'Applying cluster analysis to test a typology of homelessness: Results from the analysis of administrative data', *American Journal of Community Psychology*, 17(1): 23–43.

Lancione, M., Stefanizzi, A. and Gaboardi, M. (2018) 'Passive adaptation or active engagement? The challenges of Housing First internationally and in the Italian case', *Housing Studies*, 33(1): 40–57.

Lee, B.A., Tyler, K.A. and Wright, J.D. (2010) 'The new homelessness revisited', *Annual Review of Sociology*, 36: 501–21.

Lee, D., McGuire, M. and Kim, J.H. (2018) 'Collaboration, strategic plans, and government performance: The case of efforts to reduce homelessness', *Public Management Review*, 20(3): 360–76.

Lewis, E. (2019) *Social Housing Policy in Ireland: New Directions*, Dublin: Institute of Public Administration.

Library and Research Service (2018) *Regulation of Approved Housing Bodies in Ireland*, Dublin, Houses of the Oireachtas.

Luomanen, R. (2010) *Long-term Homelessness Reduction Programme 2008-2011: Background Report*, Helsinki: Ministry of the Environment.

Lyon-Callo, V. (2000) 'Medicalizing homelessness: The production of self-blame and self-governing within homeless shelters', *Medical Anthropology Quarterly*, 14(3): 328–45.

Mackie, P., Johnsen, S. and Wood, J. (2017) *Ending Rough Sleeping: What Works?*, London: Crisis.

Maeseele, T., Roose, R., Bouverne-De Bie, M. and Roets, G. (2014) 'From vagrancy to homelessness: The value of a welfare approach to homelessness', *British Journal of Social Work*, 44(7): 1717–34.

Manning, R.M., Greenwood, R.M. and Kirby, C. (2018) 'Building a way home: A study of fidelity in the Housing First model in Dublin, Ireland', *European Journal of Homelessness*, 12(3): 33–54.

Marcus, A. (2003) 'Shelterization revisited: Some methodological dangers of institutional studies of the homeless', *Human Organisation*, 62(3): 134–42.

Ministry of Internal and Social Affairs (2009) *The Government's Homelessness Strategy – A Strategy to Reduce Homelessness in Denmark 2009–2012*, Copenhagen: Indenrigs- og Socialministeriet and Ramboll Management Consulting.

Montgomery, A.E., Metraux, S. and Culhane, D.P. (2013) Rethinking homelessness prevention among persons with serious mental illness, *Social Issues and Policy Review* 7(1): 58–82.

Moore, J. (1994) *B&B in Focus: The Use of Bed and Breakfast Accommodation for Homeless Adults in Dublin*, Dublin: Focus Point.

Nexus Research (1992) *Promises, Promises: An Assessment of the Housing Act, 1988, in Housing Homeless People in Ireland*, Dublin: National Campaign for the Homeless.

Nielsen, S. F., Hjortøj, C. R., Erlangsen, A. and Nordentoft, M. (2011) 'Psychiatric disorders and mortality among people in homeless shelters in Denmark: A nationwide register-based cohort study, *Lancet*, 377: 2205–14.

Norris, M. (2016) *Property, Family and the Irish Welfare State*, London: Palgrave Macmillan.

Norris, M. and Byrne, M. (2017) 'A tale of two busts (and a boom): Irish social housing before and after the Global Financial Crisis, *Critical Housing Analysis*, 4(2): 19–28.

O'Brien, J. (1981) 'Poverty and homelessness', in S. Kennedy (ed) *One Million Poor? The Challenge of Irish Inequality*, Dublin: Turoe Press.

O Cinneide, S. and Mooney, P. (1972) '*Simon Survey of the Homeless*', Dublin: The Simon Community supported by the Medico-Social Research Board.

O'Flaherty, B. (2004) 'Wrong person and wrong place: For homelessness, the conjunction is what matters', *Journal of Housing Economics*, 13(1): 1–15.

O'Sullivan, E. (2012) *Ending Homelessness: A Housing-Led Approach*, Dublin: Department of the Environment, Heritage and Local Government.

O'Sullivan, E. (2016a) 'Ending homelessness in Ireland: Ambition, austerity, adjustment?', *European Journal of Homelessness*, 10(2): 11–39.

O'Sullivan, E. (2016b) 'Women's homelessness: A historical perspective', in P. Mayock and J. Bretherton (eds) *Women's Homelessness in Europe*, London: Palgrave Macmillan, pp 15–40.

O'Sullivan, E. (2017a) 'Ending homelessness in Ireland, Denmark and Finland?', *Parity*, 30(10): 17–19.

O'Sullivan, E. (2017b) 'International commentary: Family options study – observations from the periphery of Europe', *Cityscape: A Journal of Policy Development and Research*, 19(3): 207–13.

Owen, R. (2015) 'Achieving goals: Strategies to end homelessness', *Homeless in Europe*, Summer: 2–3.

Padgett, D.K. (2007) 'There's no place like (a) home: Ontological security among persons with serious mental illness in the United States', *Social Science and Medicine*, 64(9): 1925–36.

Padgett, D.K., Henwood, B.F. and Tsemberis, S.J. (2016) *Housing First: Ending Homelessness, Transforming Systems, and Changing Lives*, New York, Oxford University Press.

Parsell, C. (2017) 'Do we have the knowledge to address homelessness?', *Social Service Review*, 91(1): 134–53.

Parsell, C. and Watts, B. (2017) 'Charity and justice: A reflection on new forms of homeless provision in Australia', *European Journal of Homelessness*, 11(2): 65–76.

Parsell, C., Jones, A. and Head, B. (2012) 'Policies and programmes to end homelessness in Australia: Learning from international practice', *International Journal of Social Welfare*, 2(2): 186–94.

Parsell, C., Petersen, M. and Culhane, D. (2017) 'Cost offsets of supportive housing: Evidence for social work', *British Journal of Social Work*, 47(5): 1534–53.

Pauly, B., Carlson, E. and Perkin, K. (2012) *Strategies to End Homelessness: Current Approaches to Evaluation*, Toronto: Canadian Homelessness Research Network Press.

Pearson, C., Montgomery, A.E. and Locke, G. (2009) 'Housing stability among homeless individuals with serious mental illness participating in housing first programs', *Journal of Community Psychology*, 37(34): 404–17.

Peterson, W.J. and Maxwell, M.A (1958) 'The skid row "wino"', *Social Problems*, 5(4): 308–16.

Pleace, N. (2008) *Effective Services for Substance Misuse and Homelessness in Scotland: Evidence from an International Review*, Edinburgh: Scottish Government.

Pleace, N. (2011) 'The ambiguities, limits and risks of Housing First from a European perspective', *European Journal of Homelessness*, 5(2): 113–22.

Pleace, N. (2014) 'Fieldwork notes from the evaluation of the Finnish homelessness strategy', unpublished.

Pleace, N. (2016a) 'Excluded by definition: The under-representation of women in European homelessness statistics', in P. Mayock and J. Bretherton (eds) *Women's Homelessness in Europe*, London: Palgrave Macmillan, pp 105–126.

Pleace, N. (2016b) 'Researching homelessness in Europe: Theoretical perspectives', *European Journal of Homelessness*, 10(3): 19–44.

Pleace, N. (2017) 'The action plan for preventing homelessness in Finland 2016–2019: The culmination of an integrated strategy to end homelessness?', *European Journal of Homelessness*, 11(2): 95–115.

Pleace, N. (2018) *Using Housing First in Integrated Homelessness Strategies: A Review of the Evidence*, York: Centre for Housing Policy.

Pleace, N. and Bretherton, J. (2013) 'The case for Housing First in the European Union: A critical evaluation of concerns about effectiveness', *European Journal of Homelessness*, 7(2): 21–41.

Pleace, N. and Culhane, D. (2016) *Better than Cure? Testing the Case for Enhancing Prevention of Single Homelessness in England*, London: Crisis.

Pleace, N., Culhane, D., Granfelt, R. and Knutagård, M. (2015) *The Finnish Homelessness Strategy: An International Review*, Helsinki: Ministry of the Environment.

Pleace, N., Knutagård, M., Culhane, D.P. and Granfelt, R. (2016) 'The strategic response to homelessness in Finland: Exploring innovation and coordination within a national plan to reduce and prevent homelessness', in N. Nichols and C. Doberstein (eds) *Exploring Effective Systems Responses to Homelessness*, Toronto: Canadian Observatory on Homelessness, pp 426–42.

Quilgars, D. and Pleace, N. (2016) 'Housing First and social integration: A realistic aim?', *Social Inclusion*, 4(4): 5–15.

Quinn, A. (2018) 'Housing First and the city: How has delivery of the Housing First model in Dublin impacted and been impacted by existing practice and policy in Ireland?', *Irish Journal of Social, Economic and Environmental Sustainability*, 1(2): 111–23.

Quirouette, M. (2016) 'Managing multiple disadvantages: The regulation of complex needs in emergency shelters for the homeless', *Journal of Poverty*, 20(3): 316–39.

Rambøll & SFI. (2013) *Hjemløsestrategien. Afsluttende rapport* [*The homelessness strategy: Final report*], Copenhagen: Rambøll & SFI.

Ranasinghe, P. (2017) *Helter-Shelter: Security, Legality, and an Ethic of Care in an Emergency Shelter*, Toronto: University of Toronto Press.

Ranta, J. (2019) 'Review of Fredriksson, P. (2018) (ed) "Yömajasta omaan asuntoon. Suomalaisen asunnottomuuspolitiikan murros" ["From a shelter to my own home – Transformation of Finnish homelessness policy"]', *European Journal of Homelessness*, 13(1): 211–14.

Reilly, M. and Maphosa, P. (2018) *Homelessness and the Assessment of Housing Needs 2016: Report for Dublin*, Dublin, Dublin Region Homeless Executive.

Rhenter, P., Tinland, A., Grard, J. et al. (2018) Problems maintaining collaborative approaches with excluded populations in a randomised control trial: lessons learned implementing Housing First in France, *Health Research Policy and Systems*, 16:34. doi.org/10.1186/s12961-018-0305-1

Ridgway, P. and Zipple, A.M. (1990) 'The paradigm shift in residential services: From the linear continuum to supported housing approaches', *Psychosocial Rehabilitation Journal*, 13: 11–31.

Rooney, J.F. (1980) 'Organizational success through program failure: Skid row missions', *Social Forces*, 58(3): 904–24.

Rosenheck, R. (2010) 'Service models and mental health problems: Cost effectiveness and policy relevance', in I. Gould Ellen and B. O'Flaherty (eds) *How to House the Homeless*, New York, NY: Russell Sage Foundation, pp 17–36.

Ruonavaara, H. (2017) 'Retrenchment and social housing: the case of Finland', *Critical Housing Analysis*, 4(2):.8–18.

Sahlin, I. (2005) 'The staircase of transition: Survival through failure', *Innovation: The European Journal of Social Science Research*, 18(2): 115–36.

Saltman, R.B. and Teperi, J. (2016) 'Health reform in Finland: Current proposals and unresolved challenges', *Health Economics, Policy and Law*, 11(3): 303–19.

Serme-Morin, C. and Coupechoux, S. (2019) *Fourth Overview of Housing Exclusion in Europe 2019*, Brussels: Fondation Abbe Pierre/FEANTSA.

Shannon, D. (1988) 'The history and future of the Housing (Miscellaneous Provisions) Bill, 1985, in S. Kennedy, S. and J. Blackwell (eds.) *Focus on Homelessness: A New Look at Housing Policy*, Dublin: The Columba Press, pp 135–43.

Shlay, A.B. and Rossi, P.H. (1992) 'Social science research and contemporary studies of homelessness', *Annual Review of Sociology*, 18: 129–60.

Skifter Andersen, H. (2010) 'Spatial assimilation in Denmark? Why do immigrants move to and from multi-ethnic neighbourhoods?', *Housing Studies*, 25(3): 281–300.

Smith, C. and Anderson, L. (2018) 'Fitting stories: Outreach worker strategies for housing homeless clients', *Journal of Contemporary Ethnography*, 47(5): 535–50.

Snow, D.A., Baker, S.G., Anderson, L. and Martin, M. (1986) 'The myth of pervasive mental illness among the homeless', *Social Problems*, 33(5): 407–23.

Snow, D.A., Anderson, L. and Koegel, P. (1994) 'Distorting tendencies in research on the homeless', *American Behavioral Scientist*, 37(4): 461–75.

Somers, J.M., Moniruzzaman, A., Patterson, M., Currie, L., Rezansoff, S.N., Palepu, A. and K. Fryer (2017) 'A randomized trial examining housing first in congregate and scattered site formats', *PloS one*, 12(1) p.e0168745.

Stanhope, V. and Dunn, K. (2011) 'The curious case of Housing First: The limits of evidence based policy', *International Journal of Law and Psychiatry*, 32: 275–82.

Stark, L.R. (1987) 'A century of alcohol and homelessness: Demographics and stereotypes', *Alcohol, Health and Research World*, 11: 8–13.

Stark, L.R. (1992) 'Demographics and stereotypes of homeless people', in R.I. Jahiel (ed) *Homelessness: A Prevention Orientated Approach*, Baltimore, MD: The Johns Hopkins Press, pp 27–39.

Stark, L.R. (1994) 'The shelter as "total institution": An organizational barrier to remedying homelessness', *American Behavioral Scientist*, 37(4): 533–62.

Statistics Finland (2018) *Dwellings and Housing Conditions*. www.stat.fi/til/asas/index_en.html

Stephens, M. and Fitzpatrick, S. (2007) 'Welfare regimes, housing systems and homelessness. How are they linked?', *European Journal of Homelessness*, 1(1): 201–12.

Stern, M.T. (1984) 'The emergence of homelessness as a public problem', *Social Service Review*, 58(2): 291–301.

Stewart, J. (1975) *Of No Fixed Abode: Vagrancy and the Welfare State*, Manchester: Manchester University Press.

Tabol, C., Drebing, C. and Rosenheck, R. (2009) 'Studies of "supported" and "supportive" housing: A comprehensive review of model descriptions and measurement', *Evaluation and Program Planning*, 33: 446–56.

Tainio, H. and Fredriksson, P. (2009) 'The Finnish homelessness strategy: From a "staircase" model to a "Housing First" approach to tackling long-term homelessness', *European Journal of Homelessness*, 3: 181–99.

Tinland, A., Fortanier, C., Girard, V., et al. (2013) 'Evaluation of the Housing First program in patients with severe mental disorders in France: study protocol for a randomized controlled trial', *Trials* 14: 309.

Tsemberis, S. (2010a) 'Housing First: Ending homelessness, promoting recovery and reducing costs', in I.E. Gould and B. O'Flaherty (eds) *How to House the Homeless*, New York, NY: Russell Sage Foundation, pp 37–56.

Tsemberis, S. (2010b) *Housing First: The Pathway Model to End Homelessness for People with Mental Illness and Addiction*, Minnesota, MN: Hazelden.

Tsemberis, S. (2011) *Observations and Recommendations on Finland's "Name on The Door Project" From a Housing First Perspective*. www.housingfirst.fi/files/1242/Tsemberis_2011_-_Observations_and_Recommendations.pdf

Tsemberis, S. and Asmussen, S. (1999) 'From street to homes: The pathways to housing consumer preference supported housing model', *Alcoholism Treatment Quarterly*, 17(1/2): 113–31.

Tunstall, B. (2015) 'Relative housing space inequality in England and Wales, and its recent rapid resurgence', *International Journal of Housing Policy*, 15(2): 105–26.

Turner, A., Pakeman, K. and Albanese, T. (2015) *Discerning 'Functional Zero': Considerations for Defining and Measuring an End to Homelessness in Canada*, Toronto: The Homeless Hub.

Udvarhelyi, E. (2014) '"If we don't push homeless people out, we will end up being pushed out by them": The criminalization of homelessness as state strategy in Hungary', *Antipode*, 46(3): 816–34.

Urbanoski, K., Veldhuizen, S., Krausz, M., Schuetz, C., Somers, J. and Kirst M. (2018) 'Effects of comorbid substance use disorders on outcomes in a Housing First intervention for homeless people with mental illness', *Addiction*, 113: 137–45.

Waldron, R., O'Donoghue-Hynes, B. and Redmond, S. (2019) 'Emergency homeless shelter use in the Dublin region 2012–2016: Utilizing a cluster analysis of administrative data', *Cities*, 94: 143–52.

Wallace, S.E. (1965) *Skid Row as a Way of Life*, NJ: Bedminister Press.

Wallerstein, J.A. (2014) 'Elusive reconciliations: Ideological conflict in youth homeless shelters', *Journal of Social Distress and the Homeless*, 23(1): 19–31.

Wallich-Clifford, A. (1974) *No Fixed Abode*, London: Macmillan.

Wasserman, J.A. and Clair, J.M. (2013) 'The insufficiency of fairness: The logics of homeless service administration and resulting gaps in service', *Culture and Organization*, 19(2): 162–83.

Watson, D., Whelan, C.T., Maître, B. and Russell, H. (2018) 'Social class and conversion capacity: Deprivation trends in the Great Recession in Ireland', *Social Indicators Research*, 140(2): 549–70.

Wewerinke, D., Al Shamma, S., Dries, L. and Wolf, J. (2013) *Housing First Europe Local Evaluation Report Amsterdam*, Nijmegen: Netherlands Centre for Social Care Research and EU.

Whelan, C.T. and Nolan, B. (2017) 'Austerity and inequality in Ireland', in E. Heffernan, J. McHale and N. Moore-Cherry (eds) *Debating Austerity in Ireland: Crisis, Experience and Recovery*, Dublin: Royal Irish Academy, pp 100–114.

Ympäristöministeriö (2016) *Action Plan for Preventing Homelessness in Finland 2016–2019: Decision of the Finnish Government 09.06.2016*, Helsinki: Ympäristöministeriö.

Y Foundation (2017) *A Home of Your Own: Housing First and Ending Homelessness in Finland*, Helsinki: Y Foundation.

Index

Page numbers in *italics* refer to tables and figures. Page numbers followed by n indicate end-of-chapter notes.

A

Aarhus 48, 125–126
absolute zero 2
administrative decision-making structures *see* political and administrative decision-making structures
affordable housing *see* public housing; social housing
Assertive Community Treatment (ACT) 18, 49, 54, 112–113
austerity 127, 144, 168
Australia 13

B

B&B accommodation 43, 152
baby boomers 12
benefit sanctions 142
Brandt, Preben 147
buy-to-let (BTL) properties 135

C

Canada 19, 107, 111, 112
chronic homelessness 9, 10, 11–12
  see also long-term homelessness
congregate accommodation 13–15
  Finland 106–107, *107*–108, *109*, 111, 165
  Ireland 39–40
Copenhagen
  Assertive Community Treatment (ACT) 49, 112–113
  historic homelessness management 4
  homeless population *101*, 125
  Housing First 48
  Project Outside *(Projekt Udenfor)* 147
  public housing 30, 174
Corrigan, E. 144
cost
  B&B accommodation 43, 152
  evictions 38
  homelessness 11–12, 16–17
  Paavo programmes 87, 151
  see also public expenditure
Critical Time Intervention (CTI) 48, 49, 54, 112
cross-sectional research 8–10, 12
Culhane, D.P. 9–10, 12, 15

D

decision-making structures *see* political and administrative decision-making structures
deinstitutionalisation 8–9
Denmark
  functional zero 22
  global financial crisis 161
  historic homelessness management 4
  homeless population 10, 11, 31, 32
  homelessness counts 23, 31–32, 46, 49–50, 63, 74, 76–81, 125, 147
  homelessness policy 30–33
  homelessness strategies 23, 47–50, 54, 56–57, 63–64, 70, 148
  homelessness trends 24, 74–81, 98, 99, 100, *101*
  Housing First 20, 23, 48, 49–50, 56–57, 63–64, 111, 112–117, 164, 166–167
  political and administrative decision-making structures 146–148
  public housing 30–31, 113–115, 123–125, 136
  welfare regime 139–141, 155–156
  youth homelessness 167
domestic violence 95
Doorley, K. 146
Dublin
  emergency accommodation 99
  exits from homelessness 90–91
  family homelessness 93
  Family Hubs 69, 99
  historic homelessness management 4
  homeless population 7, 10, 42, 89, 145
  Housing First 20, 60, 62, 117, 119
  rent subsidy 134
  rough sleepers 39, 62, 94, 154
  service provision 153
  social housing 130–131

E

Economic and Social Research Institute (ESRI) 42
England 59, 64, 111
episodic homelessness 9, 10, 11–12
Europe 19–21

European Typology of Homelessness and Housing Exclusion [ETHOS] 24, *25*
European Union 4–5
evidence-based responses 21–22
Extending Housing First 63–64

F

families
  homelessness 4, 10, 32–33, 36, 86, 93
  Irish Travellers 145
  transitional accommodation 15
Family Hubs 68–69
financial crisis *see* global financial crisis
financial reports 96–97
Finland
  global financial crisis 161
  homelessness counts 34–35, 36, 46, 52, 81–83, 85, 98, 149, 175
  homelessness policy 34–39, 170–171
  homelessness strategies 22–23, 47, 50–52, 54–55, 57–59, 64–66, 70, 71, 148–152 (*see also Paavo I; Paavo II*)
  homelessness trends 24, 34, 81–87, 98–99, 100, *101*
  Housing First 21, 22–23, 39, 51, 58, 59, 104–112, 149, 151, 164–166
  political and administrative decision-making structures 148–152, 169
  public expenditure 143, 163
  social housing 120–123, 136
  welfare regime 141–143, 156, 168
  see also Helsinki
Finnerty, J. 131
Flynn, Padraig 41
France 19, 20, 112
Fredrickson, Pieter 148
functional zero 2, 22, 159
funding *see* public expenditure

G

Garland, D. 4
gender 4, 93, 144
  see also women
gender-based violence 95
global financial crisis 160–162

H

Health Act 1953, Ireland 40
health services 40
Helsinki
  affordable housing 121, 174
  emergency accommodation 37
  evictions 38
  historic homelessness management 4, 34
  homeless population 35, 86, *101*, 175
  housing development 65
  Paavo I 55
  Paavo II 59
  prevention 59, 64, 123
hidden homelessness 32, 36, 74, 77, 85, 94–95
  see also sofa surfing
Homeless HAP Place Finder Service 133
"Homeless Initiative", Ireland 43
homelessness
  20th century understanding of 5–7
  current interpretations 8–13
  exist from 90–91
  historic response 3–5
Homelessness - An Integrated Strategy (Department of Environment and Local Government, 2000) 43–44
homelessness counts
  Denmark 23, 31–32, 46, 49–50, 63, 74, 76–81, 125, 147
  Finland 34–35, 36, 46, 52, 81–83, 85, 98, 149, 175
  Ireland 42, 46, 94, 99
  see also homelessness trends
Homelessness Inter-Agency Group, Ireland 155
Homelessness Oversight Group, Ireland 95, 155
homelessness policy
  20th century 4, 29–30
  Denmark 22, 30–33
  Finland 22–23, 34–39, 170–171
  Ireland 22, 23, 39–45
  see also political and administrative decision-making structures
Homelessness Policy Statement, Ireland 60, 61, 117–118
homelessness prevention 21–22, 59, 63–64, 123, 133
homelessness services *see* service responses
homelessness strategies 22–24, 47–71
  Denmark 23, 47–50, 54, 56–57, 63–64, 70, 148
  Finland 22–23, 47, 50–52, 54–55, 57–59, 64–66, 70, 71, 148–152 (*see also Paavo I; Paavo II*)
  Ireland 23, 47, 52–54, 55–56, 59–62, 66–69, 70–71
homelessness trends 73–102
  Denmark 24, 74–81, 98, 99, 100, *101*, 125
  Finland 24, 81–87, 98–99, 100, *101*
  Ireland 24, 40, 41, 45, 53, 60, 61, 62, 87–97, 98, 99, *100*, *101*, 118–119
  see also homelessness counts

Index

house building
  Denmark 124–125
  Finland 22, 34, 59, 65, 122
  Ireland 60, 67, 126–128
housing *see* public housing; social housing
Housing Act 1966, Ireland 40
Housing Act 1988, Ireland 40–41
housing affordability 144
Housing Assistance Payment (HAP) 127, 131, 132
housing benefit 127, 132
Housing First 17–21, 103–120, 163–167
  Denmark 20, 23, 48, 49–50, 56–57, 63–64, 111, 112–117, 164, 166–167
  Dublin 20, 60, 62, 117, 119
  Finland 21, 22–23, 39, 51, 58, 59, 104–112, 149, 151, 164–166
  Ireland 62, 117–120, 164, 167
housing markets 12, 13
housing policy 172–174
housing readiness 114
Housing Ready model 6, 15–16
  see also Staircase model
housing social work services 123
housing-led approach 17, 22, 23, 60
Hungary 23–24

I

immigration *see* migration
Implementation Plan on the State's Response to Homelessness (Department of the Environment, Community and Local Government, 2014) 61–62
Intensive Case Management (ICM) 18, 49, 54, 112, 113
intentional homelessness 40
Ireland
  functional zero 22
  global financial crisis 161, 162
  homelessness counts 42, 46, 94, 99
  homelessness policy 39–45
  homelessness strategies 23, 47, 52–54, 55–56, 59–62, 66–69, 70–71
  homelessness trends 24, 40, 41, 45, 53, 60, 61, 62, 87–97, 98, 99, *100*, *101*, 118–119
  Housing First 62, 117–120, 164, 167
  political and administrative decision-making structures 152–155, 170
  public expenditure 54, 70, 96–97, 119, *128*, 152–153, 163
  social housing 126–136
  welfare regime 143–146, 156–157, 168
  see also Dublin
Irish Travellers 145–146
Italy 20, 111

J

Journeys Home study 13

K

Kaakinen, Juha 148
Kearns, K.C. 7

L

labour markets 12, 13
London 7
lone adult homelessness 29, 34, 35, 36–37, 38, *121*, 149
lone-parent households 146
long-term homelessness 16
  Denmark 70
  Finland 22, 37–38, 51–52, *83*
  Ireland 23, 53, 60, 61, 66
  see also chronic homelessness

M

mental illness 8–9
migration 142–143, 145
minority ethnic groups 145–146
Montgomery, A.E. 9

N

Name on the Door report, Finland 50–51, 55, 65, 104, 105–106, 107
National Homelessness Consultative Committee (NHCC), Ireland 154
Netherlands 20, 21
new homelessness 4–5, 8
New York 16, 17
Nolan, B. 144
normalisation 108

O

Odense 125–126

P

Paavo I 50–52, 54–55, 63, 70, 71, 83, 109, 148, 149, 150, 151, 164
Paavo II 57–59, 63, 71, 83, 123, 150–151, 164–165
Parsell, C. 3
Pathway Accommodation & Support System (PASS) 73
Pathways to Housing 16–17, 109, 110
political and administrative decision-making structures 168–171
  Denmark 146–148
  Finland 148–152, 169
  Ireland 152–155, 170
political will 169

prevention 21–22, 59, 63–64, 123, 133
private rented sector
  Finland 122
  Ireland 117, 127, 131–136, 137n, 144–145, 146, 156
Project Outside *(Projekt Udenfor)* 147
psychiatric deinstitutionalisation 8–9
public expenditure 162–163
  Finland 142, 163
  Ireland 54, 70, 96–97, 119, *128*, 152–153, 163
  see also costs
public housing
  Denmark 30–31, 113–115, 123–125, 136, 139–140, 174
  Finland 120–123, 136
  Ireland 117–118, 126–136

R

Rebuilding Ireland (Department of Housing, Planning, Community and Local Government, 2016) 66–68, 118, 130
refuges 95
Regional Homelessness Consultative Forums, Ireland 154–155
rent
  Denmark 30, 114–115
  Finland 122
  Ireland 127, 132, 133–136, 145, 168
Rental Accommodation Scheme (RAS) 127, 132
repossession 135
role conflict 14
rough sleepers
  Denmark 49–50, 78, 79, 84–85
  Finland 84
  Ireland 39, 62, 94, 99, 154

S

Sahlin, Ingrid 112
service responses
  congregate accommodation 13–15, 39–40
  evidence-based 21–22
  historic 3–5
  "Homeless Initiative", Ireland 43
  Housing Ready / Staircase model 6, 15–16, 17, 38, 104–105, 112
  Pathways to Housing 16–17, 109, 110
  see also Housing First
shelterisation 14
Snow, D.A. 8, 9
social housing
  see public housing
social integration 108–109

sofa surfing 50, 70, 79–80
Staircase model 6, 15–16, 17, 38, 104–105, 112
Stern, M.T. 8
support services *see* service responses
Sweden 20, 112

T

Tenancy Protection Service 132, 145
transitional accommodation 15
transitional homelessness 9–10, 83
Tsemberis, Sam 16, 105, 108, 109
Turner, A. 2

U

UK 20, 121
unemployment 143–144
unemployment benefits 142
US
  causes of homelessness 7, 8, 21–22
  cost 11–12
  Housing First 17–19, 106–107
  new homelessness 4
  Pathways to Housing 16–17
  private sector 113
  residential services 15
  Staircase model 104–105
  veteran homelessness 2

V

vagrant populations 3–4

W

Wallace, S.E. 7
Way Home, The: A Strategy to Address Adult Homelessness in Ireland 2008–2013 (Department of the Environment, Heritage and Local Government, 2008) 45, 52–54, 55–56
welfare regimes / welfare states 4, 24, 167–168
  Denmark 139–141, 155–156
  Finland 141–143, 156, 168
  Ireland 143–146, 156–157, 168
Whelan, C.T. 144
women 4, 5, 12, 33, 93, 145, 146

Y

young people 58, 65, 121, 140, 146
youth homelessness 4, 5, 49–50, 59, 80, 140, 167
Y-Säätiö (Y Foundation) 35, 36, 38–39, 58, 105, 163, 172, 173
  affordable housing 120, *121*, 122